U.S. Manufacturing

U.S. Manufacturing

The Engine for Growth in a Global Economy

Edited by Thomas J. Duesterberg and Ernest H. Preeg

Foreword by Robert McTeer

A Project of the Manufacturers Alliance/MAPI

PRAEGER

Westport, Connecticut
London

Library of Congress Cataloging-in-Publication Data

U.S. manufacturing : the engine for growth in a global economy / edited by Thomas J. Duesterberg and Ernest H. Preeg ; foreword by Robert McTeer.
p. cm.
"A project of the Manufacturers Alliance/MAPI."
Includes bibliographical references and index.
ISBN 0-275-98041-3 (alk. paper)
1. Manufacturing industries—United States. 2. United States—Foreign economic relations. I. Title: US manufacturing. II. Duesterberg, Thomas James, 1950– III. Preeg, Ernest H.
HD9725.U15 2003
338.4'767'0973—dc21 2003045599

British Library Cataloguing in Publication Data is available.

Library of Congress Catalog Card Number: 2003045599
ISBN: 0-275-98041-3

First published in 2003

Praeger Publishers, 88 Post Road West, Westport, CT 06881
An imprint of Greenwood Publishing Group, Inc.
www.praeger.com

Printed in the United States of America

The paper used in this book complies with the Permanent Paper Standard issued by the National Information Standards Organization (Z39.48–1984).

10 9 8 7 6 5 4 3 2

Contents

Illustrations

FIGURES

TABLES

Foreword

by Robert McTeer

Those of us who, like myself, have been advocating that America has been experiencing a New Economy that requires new ways of thinking about economic reality and policies can now quite legitimately ask several relevant and difficult questions: Was there a New Economy at all? Has globalization worked? Is free trade good for American workers and companies? Can a major economy continue to thrive by producing a greater amount of services on an ever-declining manufacturing foundation? And, New Economy or no, what about the ongoing, and growing, trade deficit between America and the rest of the world? These are all fair and important questions and, at a minimum, the beginnings of the answers are to be found in this book.

Far from being discouraged about manufacturing, productivity, and global competition, the analysts' work on which this volume rests suggests that the future of the American economy is secure, so long as we do not go off the rails because we are temporarily blinded by our current recessionary economic situation. The brief against the New Economy has by now become well known: irrational exuberance led to overinvestment in high-tech innovations, people lost their common sense and their ability to distinguish between sound investments and pure hype, criminal conspiracies to defraud investors were entwined within many New Economy businesses as the markets soared higher and higher until, for the second time in 15 years, the markets experienced a severe "crash." With the crash and the morning after effects has come the sober realization that the entire period between 1993 and 2000 was nothing but froth, a boom without substance, cheered on by analysts (*Dow 36000!*) and economists who believed—or maybe just claimed to believe—that time and space and all of the old relationships in business no longer applied to an American economy that operated in cyberspace.

Button-down suits, blue shirts, and rep ties were out, casual was in; offices with picture windows were out, telecommuting was in; golf, cigars, and martinis were suddenly back at the club, but now were consumed amid cell phones, PDAs, pagers, remote E-mails, and faxes. Where has it all gone?

It is hard to maintain faith in the transforming technologies that are shaping the modern world in this current environment, but some of us still believe. How can we? Because of the essential truth of the New Economy foundation: innovation and rapid change, increasing competitive pressures both domestically and globally, biotech and nanotech breakthroughs, decentralized capital funding, exponentially increasing knowledge, and the decreasing importance of geographically specific physical spaces. None of this has gone, nor will be going, away.

If in 1987, when the last "crash" occurred, you had refused to invest in stocks for the next decade, you would have missed one of the most substantial equities increases in history, an increase that raised overall societal wealth five times over. The same thing will happen to those who look around today and see only gloom and doom and refuse to participate in the next economic expansion, an expansion that will surely come, leaving only the question: How soon?

When it does happen, as this book points out, it likely will be led by the manufacturing sector of our economy. Regarding American manufacturing, as Mark Twain once said, "The reports of my death have been greatly exaggerated." As the authors demonstrate, manufacturing remains a dynamic and powerful economic engine for the American economy. This is not to say that some things cannot be improved, but it is to say that, being led by market forces—and assuming it is allowed to do so—manufacturing concerns will adapt and thrive in the globally competitive marketplace.

Sensible public policy will be required as we move forward, of course, and this book advocates many specific policies that the authors believe will promote a healthy future economy. Regardless of whether one agrees with all of these policy suggestions, the wealth of data and insight in this volume makes it valuable both to lay readers and to policy analysts.

Preface

by Thomas J. Duesterberg

The last decade has witnessed an apparent roller-coaster ride for the U.S. economy. From a slow start in the early 1990s, to a historic expansion that was especially strong at the end of the 1990s, to the worst recession since the second oil crisis in the early part of the new millennium, the economy has fluctuated across an abnormally wide band of performance. At the same time, foreign competition to U.S. producers and service providers has grown as more and more countries enter the successful, free market economy and international trade and investment barriers steadily fall. In this context, especially in the period of economic underperformance in the early 21st century, many analysts, politicians, and businesspeople have begun to speculate on the future of the U.S. manufacturing sector. After all, this sector has seen a steady decline in its share of the labor force since the 1970s, and it is the sector most directly and broadly exposed to foreign competition.

A number of important questions arise from this confluence of economic developments. Is U.S. manufacturing doomed to long-term decline in the face of foreign competition? Will capital markets, partly due to the perceived decline, shift resources out of manufacturing and into other sectors, as other countries have done? Is the long-term technological and managerial lead of U.S. industry waning? In short, is there a future for American manufacturing that merits continued investment and motivates workers, managers, and researchers to enter or stay in this sector? These questions are obviously related and, if answered broadly in the negative, could have the effect of a self-fulfilling prophecy.

In 2001, Rockwell Automation came to us at the Manufacturers Alliance/MAPI, a research and executive education association organized in 1933, to see what we thought about the future of U.S. manufacturing. Having had nearly 70 years of experience in research, both theoretical and practical, on this sector, and continuous interaction with senior executives working within it, we were in a good position to investigate the many issues involved in answering this question. In fact, in the early years of our organization, our chief economist, George Terborgh, wrote an influential book in response to fears about long-term economic stagnation (see George Terborgh, *The Bogey of Economic Maturity*, Chicago: Machinery and Allied Products Institute, 1945).

This book looks out over the next decade to map out how U.S. manufacturing is evolving, what role it plays in the overall U.S. economy, and how it competes on the global economic stage. We outline a vision of how U.S. technological and managerial progress has vastly changed the face of manufacturing and how the exigencies of globalization require constant change to ensure continued success. We also try to show how some non-economic factors, such as political and legal institutions and sociocultural factors, influence modern manufacturing. These noneconomic factors also play a role in determining who will succeed in the global arena. While our conclusions are generally optimistic, we do see challenges both from without and from within the country that will have to be met to produce continued success. Obviously, not all sectors or firms in the United States will share in the success we envision, so we try to outline many of the characteristics that will promote success in the global economy.

Though we consulted with a number of experts and business executives from industry and academe, the conclusions are wholly our own.

We are grateful to Rockwell Automation for supporting this book. An abbreviated version was done for Rockwell, and we benefited from helpful suggestions and criticisms from its leadership, including Don Davis, Keith Nosbusch, Michael Bless, John Cohn, and Sujeet Chand. Others with whom we consulted at Rockwell include Ted Crandell, Steve Eisenbrown, and Ron Wichter. We especially want to thank Don Davis, the Chairman and Chief Executive Officer, whose ideas and leadership inspired this project. We also received some useful suggestions on parts of the book from David Heuther, Jonathan Menes, and Kevin Stiroh. Robert Kups of Parker Hannifin Corporation and Jeffrey Price of Cincinnati Machine provided some useful ideas. Walter Kozikowski of the National Electronic Manufacturers Association and John Werling at the Institute for Economic Transformation also helped with some of the conceptual aspects of the sections on automation. Terri Daniel and Susan Sumler did yeoman work in preparing many drafts of the manuscript, compiling the bibliography, and perfecting the index.

Chapter 1

Introduction and Principal Conclusions

by Thomas J. Duesterberg

INTRODUCTION

This book is meant to counter the currently popular notion that U.S. manufacturing is in an irremediable state of decline. The summer of 2002, when the manuscript was completed, witnessed a crescendo of gloom pervading the American economy. Although most economic indicators signaled a recovery from the recession that started early in 2001, financial markets, faith in American business, and consumer and executive confidence indices all had lost considerable ground. Capital investment, a good proxy for both business confidence and future industrial growth, remained at depressed levels. More than five years of stock market gains, much of them undoubtedly the result of "overexuberance" in the first place, were rolled back and threatened the lackluster recovery. Leading the economic downturn of 2001-2002 was the manufacturing sector. Industrial production declined for 18 straight months, beginning in the fall of 2000. Although the severe recession and crisis of confidence had multiple causes—overcapacity in key industries, inventory buildup, strong global competition, and profit-killing disinflation—the convergence of these factors led to new questions about the future of manufacturing in the United States.[1]

Such questions are of course not new. In the 1980s many feared the "hollowing out" of U.S. manufacturing, the 1970s were dominated by fears of an energy crisis and overdependence on unreliable foreign suppliers, and the 1960s saw a grand debate over the "limits to growth." As far back as the late 1930s and 1940s, American economists debated whether modern industrial capitalism had reached a state of "maturity" that allowed little prospect for future growth.[2]

The undisputed success of the American economy in the late 1990s, including the manufacturing sector, apparently was not sufficient to allay the recurrence of fears about the future of that sector. Some of the reasons currently being advanced for the alleged decline in manufacturing emerged years ago, especially in the 1973-1982 period of stagflation, and some are relatively new. The "limits to growth" theory, with its underlying doctrine of resource depletion, has effectively been put to rest by the empirical experience since the 1960s, and does not figure prominently in the current debate. The same can be said for the theory of "economic maturity."

Most analysts now accept the proposition that advanced economies can grow more or less indefinitely. For many, however, the same is not the case for manufacturing. For decades the proportion of the U.S. workforce employed in the manufacturing sector has been falling: in 1960 nearly 31 percent of all workers labored in this sector, and by the height of the recent recession the proportion dropped below 13 percent. Such numbers, politically charged and viewed in isolation, led many to lament that manufacturing will follow the same path as agriculture and condemn the United States to becoming a services economy. Beginning in the 1970s and reaching a peak in the 1980s, the view that foreign competition, much of it labeled "unfair" for various reasons, was destroying U.S. industry became more widespread. This line of thinking has not disappeared, especially since the U.S. trade deficit has grown to around 4 percent of the gross domestic product (GDP) in the last few years, and more and more nations, including China, have the technical sophistication to compete with U.S. firms. But layered onto these traditional fears are newer ones arising from the increasing global integration of goods production, services, and investment. The notion is that, given the highly fluid movement of capital, technology, labor, and goods in the world today, highly paid U.S. workers and investors expecting large returns on investment in an environmentally friendly atmosphere will lose out to workers in the developing world. In many developing nations, according to this argument, workers are willing to labor for much less than in advanced economies and investors are willing to take smaller returns on capital with no concern for the environment.[3] This somewhat simplified view of U.S. manufacturing as unable to compete effectively in the era of "globalism" is often reinforced by notions that foreign competition is not fair: that foreign markets are not open, that international trade rules are flouted, that currency values are manipulated, or that proprietary technology is stolen. The common theme is that U.S. manufacturing is losing out to foreign competition. Figures on U.S. investment outside its borders are often produced as indicia of the decline in the competitiveness of domestic producers.

A final factor affecting the perception of the future of manufacturing is related to ideas advanced in the late 1990s that the United States had entered the realm of a "new economy." This economy was imprecisely associated with the rapid evolution of the Internet, its impact on traditional businesses like retailing and manufacturing, and the entirely new businesses that it engendered. This new economy was said to have its own new rules which might eventually overturn those of an "old economy," most prominently the boom and bust rhythm associated with manufacturing.[4] Even though manufacturing was the source of much of the technology creating and operating the Internet, it was tarred broadly as the symbol of the dirty, cyclical, low or no growth, old economy. Drawing a somewhat heroic implication, the rise and dominance of this new economy was seen as the eventual death knell of the old. While such an idea was rarely advanced by economists, it had a certain allure to younger generations caught up in the euphoria of the undeniable vitality of the 1990s and unfamiliar with economic history. In the late 1990s manufacturing concerns widely reported a shortage of qualified personnel to work in their plants and research labs. A survey of high school students in the Midwest, for instance, found that only 1 percent would like to work in manufacturing, tied with religion for last place among 18 possible career choices.[5]

The negative perception of the future of manufacturing could, and at times did, undermine the confidence needed by both corporate executives and financial markets to support new investment and new ventures in this sector. As George Terborgh said of the pessimism in the 1940s: "A defeatist philosophy, if widely believed, can so debilitate the economy that it helps produce the very condition it assumes."[6] Indeed, it was partly this problem that originally led to the writing of this book. In 2001 the Manufacturers Alliance/MAPI (Alliance), an executive education and economic research organization formed in 1933, was approached by Rockwell Automation for its view on the prospects for manufacturing over the next decade, and especially for its assessment of whether there were solid reasons to be optimistic about these prospects. This book is a much-expanded and broader version of the original report to Rockwell senior management.

Our largely optimistic view of the future of U.S. manufacturing is based on two principal sources of information. First is the economic history of the period since the 1980s. We have surveyed reams of empirical data, largely macroeconomic in nature, related to the actual performance of U.S. firms competing in a global marketplace. Second, the extensive executive education programs at the Alliance place us in regular contact with thousands of senior executives at firms operating in the United States, including many foreign-owned companies which have chosen to locate production, marketing, and research facilities here. Such firm-specific data give us added insight into the day-to-day strategies and operating procedures employed by firms to survive and prosper in a highly competitive global setting. Much of our insight into the evolution of manufacturing since the 1980s stems from discussions with, and observations of, senior executives devising strategies to succeed in a complex and fast-changing environment.

Our most general conclusion is that, despite some obvious problems and ever-intensifying competition, a bright future is in store for manufacturing. Most of this book is devoted to detailing the many strengths of this sector in the United States, and to how the evolution of modern global manufacturing favors the model which is most fully developed in the United States. Indeed, we find that U.S. manufacturing has been, and is likely to remain, the "engine for growth in a global economy." That is not to say that the situation will remain stable. For it is undeniable that certain types of manufacturing, especially low value-added production with little embedded intellectual property or proprietary content, will move offshore. But even when production is moved outside the country, frequently the advanced management techniques pioneered in the United States are exported, and both control and profits remain with the U.S.-based firm.

Before beginning our more detailed discussion, a few observations about the declinist argument are in order. The contention that manufacturing is shrinking is true only in the sense that its share of the workforce is eroding. Since about 1991, that is, in the era of the "new economy," manufacturing has actually grown faster than the overall economy. When measured in real, chain-weighted dollars, manufacturing grew by an average of 3.3 percent in this period, almost 10 percent faster than the 3.1 percent growth rate for the overall economy.[7] Other measures, too, show the comparative importance and growth of manufacturing: wages and profits are both higher in manufacturing than in other sectors.[8] Additionally, the value-added and technology content of U.S. manufacturing remains superior to that of most other countries. Most important, and explaining the seeming contradiction in the data, is the huge differential in productivity growth separating manufacturing from other sectors of the economy. We analyze this gap in considerable depth throughout this book.

The almost miraculous recovery of productivity growth, especially starting in the 1990s, has been led by manufacturing, and allows both increasing wages for workers and better returns for investors. Moreover, the lower unit labor costs associated with this productivity boom allow U.S. manufacturers to compete effectively in global markets. Much of the gain in productivity is derived from investments and innovation in technology, which, as we will demonstrate, are centered in the manufacturing sector. The resulting dynamism in this sector not only has allowed faster GDP growth but also has helped to attract an enormous amount of foreign investment into the United States since the mid-1970s. Foreign capital, in the form of both direct and indirect investment, has poured into the country, in part to access the large and affluent local markets, but also to carve out a place in the most innovative, technologically advanced areas for global manufacturing. The Organization for Economic Cooperation and Development (OECD) recently reported that "The importance of U.S. manufacturing as a recipient [of FDI] has been staggering": 45 percent of all foreign direct investment (FDI) inflows into the 29 OECD countries went into manufacturing industries in the United States between 1991 and 2000.[9] Altogether, over $2.5 trillion in FDI has poured into the United States since 1976, compared to about $2 trillion in FDI by U.S. firms outside the country.[10] This should come as no surprise since the United States is the source for much of the computer, semiconductor, telecommunications, aerospace, medical technology, and systems engineering advances in recent decades.

A final point related to the productivity boom is that new, productivity-enhancing technologies developed largely in the manufacturing sector, the locus for the lion's share of U.S. research and development (R&D), is the source of many of the efficiency improvements in other sectors of the economy. Can there be any doubt that U.S. agriculture would not be the efficiency juggernaut of the world without the planting, harvesting, and processing machines and other inputs developed by manufacturers? Or that the world-leading U.S. financial services sector would be so efficient without the computer and communications equipment developed by manufacturers? Without Intel microprocessors, Sun, Dell, or Hewlett-Packard servers, Corning fiber-optic lines, or Cisco and Lucent switches, could there be an Internet? These rhetorical flourishes are only meant to underscore the central role of manufacturing in the modern economy. Any distinction between old or new economy is meaningless in this context. Indeed, the case is made here that manufacturing is the core of the modern, new economy and central to the growth prospects of the entire economy.

PRINCIPAL CONCLUSIONS

This book, then, is a comprehensive look at these large questions about the future of U.S. manufacturing: Where is it going? What are its driving elements? Can it survive global competition? What role does it play in the national and global economies? It consists of an integrated set of nine chapters written by the research staff of the Alliance. It looks ahead to 2010, giving an overview of prospects for manufacturing at both the macro and selected sectorial levels. It draws not only on the academic literature and the vast research experience of the authors, but also on the network of corporate executives affiliated with the Alliance and representing a vast array of individual industries. All of the authors regularly interact with corporate leaders through the Alliance Council program, which brings together senior executives twice a year to address issues and developments of current interest to specific management disciplines, such as purchasing, strategic product development, quality improvement, new product development, and finance.

Although we see a bright future for U.S. manufacturers over the period up to 2010, there is no single or straight path to success. Global competition will continue to increase, requiring the best companies to evolve constantly to meet new situations and challenges. The pace of change will continue to be rapid, but it is our view that U.S. companies are well positioned and

Figure 1-1
Motor Vehicle Ownership and Per Capita Income, 1999

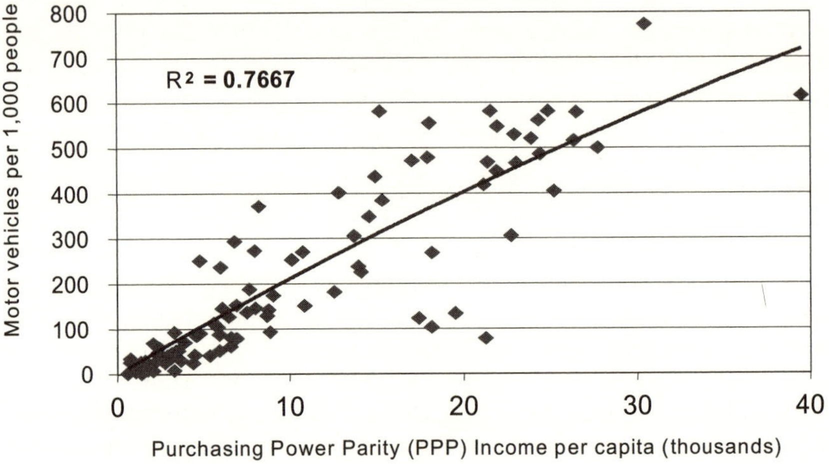

Source: World Bank, *World Development Indicators*, 2001.

flexible enough to be successful in this environment. Not all industries or companies will be able to prosper in this competitive situation. Those that are open to change, embrace new technologies and management techniques, and seek out global markets should be successful in a global economy that will grow rapidly by 2010.

We draw six principal conclusions from our analysis. While these conclusions tend to mask the underlying complexity of the data and some differences across sectors, they provide a general framework and guide for the detailed discussion in the eight chapters that follow.

The first conclusion, probably the most straightforward, is that ***world growth will remain robust in manufacturing***. This is true for both the developed and the developing worlds. In the industrialized countries such as the United States, the European Union (EU), and Japan, demand will be centered on ever more sophisticated products, often with embedded communications or control devices. In chapter 5 we review the process by which advances in wealth lead to ever-increasing demand for sophisticated goods, such as connected computing and luxury cars. In the developing world, especially in high-growth (in terms of both population and economic output) countries such as China, India, Mexico, Brazil, Turkey, and Poland, demand for traditional products such as washing machines, cars, and telephones will grow even faster as larger shares of the expanding populations move up the income scale and buy more of these products. As just one product example, figure 1-1 shows how the ownership of automobiles correlated closely with per capita income at the close of the 20th century. Personal consumption expenditures in Asia, to take a regional example, already total $4.8 trillion, compared to $5 trillion in the EU and $6.9 trillion in the United States. More rapid growth in this region means that its demand for manufactured products will soon exceed that of Europe and will rival that of the United States.[11] Demand growth in the developing countries is explored in chapter 7.

Second, we find that ***U.S. manufacturing is the principal engine for growth*** in the modern economy. Such a conclusion may appear paradoxical, given manufacturing's declining share as a proportion of employment and nominal (although not real) output. But, despite this secular decline in the relative proportion of employment, manufacturing growth has been strong since the 1980s and will continue to be a driver of growth through 2010.

Manufacturing provided 22 percent of U.S. growth in the period from 1992 to 2000, although its relative proportion of total output (when measured in constant dollars) was only around 17 percent. Moreover, in that period, growth in manufacturing averaged 4.8 percent per year, compared to only 3.4 percent in nonmanufacturing. In this entire period, manufacturing output grew by 47 percent, compared to only 34 percent for the whole economy. If the recession years of 1990 and 1991 are included, growth between 1989 and 2000 averaged 3.3 percent in manufacturing and 3 percent in nonmanufacturing.

More important, the secular change in growth in the 1990s, whereby overall economic growth accelerated to around 4 percent per year, was driven by a revival of productivity growth in manufacturing. Figure 1-2 shows how much greater productivity improvement was in the manufacturing sector, especially the durable goods industry, than in the economy at large. In the services sector, productivity growth lagged the economywide average, partly due to lack of exposure to international competition. For example, in the 1990s retail trade productivity grew by 2.3 percent and commercial banking productivity by 2.6 percent annually. Productivity growth not only improves standards of living for workers, it enables companies to succeed in the global competition which increasingly includes lower wage countries.

We also underscore the finding that improvements in productivity in the services sector, in industries like health care and financial services, derive largely from products developed in the manufacturing sector. Figure 1-3 shows R&D in the two major sectors of the economy compared to the respective shares of national output. In chapter 4 we explore in more depth the central role of manufacturing in the R&D process that leads to innovation and advances in productivity. A recent study by the National Institute of Standards and Technology (NIST) concluded: "Especially important is the fact that the service sector acquires most of its technology from manufacturing firms. . . . This fact emphasizes the substantial dependency of services on manufacturing firms for technology and thus the critical role of the myriad communications and market transactions between the two sectors."[12]

Figure 1-2
U.S. Productivity Growth, 1992–2002
(percent growth per year)

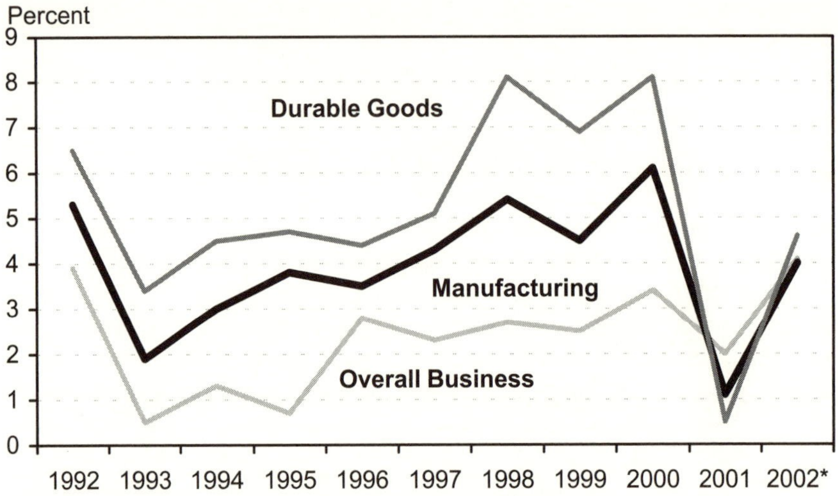

* 1st qtr 2002 data.

Source: U.S. Department of Labor.

This important theme of manufacturing driving economic growth, largely through productivity enhancements in both industry and services, is developed more fully in chapters 2 and 4.

Related to the last observation, our third conclusion is that ***technology increasingly drives economic growth*** and that the ***United States has a global technology lead*** in areas related to manufacturing. This conclusion has a number of sub-elements. In a macroeconomic sense, as chapter 4 explores in more depth, technology improvement (and associated changes in the ***management*** of technology) accounted for approximately one-third of the rapid U.S. economic growth in the period from 1995 to 1999. The contribution from technology thus accounts for much of the measured increase in growth associated with the "new economy," and is likely to continue to do so in the future.[13] Furthermore, the investment that creates and develops new technology is largely centered in the private manufacturing sector, and relatively less than in the past in the public sector. Nearly 70 percent of all U.S. R&D now is done in the private sector. About two-thirds of private-sector R&D is done by manufacturing firms, and more than 90 percent of patents are granted to researchers associated with this sector. Adoption of new technology, as chapters 5 and 6 explore, also facilitates customization of products, building of more sophisticated products, and improvements in production techniques needed to meet demand in the advanced economy

Figure 1-3
Major Industry Sector Shares of GDP and R&D Performance, 2000

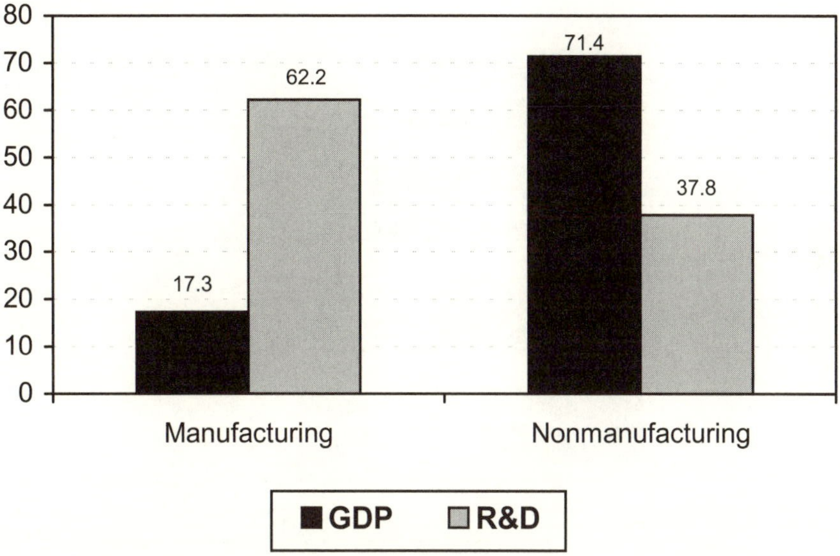

Source: National Institute of Science and Technology.

and keep pace with global competition. In a rapidly changing global economy, not all advances in technology are easily adopted and integrated into new or improved products or into improved production processes. There is a growing ***technology gap*** between those companies and plants employing the best technology and production processes and those which lag behind. Such a gap, as chapters 4 and 6 explore, offers major opportunities to capital goods producers. The cumulative effect of constant innovation, as Harvard economist Dale Jorgenson has shown, is higher productivity throughout the economy. Although the higher levels of labor productivity growth (2.9 percent annually) characteristic of the period from 1995 to 2000 are not likely to be replicated, Jorgenson estimates that sustainable productivity growth of 2.2 percent per year is achievable, a rate substantially higher than the 1.4 percent annual average between 1973 and 1995.[14] For example, productivity growth in manufacturing is about twice that of the entire economy, averaging 4.3 percent from 1995 to 2000.

Finally, for a variety of reasons U.S. firms are technology leaders, which positions them well to prosper in a global economy. To take only one broad measure, figure 1-4 sums up the total investment in advanced knowledge in selected industrial countries. Investment includes total R&D, expenditures on software, and outlays for higher education. If one were to measure growth in investment in information and communications technologies in

Figure 1-4
Investment in Knowledge in Selected Industrial Countries, 1998
(as a percent of GDP)

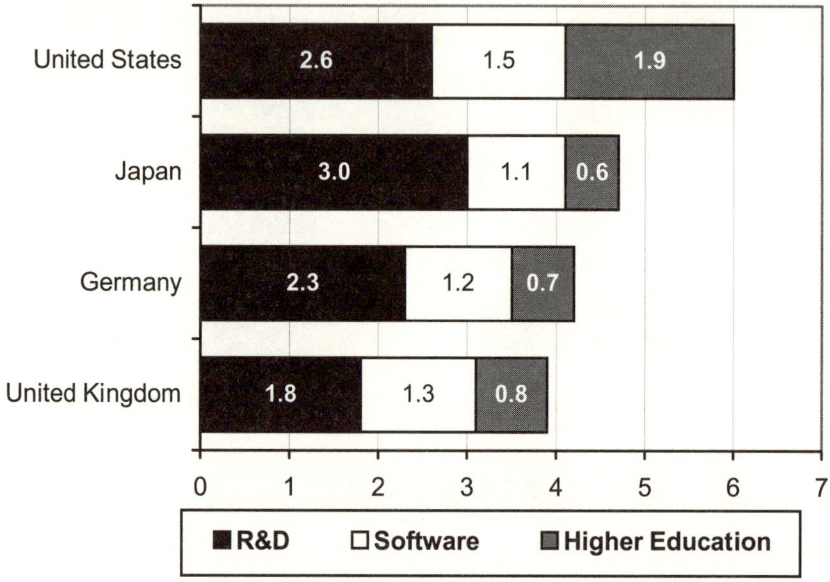

Source: *OECD Science, Technology and Industry Scorecard: Towards a Knowledge-Based Economy* (Paris: Organization for Economic Cooperation and Development, 2001).

the 1990s, as figure 1-5 does, one would also see a U.S. lead. Moreover, U.S. firms are generally more adept at employing new technologies effectively than are many competitors in Japan, EU, or the more advanced economies of Asia, such as Korea. This is because corporate organization and labor rigidities in these other countries tend to resist change, whereas American laws, institutions, and corporate culture are all open to fairly rapid change. Indeed, openness to change is one of the central pillars of modern management education, which is highly advanced in the United States in both academic settings and peer-learning programs like those offered by the Manufacturers Alliance/MAPI. Capital investment is generally more productive in the United States than elsewhere, partly because management at U.S. financial firms is more flexible and open to change than among peer competitors. Finally, the macroeconomic and cultural climates in the United States are more favorable than in most other countries to the high levels of innovation and change needed to thrive in the modern, global economy.[15] Although the United States has clear structural impediments to innovation and growth, as we explore in chapter 9, such as an overaggressive legal system, rapidly increasing health care costs, and an underperforming educational system, its culture and institutions, built on a democratic rule of

Figure 1-5
Growth in ICT Investment at Constant Prices in Selected OECD Countries, 1990–1999
(based on harmonized deflators for ICT products)*

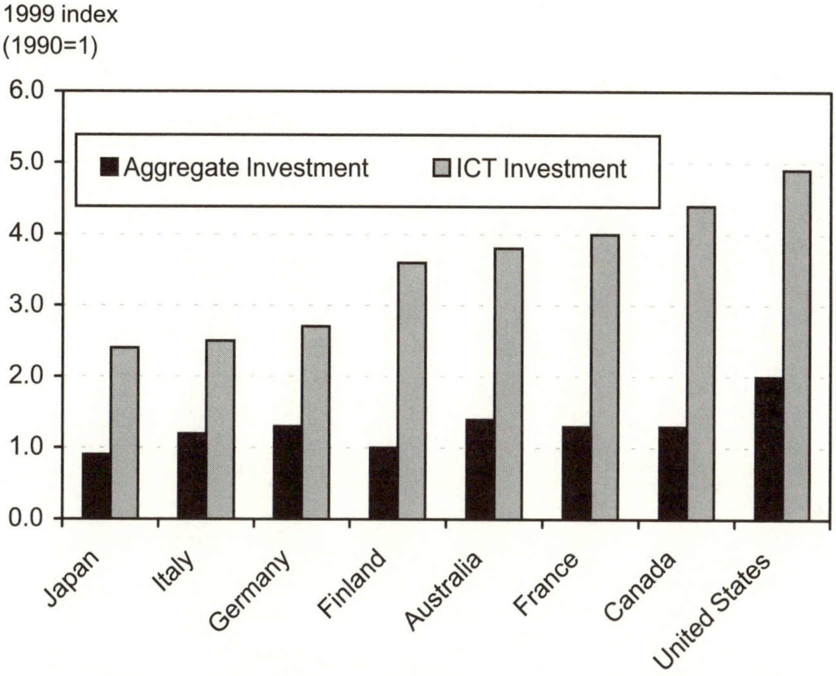

* Estimates of "harmonized" price indexes assume that price ratios between ICT and non-ICT products have the same time pattern across countries, with the United States as the benchmark.

Source: *OECD Science, Technology and Industry Scorecard: Towards a Knowledge-Based Economy* (Paris: Organization for Economic Cooperation and Development, 2001).

law, private property, and reliance on market mechanisms to direct economic activity, foster the flexibility and stable economic infrastructure required to adapt rapidly to changes in competitive conditions. Importantly, the United States does not, with some notable exceptions, protect threatened industries or try to manage and direct industrial development, allowing resources to move quickly and efficiently to their most productive uses.

These advantages have resulted in an improved competitive position for U.S. manufacturers. According to the National Science Foundation (NSF), the high-technology share of U.S. manufacturing output increased from 9.6 percent to 16.6 percent between 1980 and 1998.[16] During the same period, the U.S. share of all worldwide technology production expanded from 30 percent to 36 percent, and its share of worldwide technology exports grew

Figure 1-6
High-Tech Exports, 1980–1998

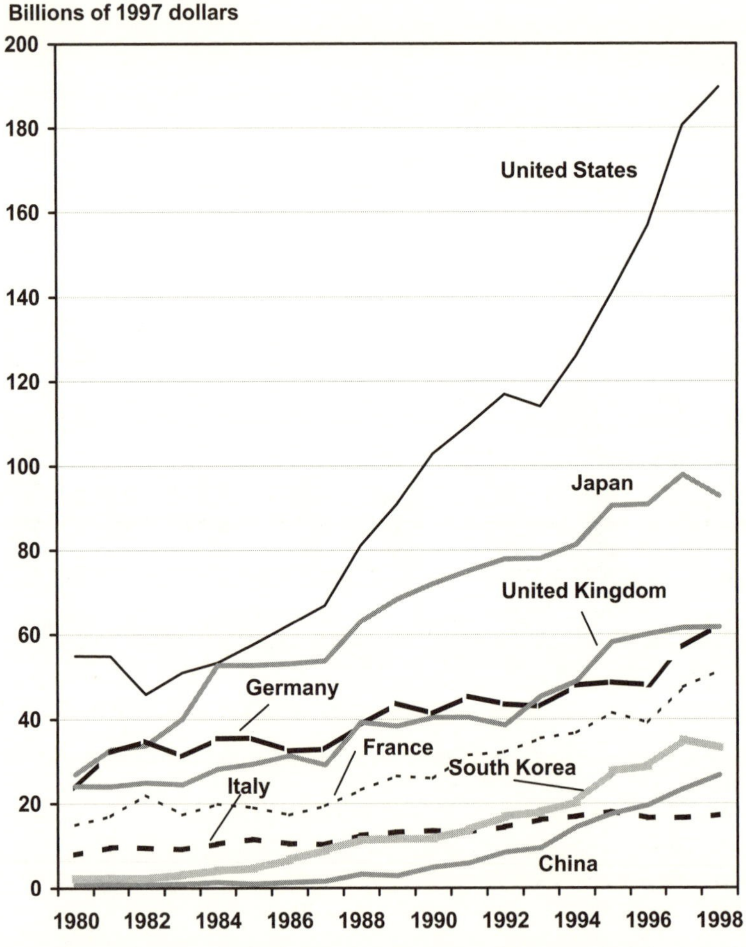

Source: National Science Foundation, *Science & Engineering Indicators—2002.*

to 20 percent, far surpassing the share of other industrialized countries, as figure 1-6 shows. The United States actually improved its competitive position in international markets for technology products compared to other advanced economies, such as Japan and Germany. Finally, the NSF notes that U.S.-based technology companies increased their share of the domestic market from two-thirds to three-fourths between the mid-1990s and the end of the century, belying the thesis that high-technology manufacturing was being "hollowed out."

The fourth major conclusion drawn from our analysis is that the ***value***

provided by manufacturing is shifting from a "production" to a "solutions" model. In the increasingly complex and competitive global marketplace, customers are demanding more than just standardized or commodity products. They increasingly require customized products and a whole array of support for that product. On the consumer side, customers want and increasingly can get customized clothes or computers or automobiles. On the production side, original equipment makers are demanding integrated modules (such as the interior or door of a car or wing of an airplane) from their suppliers rather than a single component, such as a seat or a pump. And manufacturers and other users of capital equipment want that equipment to be integrated seamlessly into their supply, production, marketing, and services operations. As explored in chapters 5, 6, and 8, this requires manufacturers to get much closer to their customers and form partnerships to offer solutions to the design and production processes of their clients, as well as to the sales and servicing of products. This is in contrast to the old model of offering products only, and asking end users to integrate them into a completed product or into a production process.

Frequently, such partnerships and customized production require better integration of supply chains and better connections from end users to producers to suppliers. Information technology is the tool that facilitates such a connection, but management expertise and flexibility are what enable it to be successful. Firms cannot simply sell isolated products; they must help create the value chain extending from sophisticated end users to a plethora of suppliers. Eastman Chemical, for example, strives to be "a company that gets paid for what it knows—not just what it makes."[17] More and more frequently, companies find that part of the value proposition they need to offer involves "services" such as logistics, product design and maintenance, and finance. All of this requires firms to be flexible, creative, and willing to change rapidly. Capital goods that enable manufacturers to achieve this flexibility, often by incorporating information technology into the production and logistics processes, will be successful in this environment. Given the flexibility and technology base of its manufacturing firms, such an evolution is favorable to producers in the United States as opposed to the production-based companies in other parts of the world, especially the developing world.

Our fifth principal conclusion is that ***globalization***, defined as the deepening and broadening of cross-border trade in goods, services, capital, and labor, ***provides*** both increased ***competition and opportunity*** to U.S. manufacturers. Chapter 7 provides details on the direction and metrics of trade and investment since the 1980s. Currently, over 60 percent of all global trade is in manufactured goods and 70 percent of trade is by industrialized countries. Competition among industrialized countries rewards those who can utilize new technology, innovate rapidly, use capital efficiently, and meet sophisticated customer demands. Earlier conclusions have been that U.S.

manufacturers excel at these strategies, and the productivity boom in manufacturing has helped to keep its unit labor costs competitive.

A growing share of trade, however, is with the developing world, especially the Pacific Rim, China, India, Eastern Europe, and Latin America. While competition based on labor prices is obviously important as these regions become industrial powerhouses, the labor content of manufactured goods continues to decline. Production is frequently organized as partnerships between firms providing high value-added functions such as R&D, management, customized production, and finance, which often are performed in the United States, Japan, or Europe, and those providing lower value functions such as parts production or assembly, which can be done in developing countries like Mexico and China.

As both consumer demand and production expand into new markets like China and India, all production becomes essentially global. Product standards are increasingly global and production, supply, and sales functions will have to be organized globally. Already leading industries like automobiles, cellular phones, aerospace, and televisions are moving in this direction. The capital goods industry, too, will benefit by the expansion of production in the developing world, but it will have to adapt to global standards and competition from new entrants.

The sixth principal conclusion in our study is that ***automation leaders have new opportunities to thrive in the global economy.*** The United States has, and we believe it will continue to have, a competitive position in the capital goods sector. Not only is manufacturing growing around the world, but the role of automation is becoming more vital. Automation, especially when it embeds modern information and communication technology, is a key to the type of flexible production and integrated supply chains needed to compete in the globalized economy. As is discussed in chapter 3, U.S. Department of Labor projections show that U.S. demand for automation equipment will grow faster than the economy as a whole and than manufacturing in particular. This is not because its end markets are growing more rapidly than the norm, but because it will take more market share in capital goods spending. That is, automation is becoming more vital to the production process for a whole host of reasons discussed earlier. Automation today differs significantly from the simple, labor-saving assembly-line improvements of yesteryear. Today it improves production processes and helps integrate the supply chain with real-time information as well as reducing labor inputs. Automation equipment enables manufacturing firms to provide the low cost, quality, fast delivery, rapid innovation, and feasibility needed to thrive in the modern, global economy. This is discussed more fully in chapter 6.

In the developing world, a number of "newly industrialized" economies are beginning to produce more advanced industrial products—for both home and export markets. They also will gradually incorporate the many other functions—design, servicing, logistics, marketing, and finance—needed to provide "solutions" to their customers and partners. Hence, they will begin to use more and more sophisticated automation products, just as their competitors in the United States, the EU, or Japan do. If U.S. capital goods firms continue to invest, innovate, adapt, and integrate into the global markets, there is no reason to believe they cannot be successful in expanding market share in foreign as well as domestic markets.

If our six principal conclusions are correct, as we believe they are, then the period up to 2010 should be a positive one for U.S. manufacturing as a whole and for the automation sector in particular. The following chapters develop these themes in much more detail, and provide considerably more nuance and subtlety than is possible in a brief summary. Finally, it would be a grave error simply to outline the current strengths of U.S. manufacturing and assume continued evolution in a positive trajectory. As alluded to earlier, there are structural problems, largely in the policy arena, that can impede and are impeding the growth and efficiency of U.S. manufacturing. If they are not addressed in a systematic way, the growth model presented here could be eroded or undermined to some extent. The issues include an underperforming educational system and an overzealous tort system, among others. Our final chapter outlines the most pressing of these problems and suggests paths to alleviating them.

Chapter 2

The Transformation of U.S. Manufacturing: A Broad Analytic Framework

by Ernest H. Preeg

This chapter presents a broad analytic framework for the process of radical change under way within U.S. manufacturing industry; indeed, a veritable metamorphosis in how such manufacturing is conducted. The ensuing chapters then assess, within this framework, key specific areas of change in greater depth.

It is a highly dynamic framework developed in terms of three interacting dimensions. The first dimension consists of the surging, mutually reinforcing trends in productivity growth and globalization. These stark quantitative indicators establish the broad parameters within which the many-faceted process of change is proceeding. The second dimension is the more qualitative phenomenon of a macro/microeconomic synergy within the U.S. economy for stimulating innovation and growth which is far more favorable than that in other regions of the world, including Europe and Japan. The third dimension is the continued role of U.S. manufacturing as the principal engine for economic growth despite a paradoxical secular decline in its share of the labor force and gross domestic product (GDP). This final dimension is largely derivative from the first two, and is presented in broader historical perspective in order to provide a critical understanding of the future course of both the U.S. and the global economies.

TWO SURGING, MUTUALLY REINFORCING TRENDS: PRODUCTIVITY GROWTH AND GLOBALIZATION

Exhaustive analysis of the "new economy" has rightly emphasized the surge in productivity growth since the second half of the 1990s and the concurrent rapid globalization of markets. Unfortunately, however, the focus has been on the aggregate U.S. economy. Relatively little attention has been given to the distinctive and central role of the manufacturing sector for both productivity growth and globalization. The starting point for understanding the transformation under way for U.S. manufacturing is thus to present the basic facts about these two upward surging trends, which together define in broadest terms where the U.S. manufacturing sector is headed. The presentation also highlights the sharp sectorial contrasts between the manufacturing and services sectors within the overall U.S. economy, and the inherent interaction between productivity growth and economic globalization.

Surging Yet Volatile Productivity Growth in Manufacturing

Growth in U.S. labor productivity was much higher in manufacturing than in other nonfarm business—almost all services—in each year from 1990 through 2000, as shown in table 2-1. For 1990–1994, the average annual productivity growth for manufacturing was 3.0 percent compared with 1.3 percent in other nonfarm business; for 1995–2000, it was 4.3 percent versus 1.7 percent. The annual productivity growth for all nonfarm business shows the familiar acceleration from 1.6 percent in 1990–1994 to 2.2 percent in 1995–2000. The issue emphasized here is the sectorial divide, wherein the manufacturing sector was the leading edge throughout the decade, with productivity growth two to three times that of services.

The figures for 2001–2002 show a small, temporary reversal of the sectorial relationship, with productivity growth in manufacturing slightly lower than other nonfarm business. This was the result of the exceptionally sharp drop of 7 percent in industrial production during 2001, together with the usual time lag for laying off workers during a recession. More relevant for the overall engine for growth path was that productivity growth in both sectors continued on a positive track throughout the recession, albeit with greater cyclical volatility in the manufacturing sector compared with past recessions.

The central questions raised by table 2-1 are: Why the much higher productivity growth in manufacturing, and will it continue? The answers constitute much of the content of this entire volume. New technology development and application is a major component, as analyzed throughout the new economy debate and updated in chapter 4. Over 90 percent of American patent grants and more than 60 percent of private-sector research and development (R&D) are in the manufacturing sector, while the productivity-enhanced products embodying the new technologies are almost all manufactured products. The concentration of resulting productivity gains in manufacturing is particularly strong for information technology products.

Another broad cause for exceptionally high productivity gains has been

Table 2-1
Growth in Labor Productivity
(percent)

	All Nonfarm Business	Manufacturing	Other Nonfarm Business
1990	1.1	2.5	0.8
1991	1.6	2.3	1.4
1992	3.7	5.3	3.3
1993	0.5	1.9	0.2
1994	1.3	3.0	0.9
1995	0.9	3.8	0.2
1996	2.5	3.5	2.3
1997	2.0	4.3	1.4
1998	2.6	4.9	2.1
1999	2.4	5.1	1.7
2000	2.9	4.1	2.6
2001	1.1	0.9	1.2
2002	4.8	4.5	4.9
1990–1994	1.6	3.0	1.3
1995–2000	2.2	4.3	1.7

Source: Bureau of Labor Statistics, U.S. Department of Labor (DOL) Web site, for manufacturing sector; nonfarm business other than manufacturing is estimated on the basis that manufacturing accounts for about 20 percent of nonfarm business output. (The DOL reports that nonfarm business accounted for 76 percent of GDP in 1996; the manufacturing share was 16 percent in 1998.)

the widespread adoption in recent years of productivity-enhancing corporate strategies, such as "lean manufacturing," to cut costs across the board. The Six Sigma technique developed and popularized by General Electric (GE) is the most familiar, but other approaches abound throughout manufacturing industry. Moreover, the severe squeeze on profits during 2001–2002 was a strong catalyst for intensifying such systematic cost cutting. Chapters 5, 6, and 8 provide numerous examples of how this is being achieved.

The third major reason for accelerated productivity gains in U.S. manufacturing is the rapid pace of globalization of markets. This is the least well understood because it is the most difficult to measure. And yet it is very real and perhaps the most important of all. Traditional comparative cost gains through U.S. exports of capital- and skill-intensive products and imports of labor-intensive components and products have grown exponentially. In addition, large new international economies of scale, beyond classic assembly-line gains, have proliferated in industries characterized by large R&D and initial investment expenditures. If half of the final product is exported, such per unit expenditures are likewise half of what they would be based on the domestic market alone, a relationship of great benefit to the semiconductor, software, telecommunications, and pharmaceutical industries, among others. The least clear yet perhaps largest gains from economic globalization come from integrated cross-border initiatives involving foreign direct investment (FDI) with embedded new technology, trade, and more efficient, "leaner" production operations. This integrated approach plays a major role in the "economic convergence" under way between the industrialized and emerging market economies, epitomized by the U.S.-Mexican relationship within the North American Free Trade Agreement (NAFTA).

The analysis of this complex set of international economic forces in play is left for chapter 7. The introduction here is limited to presenting the broad trends of "economic globalization" and the central role within it of the U.S. manufacturing sector.

The Accelerated Globalization of Markets

"Globalization" is a much abused catchphrase, and it is defined throughout this chapter in simple yet precise economic terms as growth in trade, investment, and other economic activities across national borders at a more rapid rate than growth in national economies, resulting in deeper linkages between national economies and international markets.[1] Based on this definition, the process of globalization has been going on for half a century, but something happened during the 1980s that greatly accelerated the pace of economic globalization, with central impact on the manufacturing sector. Table 2-2 presents key indicators of this acceleration. Trade grew 20 percent faster than global GDP in 1974–1984 (i.e., the 1.2 ratio in line 1 of the table), then accelerated to 70 percent faster in 1985–1990, and to an extraordinary 250 percent faster rate in 1990–2000. A more than quadrupling of FDI as a percentage of global GDP also took place during this period. The other listed indicators are proxies for an even more spectacular acceleration in globalization related to technology transfer and to cross-border financial and telecommunications services which provide much of the infrastructure for the rapid growth in trade and investment.

The central impact of this accelerated globalization on U.S. manufacturing is most important in terms of trade. The manufactures' share of total world trade has grown steadily over the decades. It was less than half in 1960. Recently, however, as shown in table 2-3, the manufactures' share increased from 58 percent in 1990 to 61 percent in 2001, while the share of trade in services was flat at 19–20 percent and that for agriculture declined from 11 percent to 8 percent. Moreover, this rising share of total trade in manufactures has taken place in the context of the very rapid growth of total trade. The net result is that global export of manufactures increased from $2.4

Table 2-2
Economic Globalization: Sharp Acceleration Since the Mid-1980s

	Before	After
1. Ratio of growth in merchandise trade to growth in global GDP	1.2 (1950–64) 1.6 (1964–74) 1.2 (1974–84)	1.7 (1985–90) 3.5 (1990–2000)
2. FDI as a percentage of global GDP	0.4–0.6 (1970–85)	0.9–1.2 (1990–95) 1.2–3.8 (1996–2000)
3. Royalty and licensing fees to U.S. companies	$4 billion (1975) $7 billion (1980) $7 billion (1985)	$17 billion (1990) $38 billion (2000)
4. International telephone calls to and from the United States	500 million minutes (1975) 3 billion minutes (1980) 6 billion minutes (1985)	12 billion minutes (1990) 47 billion minutes (2000)
5. Foreign exchange transactions, daily	$10–20 billion (1973) $60 billion (1983)	$700 billion (1990) $1.5 trillion (1998)
6. Worldwide number of Internet users—% in the United States	World Wide Web did not exist prior to 1991	3 million (1993) 26 million—75% (1995) 171 million—56% (1999) 538 million—31% (2002)

Source: Ernest H. Preeg, *From Here to Free Trade: Essays in Post-Uruguay Round Trade Strategy* (Chicago: University of Chicago Press, 1998), p. 18, with some updates.

trillion in 1990 to $4.5 trillion in 2001. As with the productivity trend described in the previous subsection, trade in manufactures experienced an unusual though slight decline in 2001, but then began to recover growth in 2002.

The impact of this rapid expansion of world trade in manufactures on U.S. manufacturing industry has been to more than double industry engagement in global markets, or its "economic globalization" as defined here. As shown in table 2-4, U.S. exports of manufactures as a percent of manufacturing output doubled from 22 percent in 1982 to 44 percent in 2000, while the import ratio more than doubled from 23 percent to 56 percent. The economic impact of these ratios in terms of value added within and among industries involves complicated calculations, but this does not change the basic fact that the degree of international engagement for manufacturing industry as a whole has more than doubled over a period of 20 years.

The equally striking figures in table 2-4 are the very low levels of trade engagement for the U.S. service industry, only 3 percent to 4 percent in 2000, less than one-tenth that for manufactures. There are several reasons

Table 2-3
Sectorial Shares of World Exports, 1990–2000
(percentage)

	1990	2000	2001
Manufactures	58	62	61
Agricultural products	11	8	8
Mineral fuels	9	9	9
Nonagricultural raw materials	3	2	2
Services	19	19	20

Source: World Trade Organization, *International Trade Statistics.*

for this contrast. A principal reason is that the international engagement in some service industries, including financial and telecommunications services, tends to be more investment- than trade-related.[2] The pattern of U.S. FDI bears this out. In 2000, U.S. direct investment abroad in manufacturing was $44 billion, 32 percent of the total, compared with 42 percent for "finance, investment and real estate," and 7 percent for petroleum. International investment relationships, in any event, are more difficult to measure and assess than trade relationships, and this assessment is left for chapter 7.

* * *

These are the two broad quantitative parameters for defining the fundamental change under way in U.S. manufacturing industry—high productivity growth and rapid globalization of markets. As explained at various points, the two trends are mutually reinforcing. Productivity-enhancing new technologies and leaner manufacturing processes offer extraordinarily large gains from increased international trade and investment, while the resulting more open markets stimulate such innovation further through more intense global competition and new opportunities for cross-border innovating joint ventures. This interactive global process, moreover, is driven principally by initiatives from within the U.S. manufacturing sector, emanating from what is referred to here as the macro/microeconomic synergy.

THE MACRO/MICROECONOMIC SYNERGY

Economic performance is normally analyzed in terms of macro and micro behavior, the former related to the workings of the economy as a whole and the latter to decision-making by individual firms, households, and specific industries. A parallel distinction is made for macroeconomic and microeconomic policies. An explanation of the causes of the high productivity growth in U.S. manufacturing and related positive developments since the 1980s similarly needs to be addressed at both the macro and the micro levels, while including important relationships between the two. The overall U.S. expe-

Table 2-4
U.S. Trade as a Share of Output: Manufactures Versus Services
(percent)

	1982	1998	2000*
Exports of manufactures as a percent of manufacturing output	22	39	44
Imports of manufactures as a percent of manufacturing output	23	54	56
Exports of services as a percent of services output	—	3	3
Imports of services as a percent of services output	—	4	4

*Estimated based on 1998 relationships.

Source: *U.N. International Trade Statistics Yearbook.*

rience has been highly favorable, both in absolute terms and relative to other economies around the world. Indeed, a unique synergy has emerged between the macro and micro forces in play for stimulating innovation, economic growth, and job creation.

The Favorable Macroeconomic Playing Field for Stimulating Innovation and Growth in Manufacturing

The U.S. macroeconomic setting for stimulating technological innovation and productive investment is a combination of a public policy framework oriented toward economic freedom and a private-sector culture well-prepared and accustomed to rising to the challenge—with considerable interaction between the two. The American economy—now being expanded to an integrated continental market including Canada and Mexico—meets these criteria in unprecedented fashion and, even more relevant for the course ahead, on considerably more favorable terms than prevail elsewhere, not only in developing countries but in the industrial economies of Western Europe and Japan as well.

These international competitive relationships, however, are not static but in a state of constant change, with the United States working to improve its macroeconomic setting, while others, for the most part, seek to catch up. In this comparative context, seven basic dimensions of the macro setting are offered as benchmarks for the overall positive assessment. The focus remains on the manufacturing sector, with particular reference to areas where the current U.S. setting can be improved. Specific recommendations for improvement, however, are left for chapter 9.

1. Financing.—Financing new productive investment is at the center of the economic growth process, and U.S. financial services are clearly at the forefront in providing responsive, lower-cost funding to changing investment opportunities. The unique U.S. venture capital market is only one example of such responsiveness. Moreover, investment financing goes well beyond banks and brokers, and much financing is generated from within manufacturing companies. As for improvements, the U.S. tax system is exceedingly complex and in some ways distortive in its impact. Corporate profits, unusually among advanced nations, are taxed twice. The need for greater transparency for investments, particularly related to accounting practices, is agonizingly apparent in light of the Enron and other recent scandals, and should become an example of how American companies are quick to respond once they recognize a problem and set their minds to resolving it.

2. *Science and technology.*—The United States is the clear leader in basic scientific research and the development of new technologies, as is evident in the surge of information and related technology development and application during the 1990s. More patents are granted in the United States than in the rest of the world combined, and the number of patents granted annually in the United States has doubled since the late 1980s. Science and technology leadership is a symbiosis of public- and private-sector innovation, including national laboratories, university research, and more targeted corporate R&D programs. A particularly helpful American development has been the evolution of geographic "clusters" of concentrated private-sector interaction in particular high-technology sectors, such as computers and more recently biotechnology around Boston, semiconductors in Silicon Valley, and software in northern Virginia. Two broad areas for further improvement are deregulation, particularly in the telecommunications sector, and curtailment of debilitating lawsuits.

3. *Human resources.*—The United States again stands out in the quality and flexibility of its labor force to adapt to continually changing requirements. University training in science, engineering, business, and economics attracts students worldwide. Corporate training programs, especially in the manufacturing sector, have grown along with skill requirements in the labor force. Private/public initiative is noteworthy in community college programs focused on job-related technical skills. The need for improvement, however, is equally stark in this area. American primary and secondary school performance compares poorly with other countries on reading, science, and math. Teacher training at the university level is a related weak component. Greater labor market flexibility, including increased mobility for pension and health care programs, would be useful. In broadest terms, human resource development is an issue of economic freedom, from the freedom of parents to do the best for their children to that of workers seeking to improve their productive abilities and apply them to maximum gain.

4. *Economic infrastructure.*—This is a wide-ranging area, from more traditional transportation, telephone, and electric power capabilities to rapidly expanding new economy telecommunications and financial services needs. The United States, in most respects, provides a relatively favorable infrastructure for productive investment, but there are also obvious weaknesses. The

central new economy themes for improvement are deregulation and privatization, not only within the United States but throughout the world. Among U.S. weaknesses in this context are marine transportation and broadband telecommunications. The energy sector is another important challenge, and full and effective deregulation is the rational way, with recent problems in California and energy companies like Enron providing useful lessons in the pitfalls of less than full, ineffective deregulation.

5. *Market size.*—The U.S.—now North American—market offers the broadest scope and depth for new productive investment and revenues, as is clearly evident in the accelerating movement of foreign companies to establish production in North America. The large market incentives, moreover, are particularly attractive for advanced technology products, for which affluent American consumers provide a very large initial customer base and more customized products benefit from customer proximity. The only other market of comparable size is the European Union, recently enhanced through a single currency, but regulatory restrictions on continentwide marketing in Europe still abound.

6. *Open trade and investment.*—The U.S. market is also the most open internationally, particularly for the manufacturing sector, which adds to the competitiveness and quick adaptability of American industry. American agriculture is a glaring contrast of high and rising protection through agricultural subsidies and import restrictions, but this sector is of declining importance in world trade, in part because of such high protection throughout the world. The international Achilles' heel for the U.S. manufacturing sector, however, is the chronic, record trade deficit, an issue addressed in chapter 7.

7. *A stable, transparent, and business-friendly rule of law.*—The absence of such a legal framework for private property and commerce is central to the definition of a "less developed" country, while the U.S. legal system, developed over more than two centuries of rapid industrialization, is among the most responsive. Longer-term investment strategies based on innovation and change can proceed only within a reasonably predictable legal framework, which generally prevails in the United States. The legal frameworks in Europe and Japan, in contrast, are less certain, particularly with respect to labor laws and technical standards. Once again, however, there is considerable scope for improvement in the legal setting for business in America, including in the areas of tort litigation, antitrust, and environmental laws.

* * *

These are the broad lines of the macroeconomic setting, which at this point are, on balance, highly favorable for the United States compared with other parts of the world. In Europe, the Macroeconomic Policy Group of the Center for European Policy Studies in Brussels concluded in June 2002:

> Restoring productivity growth in Euroland can only be achieved through a removal of supply-side distortions, particularly through progress in labor market reforms. The complicated EU-wide processes that are supposed to foster this progress . . . are at best useless and may even make matters worse. . . . [Meanwhile], the "new economy" seems alive and well in the U.S. Output per man-hour continued to rise throughout the recession, and the rebound of early 2002 sent productivity growth to a record pace (+8% in Q1). By contrast in Europe, productivity growth has fallen to close to zero.

For Japan, there is consensus that renewal of economic growth requires structural reforms related to deregulation and economic freedom, but the Japanese political system remains largely incapable of responding. As for the emerging market economies of Asia, Latin America, and Central Europe, macroeconomic reform objectives follow similar lines, largely based on the U.S. paradigm, but progress is highly uneven. The relative paths of such systemic "convergence" are addressed in chapter 7 as an important consideration for U.S. corporate strategy in the decade ahead.

Given this overall macroeconomic picture, the central question becomes how individual companies are responding to the new economy setting of rapid change in technological prowess and market orientation, or in other words, the microeconomic response.

Microeconomic Response of U.S. Companies to This Favorable Macro Setting

The wide-ranging micro response is examined throughout the ensuing six chapters and is not elaborated here. Needless to say, this is where the real action takes place for raising productivity, stimulating growth, creating higher skill jobs, and transmitting the benefits of the U.S. new economy throughout the world. Among the specific issues addressed in what follows are the shifting structure of the U.S. manufacturing labor force toward professional and high-skill technical workers, the ever more central role of new technology development and application, the broadening of value added to include customized products and product services, outsourcing up and down the supply chain, broadened application of automated equipment, and streamlined management organization.

* * *

The synergy between the favorable macroeconomic and microeconomic forces in play are self-evident in conceptual terms but difficult to measure with specificity. The bottom-line engine for growth result, however, is without doubt, although it needs clarification with respect to the parallel secular decline in the manufacturing share of U.S. GDP.

U.S. MANUFACTURING REMAINS THE PRINCIPAL ENGINE FOR ECONOMIC GROWTH DESPITE A PARADOXICAL SECULAR DECLINE IN ITS SHARES OF THE LABOR FORCE AND GDP

The U.S. manufacturing sector remains the principal engine for growth within a new technology-driven economy, as explained throughout this study, and is its most important conclusion. Nevertheless, this critical assessment is not well understood, and highly misleading statements to the contrary about the "hollowing out" of U.S. manufacturing abound. One cause of confusion is the apparent paradox of a secular decline in the manufacturing shares of the labor force and GDP proceeding in parallel with a continued central role of manufacturing as the engine for growth. It is therefore helpful to describe first the secular decline, and then, from this highly dynamic trend, to explain how the manufacturing sector emerges as a more compact and even more powerful engine for growth.

Declining Shares of U.S. Labor Force and GDP

Increased labor productivity, by definition, means achieving the same quantity of economic output with less labor. The record 4.1 percent productivity increase in U.S. manufacturing in 2000 meant that the same amount of goods could be produced in 2000 as in 1999 with 4.1 percent less labor or, in a more positive growth context, the same labor force could increase output 4.1 percent above the previous year. In fact, during 2000 manufacturing output rose 5.7 percent while hours worked fell by only 0.9 percent. This same heavy skewing of productivity gains toward increased output rather than decreased employment prevailed throughout the high-growth 1990s, when labor productivity in manufacturing grew almost 4 percent per year, while the labor force in the sector declined only slightly, by 4 percent, over the entire decade.

Even with such sustained growth in output, however, a secular decline in the share of the labor force in manufacturing has been under way since the 1950s, as a direct result of relatively higher productivity gains—and thus relatively lower costs and prices—in manufacturing compared with the rest of the economy. During the first half of the 20th century, the manufacturing share of total employment ranged between 25 percent and 30 percent, down somewhat during the Great Depression and up again during World War II and the immediate postwar years. Then, beginning about 1950, as shown in table 2-5, the manufacturing share declined steadily from 29.0 percent in 1950 to 20.4 percent in 1980 to 13.7 percent in 2000. In absolute terms, the number of employees in manufacturing declined only moderately, from a high of 20.3 million in 1980 to 18.5 million in 2000, but this was in the context of total U.S. employment rising from 99 million to 135 million.

Table 2-5
The Declining Manufacturing Share of U.S. Employment

Year	Total Employment (millions)	Manufacturing Employment (millions)	Manufacturing Employment as a Percentage of Total
1950	52.4	15.2	29.0
1960	60.7	16.8	27.7
1970	78.7	19.4	24.7
1980	99.3	20.3	20.4
1990	118.8	19.1	16.1
2000	135.2	18.5	13.7
2001	135.1	17.7	13.1
2002	136.4	16.5	12.1

Source: U.S. Department of Labor, Bureau of Labor Statistics, *Employment and Earnings*, Tables A1 and B1.

One related result of the consistently high gains in manufacturing labor productivity is that production worker wages as a percent of value added have dropped sharply, from 39 percent in 1950 to 26 percent in 1980 to about 18 percent in 2000. This decline has important consequences for the domestic labor market, with employment opportunities shifting to higher-skill, nonproduction workers, and for international competition, where labor cost differentials among nations are a declining factor for determining trade patterns.[3]

The downturn in 2001–2002, of course, had a severe, short-term adverse impact on employment in manufacturing. Labor productivity increased by 1 percent together with a 7 percent decline in industrial production, with a resulting loss of two million jobs, thus bringing the share of the labor force in manufacturing down sharply from 13.7 percent in 2000 to 13.1 percent in 2001 and to 12.1 percent in 2002. This abrupt decline is again related to the greater cyclical volatility of manufacturing in the "new economy," and should reverse in similar fashion to a relatively higher pace of job creation as the economy resumes healthy growth. But whatever the short-term cyclical swings, the secular decline in the share of jobs in manufacturing continues and appears to have accelerated since the mid-1990s, principally as a result of more rapid growth in labor productivity. On the current course, the share of the labor force in manufacturing will be 10 percent to 11 percent by 2010, compared with over 80 percent in services.

The share of U.S. GDP in manufacturing has been on a similar secular decline, as is shown in table 2-6, and for the same reasons. The GDP share has fallen steadily from 27.7 percent in 1959 to 22.8 percent in 1977 to 15.9 percent in 2000 and was about 15 percent in 2002. The principal cause

Table 2-6
Manufacturing Share of Gross Domestic Product
(percent, in current dollars)

1947	26.9	1987	18.7
1959	27.7	1997	16.6
1977	22.8	2000	15.9

Source: *Survey of Current Business*, June 2000 and November 2001.

of the decline was again the relatively higher growth in productivity in manufactures compared with the rest of the economy. And again, a 15 percent GDP share for manufacturing compares with 80 percent in the services sector.

But No Decline in Manufacturing Output

The declining shares of the labor force and GDP in manufactures, however, do not mean that U.S. manufacturing industry is producing less goods, but rather that, as a result of faster productivity growth, manufactured products are being produced at lower cost—and price—compared with services, and thus relatively fewer dollars to GDP accounts.[4] In fact, during the 1990s, manufacturing output in quantitative terms grew faster than all nonfarm business (4.1 percent versus 3.9 percent), while the average price changes for 1994–1999 were –0.4 percent for manufacturing, compared with +1.5 percent for all private business. This critical distinction between relatively higher growth in the quantity of manufacturing output and a productivity-induced decline in the share of current-dollar GDP can be illustrated even more sharply with reference to earlier, similar trends in the agricultural sector.

The Half-True Analogy with Agriculture: No Hollowing Out

The same productivity-induced decline in the shares of the labor force and GDP took place in the agricultural sector beginning in the late 19th century. Extraordinary gains in agricultural productivity resulted in a sharp decline in the agricultural share of U.S. employment from 41 percent in 1900 to 12 percent in 1950 to 2 percent in 2000. The share of GDP in agriculture, forestry, and fishing showed a similar decline, from 8.5 percent in 1947 to only 1.4 percent in 2000. In parallel, however, and in spite of these massive declines in the share of labor and GDP, American farmers continue to feed—indeed, overfeed—the U.S. population, export a third or more of production, and accumulate large surpluses that the government is obliged to dispose of.

The central and overwhelmingly positive conclusion is that there has been no "hollowing out" of American agricultural production. Rather, an amazing transformation has occurred in how farming is conducted, to the point where 2 percent of the population produces far more food than over half of the U.S. population did in the 19th century, in broader historical perspective, more than 80 percent to 90 percent of the world population throughout most of human history.

The analogy of this productivity-driven growth in agricultural output with more recent events in the manufacturing sector is valid. ***There has been no hollowing out of U.S. manufacturing industry.*** The output of manufactured goods, as earlier for agricultural goods, has continued to rise at least as fast as the overall economy, but at ever lower relative costs and with relatively less labor. U.S. domestic steel shipments rose from 84 million tons in 1980 to 108 million tons in 2000, during which time the number of man-hours needed to produce a ton of steel declined from ten to four, with a corresponding decline in the value of steel production to less than 1 percent of GDP. Even more dramatic relative cost declines are reported regularly in the semiconductor and computer sectors.

The analogy with agriculture, however, is frequently overdrawn, with misleading conclusions as to the central role of manufacturing industry for overall growth, and, even more important, for where the sector is headed in the decade ahead.

The Half-False Analogy: A Distinctive Structural Transformation in Manufacturing

The half-wrong part of the analogy with agriculture is that whereas farmers remain farmers, manufacturing industry is going through a structural transformation to something very different from what it was a half-century ago.

Farm size grew and farms became far more mechanized, but farmers today remain devoted almost entirely to raising their on-site crops. The R&D that led to massive productivity gains in agriculture was conducted off the farm, in government and nonfarm private research centers. The application of new technologies to supply farmers with machinery, fertilizers, and new varieties of seed was likewise carried out by other businesses, principally in the manufacturing sector. The processing and marketing of farm commodities were again the domain of other sectors of the economy. And "globalization" for farmers remains limited to selling the home product to other companies for export. Today's American farm is a bigger and higher-tech business than the family farm of yore, but the new economy farmer is still on the farm, limiting himself to raising a maximum crop for market.

The manufacturing firm today, in fundamental contrast, is very different from what it was, and is in rapid process of further fundamental change. Production is more R&D- and investment-intensive. Product cycles are shorter, with a premium placed on innovation and the introduction of new products. The labor force is of higher skill with relatively fewer production workers. Deeper supplier relationships up and down the production line proliferate. New within-the-firm activities in the areas of financing, marketing, and product service broaden the scope of corporate value added. Direct participation in globalization is multifaceted. The net consequence is that corporate organization is being reformulated, in some extreme instances toward an ill-defined "virtual company."

Thus, the new economy manufacturing company is on a very different and more expansive restructuring track than was agriculture. The manufacturing sector will never contract to 2 percent of the labor force or 1 percent of GDP, as agriculture has. Rather, it could, over time, metamorphose itself into something with a larger share of labor and GDP, perhaps even with a new appellation. In any event, the transformation under way within manufacturing is far more complex than the agricultural experience, and therefore needs more searching analysis.

* * *

There should be no doubt, however, that the manufacturing sector remains the principal engine for growth, albeit in more compact and continually changing form. R&D, patent applications, and investment in new plant and equipment comprise an ever larger share of value added within the sector. The application of growth-inducing new technologies throughout the economy—including in the health care, telecommunications, transportation, finance, and retail service sectors—derives from products innovated and produced in the manufacturing sector. As described in subsequent chapters, new technology-intensive products are becoming more customer-oriented and require broader application services, including training, all of which are increasingly provided by the manufacturing companies that develop the products. And the global transmission of new growth-generating and job-creating products is the domain of the manufacturing sector, accounting for over 60 percent of U.S. trade and a third of foreign direct investment. The declining shares paradox can thus be explained as doing a lot more with a lot less, with 13 percent rather than 29 percent of the labor force, while having an even more powerful impact on economic growth at home and abroad.

THE PROSPECT AHEAD FOR U.S. MANUFACTURING: A MORE CONCENTRATED AND DYNAMIC ENGINE FOR GROWTH OPERATING ON AN EVER MORE GLOBAL SCALE

This analytic presentation of the transformation of U.S. manufacturing industry up to the present is highly dynamic, subject to constant change driven by technological and organizational innovation. Looking ahead, such a dynamic model is extremely difficult to project. The manufacturing sector is also far from monolithic, and circumstances will vary greatly among sectors and subsectors. Nevertheless, four broad directions of change are relatively clear, at least through 2010 and probably 2020:

1. **High-impact concentration.** The decline of the relative size of the manufacturing sector, down to 15 percent of GDP and 12 percent of the labor force, will continue, probably by another couple of percentage points by 2010 or 2015. This smaller share of the overall economy, however, is more concentrated for creating and bringing to market new products with high-growth impact throughout the U.S. economy, and globally through international trade and investment. Work on the assembly line is of decreasing relative importance, while value added is more concentrated in high-skill employees, R&D, and capital investment. This again is the "engine for growth" phenomenon, with a more compact manufacturing sector as the principal source for rapid technological advance and overall economic growth.
2. **Constantly shifting product lines.** With notable exceptions, manufacturing companies are in a steady state of new product development at home and abroad. High-tech companies, by definition, are creating new products, while others upgrade and reorient product lines and have enhanced technical capability to do so quickly. Proliferating information available to consumers and the globalization of markets increase the importance of relating changing patterns of potential customer demand to product line decisions. The whole process puts a premium on companies being at the leading edge of lower-cost production processes and in responding to shifting customer preferences.
3. **More volatile cyclical swings.** The 2001–2002 experience demonstrated greater downside cyclical volatility for manufactures, compared with the services sector, within the new technology-intensive and more globalized economy, while 2003 promises a similar upside volatility. International trade entails much wider cyclical swings than occur within the U.S. economy, and U.S. manufacturing industry is twice as deeply engaged in trade as it was in the early 1980s. The more concentrated manufacturing sector is also more heavily impacted than in the past by cyclical waves of new technology application. Successful manufacturing companies, as a consequence, need to be more agile and flexible than in the past in responding to cyclical ups and downs.
4. **Proactive, forward-thinking management.** All of the foregoing comes together in what will be a natural market selection of successful proactive and forward-thinking management teams. Corporate strategies are more complex and subject to constant change. Firms that can rest on their name brand laurels are increasingly rare. American corporate culture, in this critical regard, demonstrates a superior managerial response compared with competitors in other parts of the world. The favorable macroeconomic setting has long engendered a more agile and innovative response by American companies to changing circumstances. One distinctive manifestation of this facility to adapt is the high degree of peer interaction among American managers seeking to improve performance, especially

intensive within the geographic clusters of high-tech companies noted earlier. Wide-ranging industry associations highlight forward-thinking discussion about how to deal with emerging problems and opportunities.[5] A more agile management response to ever more complex market opportunities also has a technology dimension in the need for more powerful information systems keyed to decision-making at all levels of management.

* * *

This is the broad prospect for U.S. manufacturing industry in the decade ahead, as examined in greater detail in the following chapters. How much beyond a decade these patterns will prevail is not foreseeable. The pace of change in terms of technology, global market scope, and corporate organization is simply too rapid and uneven. The rates of change, in any event, cannot be projected by straight or even exponential lines, and thus the most sophisticated econometric models fall by the wayside. The economic path ahead will rather be determined by wide-ranging micro decisions in corporate boardrooms, and within manufacturing boardrooms most of all.

Chapter 3

The Changing Structure of U.S. Manufacturing and Its Labor Force

by Daniel J. Meckstroth

The first decade of the new century will be both promising and challenging. Basing our analysis on projections issued by the U.S. Department of Labor,[1] we think economic growth should be robust and capital goods manufacturers can expect investment spending to grow faster than consumer demand and the general economy. Other important trends to expect are the following:

- A shortage of workers in their prime working age (25 to 54 years old) will have to be filled by younger and older workers. Manufacturing occupations are shifting toward professional and technical workers, raising the educational requirements of the sector.
- The manufacturing sector will use less of the economy's resources, but provide physical output that grows about as fast as the total economy.
- The trade deficit in manufactured goods was 10 percent of consumption in 2000. The rising trade deficit explains most of the decline in manufacturing's share (measured in current dollars) of the domestic economy.
- Fast-growing industries within manufacturing tend to be new industries or established industries producing new products. The industries that seem to thrive are ones where competition leads to new products.
- Exposure to foreign competition by itself cannot differentiate between fast- and slow-growing industries. Many fast-growing industries seem to thrive amid intense foreign competition. One success factor is that fast-growing industries counter import competition with a higher rate of exports.
- The exposure to intense foreign competition, continuing waves of innovative products and production methods, and outsourcing and downsizing will lead to strong

productivity growth through 2010. Manufacturing is not expected to generate many new jobs.

MAJOR TRENDS IN THE U.S. ECONOMIC OUTLOOK

The U.S. Department of Labor, Office of Occupational Statistics and Employment Projections, in late 2001 issued its output and employment projections for the U.S. economy and detailed industries. The general economic growth and industry growth projections were prepared in the summer of 2001, based on simulations from the DRI-WEFA macroeconomic model.[2] The models use long-term economic growth assumptions in the simulation with no attempt to forecast business-cycle fluctuations. For this reason, the recession that began April 2001 should not materially change the forecast for 2010. In every post-World War II decade, the U.S. economy has faced one or more economic recessions. Short-term business recessions are accompanied by relatively quick recoveries, so in a ten-year forecast the long-term projections do not change very much.

Table 3-1 summarizes the economic projections for inflation-adjusted gross domestic product (GDP). GDP grew at a 3.0 percent annual rate from the peak in the economic cycle in 1979 to the next cyclical peak in 1989, and at a 3.1 percent annual rate from 1989 to the current cyclical peak in 2000. Forecasters expect inflation-adjusted economic output will expand at a faster 3.4 percent annual rate in the period from 2000 to 2010.

Several major factors that are driving the general economic forecast will lead to changes at the industry level. One factor is that low inflation and interest rates, combined with a relatively strong job market, will improve U.S. consumers' finances and enable them to expand spending at a slightly faster rate in 2000–2010 than in the previous decade. Nevertheless, technological innovation and changing lifestyles in the United States will alter the mix of goods and services purchased. Currently, over half of all homes have a personal computer, and the use of the Internet is expanding rapidly. As a result, sales of computers and software are expected to have strong growth. The rapid expansion of Internet usage is also increasing the number of telephone lines per household. Telephone service is expected to grow rapidly because of consumer and business demand for mobile communication with cellular phones.

Another factor that influences the economic outlook is demographic changes in the population that will lead to adjustments in the mix of consumer spending. The 45–54-year-olds will replace the 35–44-year-old age group as the largest age cohort by 2010. A higher proportion of the population in the peak earning and spending age bracket should lead to strong growth in the purchases of furniture and household items. The aging of post-World War II baby boomers should also expand the market for health care—particularly for prescription drugs and over-the-counter medicine industries.

Table 3-1
Gross Domestic Product by Major Demand Category

	Billions of dollars	Inflation-adjusted average annual rate of change		
	Actual 2000	*Actual 1979–1989*	*Actual 1989–2000*	*Projected 2000–2010*
Gross domestic product	9,873	3.0	3.1	3.4
Personal consumption expenditures	6,728	3.2	3.3	3.5
Gross private domestic investment	1,768	2.4	6.0	5.2
Government spending	1,741	3.0	1.4	2.1

Source: U.S. Department of Labor, Bureau of Labor Statistics, November 2001.

Rising affluence, earlier retirement, and increased leisure time for the aging population in the United States explain why there should be above-average growth in recreation goods and services.

The drive for productivity improvements in the first decade of the 21st century should lead to inflation-adjusted business investment spending growing faster than consumer spending. The rate of growth in investment, however, is likely to be less robust than in the 1990s. The deceleration in the rate of investment is attributable to slower growth rates in purchases of computers and communications equipment. Both types of equipment are now closer to the saturation point than they were in the 1990s. Inflation-adjusted computer purchases by business are expected to increase 15 percent a year in 2000 to 2010 versus a 35 percent annual rate of growth in the previous ten years. Similarly, inflation-adjusted spending on communications equipment is projected to grow 4.5 percent annually through 2010, versus growth of about 12 percent a year in the 1990s.

DEMOGRAPHIC CHANGES THAT INFLUENCE THE OUTLOOK

The demographic changes that will affect the working age population by 2010 have, for the most part, already occurred. In fact, events that took place decades ago will drive population and labor force changes. These events include the post-World War II baby boom from 1946 through 1964; children born to baby boomers, which resulted in increased births from the late 1970s through the early 1990s; and the massive increase in migration into the United States from abroad that started in the 1970s and continues today.

Table 3-2
Total Population and Civilian Noninstitutional Population by Age, Sex, and Race

	Thousands of people		Average annual rate of change		
	Actual 2000	*Projected 2010*	*Actual 1980–1990*	*Actual 1990–2000*	*Projected 2000–2010*
Total, all ages	275,700	300,300	0.9	1.0	0.9
Total, 16 years & older	209,699	233,658	1.2	1.0	1.1
16–24	34,453	39,201	−1.1	0.3	1.3
25–54	118,927	122,716	2.2	1.2	0.3
55–64	23,615	34,846	−0.4	1.3	4.0
65–74	17,809	20,591	1.4	0.1	1.5
75 and older	14,896	16,304	2.6	2.5	0.9
Men	100,731	112,319	1.3	1.1	1.1
Women	108,968	121,338	1.1	1.0	1.1
White non-Hispanic	152,035	159,153	0.6	0.5	0.5
African American	25,218	29,877	1.9	1.6	1.7
Hispanic	22,393	30,359	5.2	3.5	3.1
Asian and others	10,054	14,269	6.3	3.6	3.6

Source: U.S. Department of Labor, Bureau of Labor Statistics, November 2001.

Population Growth

Rapid population growth is expected to occur at both ends of the age distribution scale, but not in the middle. The total population, age 16 years and older, shown in table 3-2, is projected to grow at a 1.1 percent annual rate from 2000 to 2010, very close to the 1.0 percent annual growth achieved in the previous ten years. There are, nevertheless, important differences in the composition of the population growth. The youth cohort, 16 to 24 years, grew at a below-average 0.3 percent annual rate in the 1990s, but those persons are expected to increase at a 1.3 percent annual rate in 2000–2010. At the other end of the working age population, the number of people between the ages of 55 and 64 years old grew at a 1.3 percent annual rate in the 1990s and should expand at a 4.0 percent annual rate in 2000–2010. This leaves the prime working age population age group (25–54 years old) rising at a slower-than-average 0.3 percent annual rate from 2000 to 2010.

Most of the growth in the prime working age population will come from immigration. The Hispanic population is predicted to increase at a 3.1 percent annual rate in 2000–2010, and the Asian population should increase at an even faster 3.6 percent annual rate. By 2010, the working age Hispanic population will be larger than the African American population.

There are important implications of the population changes:

- Older people have more assets and will demand higher value goods and services.
- An aging population will accelerate the preference for services since those over 55 have already accumulated many long-lived durable goods.
- A high portion of older people's budgets will be devoted to medical care and elder care.
- College enrollments will grow rapidly because the 16–24 age bracket will grow faster than average.
- The Hispanic culture will become more prominent in the United States and marketing campaigns will increasingly target this minority group.

Labor Force Participation

The labor force participation rate is the proportion of the population that decides to work. In 2000, the overall labor force participation rate was 67.2 percent.[3] In other words, 67.2 percent of all people 16 years of age and older were working full-time, working part-time, or looking for work. One of the long-term trends in the participation rate is that the rate is declining for men, while increasing for women. In terms of the structure by age, participation rates of the 16–24 year old group have been declining as young people stay in school longer to pursue a higher education. The peak age for labor force participation is between the ages of 25 and 54. After age 55, and particularly after age 65, the proportion of people who choose to work declines sharply. The labor force participation rate is substantially higher for Hispanic men than for men of other races, and for African American women than for women of other races.

Policies and attitudes toward working at an older age are now in a period of transition. Private pension plans are changing from defined benefits to those based on defined contributions, increasing the incentive to work more years in order to accumulate retirement assets. Federal Social Security policy is also changing in ways that favor postponing retirement. The full benefit retirement age will increase in phases from age 65 to age 67. In addition, the earnings penalty or tax on workers who collect Social Security benefits at age 65 and older, but continue to work, has been eliminated.

Figure 3-1 shows the labor force participation rates by age and sex for 2000 and projections for 2010. The outlook is for male participation to continue to decline slightly from age 16 through age 64. A rising retirement age for Social Security and other incentives to work longer will push up the participation rate for men in the 65–74 age cohort versus the group's participation rate. The participation rate for women is expected to continue to

Figure 3-1
Labor Force Participation Rates for Men and Women by Age Cohort, 2000, and Projected 2010 Labor Force as a Percent of the Population

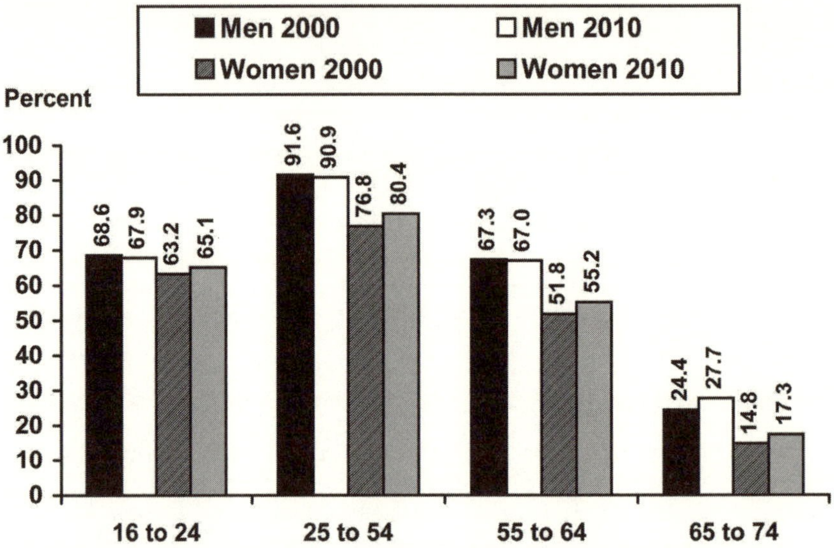

Source: U.S. Department of Labor, Bureau of Labor Statistics, November 2001.

approach the rate for men at every age cohort. Overall, the total participation rate is projected to increase slightly over the decade, rising by 0.3 percentage point to 67.5 percent in 2010.

Labor Force Growth

The growth of the labor force reflects changes in population and participation rates. Over the decade 2000–2010, the labor force is projected to increase at a 1.1 percent annual rate—the same as the rate of increase in the population. An important finding is that workers in the prime working ages of 25 to 54 will likely be in short supply. The labor force growth rate for 25–54-year-olds is expected to be only 0.5 percent a year.

Younger and older workers will fill the shortage of prime working age people. The cohort of workers aged 16–24 years old is expected to grow at a 1.4 percent annual rate. However, the fastest labor force growth will have to come from older workers. The pool of 55–64-year-old workers should expand at a 4.3 percent annual rate; 65–74-year-olds, at a 2.9 percent annual rate; and 75 and older workers, at a 1.3 percent annual rate.

It is important to keep in mind that changes in the labor force are a flow process. The number of people in the labor force in 2010 will consist of those who were in the labor force in 2000 plus the new entrants, less those leaving over the ten-year period. From 2000 to 2010, 20 million men are expected to join the labor force and 13 million men will leave the labor force, resulting in a labor force of 82 million men in 2010. Over the same time period, 21 million women are expected to enter the labor force, while 11 million women are projected to leave. The net result of these labor flows is a labor force of 76 million women in 2010.

The challenges for business to attract a productive workforce in the future include the following:

- Managing and motivating a diverse workforce that will be more diverse in terms of race and will include a higher proportion of women.
- Retaining an older and younger group of workers by being imaginative in structuring hours, providing part-time work opportunities, and offering flexible benefit programs.
- Developing extensive training programs to prepare young people for skilled jobs.
- Making the content and compensation of jobs more attractive.

G-7 Demographic Projections

Aging of the population and potential future labor shortages are not a problem only in the United States; rather they are symptomatic of the developed nations of the world. Table 3-3 shows the projected annual rate of growth in population over the period 2000 to 2010 by age cohorts for the G-7 nations. Populations in the United States and Canada are expected to grow 0.9 percent a year in the decade, but the major countries in continental Europe and Japan can expect very little growth in their overall populations. Annual population growth projections call for no growth in Italy, 0.1 percent annual growth in Japan, 0.2 percent a year growth in Germany and the United Kingdom, and 0.3 percent growth in France.

The main reason for the slow population growth in developed countries is that fertility rates have plummeted. In the early-to-mid-1960s, every developed nation had a fertility rate at or above the replacement rate (2.1 children per woman) that is needed to maintain a stable population in the future. Since about 1965, every developed nation's fertility rate has dropped to or below the replacement rate. The average fertility rate from 1995 to 2000 in the United States was 2.0 children per woman, but only 1.6 children in Canada. In continental Europe and Japan, however, the fertility rate is drastically low. The average fertility rate in the latter part of the 1990s in Japan was 1.4 children, in Germany it was 1.3 children, and in Italy and much of Southern and Eastern Europe it was only 1.2 children.[4] Many of these countries are less friendly than the United States toward immigration, and hence cannot make up the shortfall in indigenous growth.

The combination of falling fertility in developed countries and the fact that the post-World War II baby boom will be moving out of the working

Table 3-3
Population Growth by Age in G-7 Countries, 2000 to 2010
(Annual average percentage change)

	Canada	France	Germany	Italy	Japan	United Kingdom	United States
Total, all ages	0.9	0.3	0.2	0.0	0.1	0.2	0.9
15–24	0.8	−0.2	0.6	−1.6	−2.5	0.8	1.1
25–54	0.4	−0.3	0.0	−0.2	−0.7	−0.2	0.2
55–64	4.2	3.7	−0.7	0.8	1.2	2.0	4.0
65–74	1.8	−0.7	2.1	0.1	1.4	0.8	1.5
75 and older	2.4	2.3	2.3	2.5	4.1	0.9	1.1
65 and older, percent of total							
2000/ 2010	12.7/ 14.2	16.0/ 16.8	16.2/ 19.7	18.1/ 20.6	17.0/ 21.8	15.7/ 16.7	12.6/ 13.2

Source: U.S. Department of Commerce, Bureau of the Census, International Database.

age cohort by 2010 results in an actual decline in the prime working age population in many developed countries. In all the G-7 countries, the prime working age cohort (ages 25 to 54) growth is substantially below that of the general population. Canada has the fastest prime working age population growth in the 2000s (0.4 percent), followed by the United States (0.2 percent). The prime working age population growth is projected to be zero in Germany and actually to decline in France, Italy, and the United Kingdom. In Japan, the prime working age population should decline the fastest of any G-7 country, 0.7 percent a year from 2000 to 2010.

The population is aging in all the G-7 countries. The bottom row of table 3–3 shows the percent of the population in each country that is aged 65 and older in the year 2000 and projected for 2010. In the United States, 12.6 percent of the population was elderly in 2000, and that percentage is expected to rise to 13.2 percent in 2010. In all the other G-7 countries, the aging is much worse. In Italy, for example, 18.1 percent of the population is already elderly, and those 65 and older will rise to 20.6 percent in 2010. The country with a severe aging crisis on its hands is Japan. The percentage that are elderly is expected to increase 4.8 percentage points, from 17.0 percent in 2000 to 21.8 percent in 2010. This is both the highest percentage of elderly in the G-7 and the largest percentage increase in older people over the ten-year period.

There are serious implications for the United States' major competitors in Western Europe and Japan coming from demographic changes. One is that economic growth in Western Europe and Japan may slow dramatically because their working age population is declining. The Organization for Economic Cooperation and Development (OECD) estimates that the declining labor force will subtract 0.4 percent a year from potential economic growth in the European Union (EU) and will reduce potential growth 0.7 percent a year in Japan between 2000 and 2025.[5] While the declining working age population problem could be mitigated if older people delayed retirement, the fact is that the trend in Europe, as well as in the United States, is for men to retire earlier, not later. With very generous public pension and welfare benefits in Europe that are paid for on a "pay-as-you-go" basis with social taxes, all G-7 countries except the United Kingdom are expected to face a severe crisis in their public retirement and health benefit systems.[6]

A second consequence of the demographic changes in developed countries is that there simply will not be enough people working for governments to be able to pay the promised benefits to retirees. In most Western European countries, the adjustment will require major increases in already high taxes, increased government debt, and/or significant cuts in social benefits. The ability to carry more government debt is limited by the rules of the EU. Since it is very unlikely that European governments will renege on promised pension and welfare benefits, large tax increases will be needed to pay future benefits. The shifting of additional economic resources away from the private sector to nonproductive uses should depress economic growth prospects for Western Europe.

The United States may achieve a competitive advantage as Western Europe continues to struggle with Eurosclerosis. First, public pensions are less generous in the United States than in most of Western Europe. And second, the dependency statistics are not as serious in the United States vis-à-vis Western Europe and Japan. Nevertheless, the declining working age populations in Western Europe and Japan mean there will be declining numbers of affluent consumers in the developed nations. Slow growth among our G-7 trading partners limits export growth opportunities and the growth prospects for foreign affiliates of U.S. multinational corporations. Slower growth in developed countries may accelerate the effort by U.S. business to look more to Asia (excluding Japan) for rapidly growing markets.

THE RELATIVE PERFORMANCE OF THE MANUFACTURING SECTOR

There are several ways to measure the relative performance of the manufacturing sector in the economy. Manufacturing's share of the economy can be measured by gross output, value added, and jobs. Gross output is the dollar value of sales of all firms in the sector. By summing the sales of all firms in the sector, the gross output measure overstates the sector's economic contribution because intermediate purchases are double-counted.[7] Although gross output as a percent of GDP overstates manufacturing's importance, the changes in the ratio over time do reflect changes in relative importance.

Figure 3-2
Manufacturing's Share of the Economic Output and Gross Output, 1972–2010, and Value Added, 1987–2000
(percent of GDP)

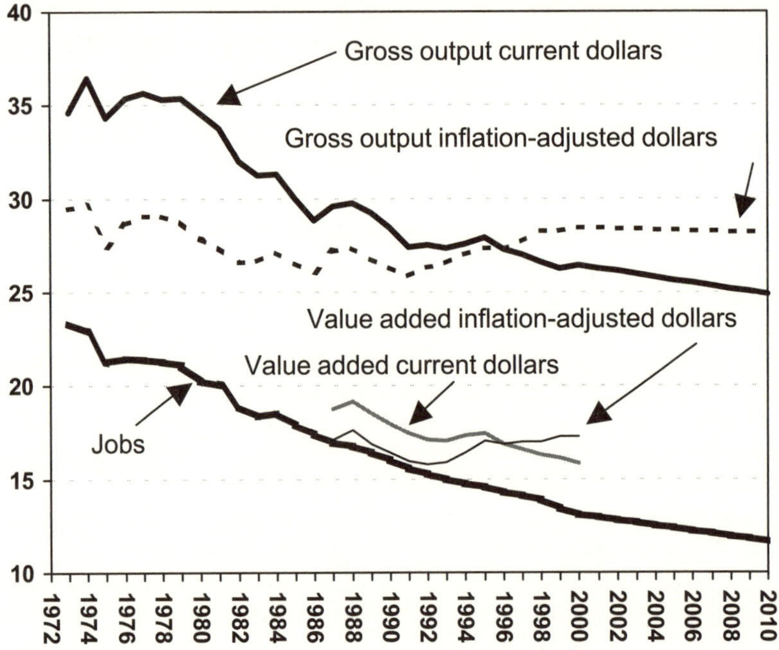

Source: U.S. Department of Commerce, Bureau of Economic Analysis, and U.S. Department of Labor, Bureau of Labor Statistics, November 2001.

Value added in manufacturing is a better measure of the sector's contribution to the economy. Value added is the dollar value of gross output minus intermediate inputs or purchased goods and services. Since purchased inputs are not counted in value added, the measure does not overstate the sector's contribution.

The interpretation of trends in manufacturing is affected by whether the dollar figures are adjusted for the effects of inflation. Current-dollar gross output, current-dollar value added, and employment show whether the manufacturing sector's use of the economy's resources is increasing or decreasing over time. Changes in inflation-adjusted gross output or inflation-adjusted value-added measures, on the other hand, indicate how fast manufacturing's physical output is growing relative to other sectors or the economy as a whole.

Manufacturing uses less and less of the economy's resources. Figure 3-2 shows that manufacturing value added in current dollars was 18.7 percent of the economy in 1987, 18.4 percent in 1989, and 15.9 percent in 2000. The same declining trend is apparent in gross output. Manufacturing gross output in current dollars was 34.6 percent of the economy in 1973 and rose to 35.4 percent in 1979 before falling to 29.2 percent in 1989 and 26.4 percent in 2000. Gross output in manufacturing is projected to continue to lose share over the next decade, falling to 24.9 percent in 2010.

Another indicator of manufacturing's declining use of the economy's resources is the sector's share of labor. In 1987, manufacturing jobs represented 17.0 percent of all jobs economywide. The share of manufacturing jobs fell to 16.4 percent in 1989, and by the year 2000 manufacturing accounted for only 13.1 percent of jobs.[8] It is expected that in 2010 only 11.7 percent of all jobs will be in the manufacturing sector.

An important finding is that while the manufacturing sector uses less of the economy's resources, it provides physical output that grows about as fast as the total economy. Inflation-adjusted value added in manufacturing grew slower than the overall economy in the early 1990s (primarily due to the 1990–1991 recession). Manufacturing inflation-adjusted value added was 17.1 percent of GDP in 1987 and 16.9 percent in 1989. It fell to a low of 15.8 percent in 1992, but rebounded sharply from the recession until 1995 and then continued to rise more gradually. In 2000, inflation-adjusted manufacturing value added was 17.3 percent of inflation-adjusted GDP. The relatively flat trend in inflation-adjusted gross output, shown in figure 3–2, provides additional confirmation that real manufacturing output has matched the pace of growth in physical output for the economy as a whole.

Manufacturing Is Intertwined with Other Industries

The manufacturing sector represents about 16 percent of the GDP of the United States, but it has a greater than proportional influence on business activity. Manufacturing's contribution to GDP is the total value added by the sector less all of the intermediate transactions that go into manufactured products. These intermediate transactions, though, come from doing business with virtually every nonmanufacturing industry in the economy and the back-and-forth transactions among industries within the manufacturing sector. Manufactured items are complex. Increasingly, components that are required in end-use products require the specialized technology of another industry. For example, the motor vehicle industry purchases steel from the steel industry, glass from the glass industry, insurance from the insurance industry, and parts or services from many other industries. The movement away from vertical integration through outsourcing components and service functions in manufacturing, and the sheer number of stock-keeping units in manufacturing creates huge numbers of transactions.

One way to measure the greater degree of linkages that the manufacturing sector has relative to other sectors of the economy is to compare manufacturing's share of GDP with its share of total transactions value or gross duplicated output (gross output). Figure 3–2 shows that the manufacturing sector generated 26 percent of the total value of economywide transactions yet provided only 15.9 percent of GDP (value added) in the year 2000. The service sector, on the other hand, does not have the degree of transactional engagement with the economy that the manufacturing sector does. For example, finance, insurance, and real estate industries made up 19.6 percent of GDP in 2000 but had gross output that was only 11.7 percent of the economywide total. Another large industry within the service sector, the services industry, accounted for 21.9 percent of GDP in 2000 but only 19.9 percent of gross output.[9] These examples show that service sector industries generally have transaction values that are less than their value-added proportion of the economy.

An alternate way of demonstrating the importance of the manufacturing sector in generating business activity is through its "backward linkage." The U.S. Department of Commerce's Bureau of Economic Analysis creates input-output tables of the economy that map the structure of production and distribution of industries and commodities in the economy. A measure created in this analysis is the total output required from all industries to supply $1 of final demand for a commodity, or what is called the backward linkage.

Analysis of backward linkages from the input-output tables leads to an important finding. Most manufactured goods have backward linkages that exceed those of services. A $1 increase in consumer, investment, or government spending for a manufactured good results in at least another $1 of demand for goods and services from the supplying industries.[10] The backward linkages for goods generally are greater than 2.0. The passenger car and truck industry's backward linkage, at 2.82, is one of the highest in manufacturing, indicating that a $1 increase in end user purchases of cars and trucks will create a $1.82 increase in transactions for goods and services from all other industries in the economy. Most service sector purchases, however, have backward linkages that are less than 2.0. For example, $1 of end-user spending on financial services generates only a $0.72 increase in demand for goods and services from all other industries. The backward linkage for wholesale and retail trade is a little less than 1.6, and the backward linkage is 1.7 for health services.[11]

The manufacturing sector is an important element in the U.S. economy. Its size is large enough for it to be important in its own right; about one-sixth of the total value of all goods and services produced comes from the manufacturing sector. In addition, the number and complexity of the products in manufacturing causes manufacturers to engage in more transactions relative to their value added and to have higher backward linkages than the service sector.

Productivity in Major Sectors of the Economy

Manufacturing has achieved parity in growth with the general economy, yet draws on a declining portion of the nation's resources (land, labor, and

Table 3-4
Productivity by Major Sectors of the Economy, Output per Man-Hour

	Average annual rate of change			
	1973–1979	1979–1989	1989–2000	Projected 2000–2010
Total	0.7	0.7	1.8	1.9
Agriculture	1.9	2.1	3.4	1.3
Mining	−5.6	2.5	2.8	1.6
Construction	−2.0	−0.7	−0.5	1.5
Manufacturing	1.7	2.1	4.3	2.7
Service producing	1.0	0.6	1.3	1.8
Transport, communications, utilities	2.8	0.5	1.0	2.6
Retail trade	0.7	0.5	1.6	2.3
Finance, insurance, and real estate	1.9	1.3	2.8	2.3
Services	−0.1	−0.3	0.8	1.2
Federal government	−0.4	1.0	0.0	0.8
State and local government	−0.7	0.6	0.4	0.4

Source: U.S. Department of Labor, Bureau of Labor Statistics, November 2001.

capital). Manufacturing's labor productivity has grown faster than output per man-hour in the economy as a whole and, for that matter, manufacturing productivity has grown faster than other major sectors of the economy. Table 3-4 shows that manufacturing labor productivity has consistently grown two to three times faster than the overall rate from 1973 to 2000.

A significant portion of the productivity growth in manufacturing has occurred in the computer, communications equipment, and semiconductor industries. While the high-tech industries will continue to lead manufacturing productivity until 2010, they are not likely to grow at the pace of the 1990s. The U.S. Department of Labor projects that manufacturing productivity will grow at a 2.7 percent annual average rate from 2000 to 2010. This forecast of the productivity growth rate is less than the 4.3 percent rate achieved from 1989 to 2000, but faster than that achieved in the 1970s and 1980s.

Impact of Foreign Trade on Manufacturing

The impact of foreign trade on the manufacturing sector is understated when trade is measured as a percent of GDP. The reason for the understatement is that much of nonmanufacturing output is not tradable. In 2000, for

Figure 3-3
Trade in Manufactured Commodities: Imports, Exports, and Trade Balance as a Percent of Manufacturing Consumption

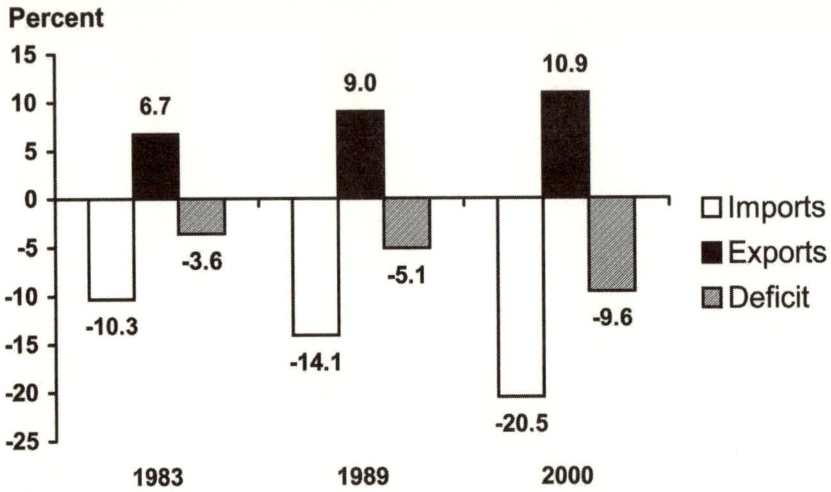

Source: U.S. Department of Labor, Bureau of Labor Statistics, November 2001.

example, 60 percent of exports and 82 percent of imports were manufactured goods, yet the manufacturing sector is responsible for only 16 percent of total economic output.

To grasp firmly how foreign trade impacts the manufacturing sector and the individual industries within manufacturing, it is best to measure trade as a percent of domestic consumption.[12] As shown in figure 3-3, imports of manufactured commodities made up 14.1 percent of manufacturing goods consumed in 1989. Manufactured imports rose to 20.5 percent of manufacturing consumption in 2000. Domestically produced manufactured goods for export were equal to 9.0 percent of consumption of manufactured products in 1989. The export ratio rose only to 10.9 in 2000.

The unfortunate consequence of imports taking a larger share of domestic consumption relative to production for export is that the trade balance becomes a larger negative number. In 1989, the trade deficit in manufactured goods was equal to 5.1 percent of consumption. By 2000, the trade deficit was up to 9.6 percent.

The rising trade deficit explains most of the decline in manufacturing's output in the domestic economy. As shown in figure 3–2, manufacturing's current-dollar value-added share of GDP was 18.5 percent in 1989 and dropped to 15.9 percent in 2000. If the trade in manufactured goods had been balanced in 2000, rather than a deficit of $523.8 billion, the additional

$523.8 billion in domestic output would have yielded $210.3 billion more in domestic value added. Under a balanced trade scenario, manufacturing's value-added share of GDP would have been 18 percent in 2000—only a 0.5 percentage point drop as a percent of GDP rather than the actual 2.6 percentage point decline.

CHANGES WITHIN DETAILED MANUFACTURING INDUSTRIES

Technology and innovation are important indicators in determining how fast industries will grow over time. An analysis of 98 manufacturing industries finds that many of the fast-growing industries in the 2000s are new industries or established industries producing new products. The industries that seem to thrive are ones where competition leads to new products being introduced into the market. Those industries where growth will be slow are, in general, trailing because technology or buyer preference has shifted away from the industry.

Manufacturing industries expected to experience the fastest rate of current-dollar output growth from 2000 to 2010 and which had a combined one-third of total manufacturing output in 2000 are shown in the top third portion of table 3-5. While the manufacturing sector as a whole is expected to have a 4.8 percent annual output growth from 2000 to 2010, the 27 fast-growth industries together have a projected expected annual growth rate of 7.1 percent. Individually, these industries are expected to grow from 6.0 percent to 10.6 percent a year. The fast-growth industries produced one-third of manufacturing output in 2000. These industries' share of manufacturing is rising over time. The 27 fast-growth industries accounted for only 28 percent of total manufacturing output in 1989; however, they are expected to make up 41 percent of manufacturing output in 2010.

The manufacturing industries that are forecast to grow the fastest in the 2000s are a collection of industries featuring innovation. Many of the fast-growth industries are miscellaneous pieces of larger industries and catch-all categories with "not elsewhere classified" (nec) trailing the title. New technology frequently does not fit into the old Standard Industrial Classification (SIC) system and is, therefore, lumped into "miscellaneous" and "nec" industries. For example, industrial machinery nec includes amusement park equipment in addition to fluid power pumps, actuators, and motors. Miscellaneous publishing includes database publishing, technical manuals, and books. Miscellaneous plastic products nec contains subindustries like plastic film and sheet, plastic bottles, plastic pipe, and polystyrene foam products. Miscellaneous fabricated textiles include drapes and curtains as well as automotive seating and interiors. Miscellaneous fabricated metal products comprise valves and fittings, springs, and aluminum foil for packaging, in addition to powdered metal.

Table 3-5
Output, Jobs, and Productivity by Detailed Manufacturing Industry

	Current-dollar output			Inflation-adjusted output		Total jobs			Inflation-adjusted output per man-hour	
	Billions of dollars	*Annual percentage growth*		*Annual percentage growth*		*Thousands of jobs*	*Annual percentage growth*		*Annual percentage growth*	
Industry	2000	1989–2000	2000–2010	1989–2000	2000–2010	2000	1989–2000	2000–2010	1989–2000	2000–2010
Toys & sporting goods	16.2	4.3	10.6	3.2	8.4	109.1	−0.3	0.8	3.5	7.5
Industrial machinery, nec	38.1	4.4	9.3	3.0	7.0	380.0	1.4	1.0	1.5	5.9
Metal coating, engraving, allied services	17.3	5.7	8.8	4.6	6.8	146.4	1.7	2.7	2.9	3.7
Railroad equipment	9.6	6.8	8.0	5.3	5.0	35.8	0.6	0.7	4.8	4.1
Drugs	117.4	8.8	7.9	4.5	5.6	315.1	2.8	2.2	1.5	3.5
Farm & garden machinery	24.5	5.3	7.9	3.5	5.3	96.3	−0.7	1.0	4.5	3.9
Electrical industrial apparatus	31.8	5.4	7.7	3.6	5.2	151.0	−1.5	−1.6	5.1	6.7
Agricultural chemicals	23.0	2.9	7.3	1.7	3.7	51.1	−0.6	0.9	2.4	2.3
Wood buildings & mobile homes	10.4	5.2	7.2	1.6	5.1	91.7	3.3	3.3	−1.1	0.7
Motor vehicles & equipment	428.2	6.3	7.2	5.1	4.4	1017.6	1.5	0.8	3.3	3.4
Measuring & controlling devices	47.4	4.8	7.2	3.1	4.9	302.4	−0.8	−0.1	3.9	4.9
Plastic materials & synthetics	65.0	2.3	7.1	2.4	4.0	155.2	−1.5	−1.8	4.1	5.4
Screw machine products, bolts, rivets	25.8	10.1	7.0	9.0	5.0	116.0	1.4	1.0	7.7	3.5
Communication equipment	102.2	10.4	7.0	10.1	5.0	276.2	0.0	0.5	10.1	4.2
Office & misc furniture & fixtures	38.9	8.2	6.8	6.4	4.3	181.2	1.6	2.8	4.6	1.3
Miscellaneous publishing	20.2	9.0	6.6	4.6	4.3	99.5	1.2	0.9	3.5	3.1
All other primary metals	11.1	0.8	6.6	1.3	4.4	44.6	−0.3	−0.3	1.3	4.8
Miscellaneous plastic products, nec	130.4	5.9	6.5	4.7	4.2	746.3	1.6	1.9	3.1	2.2
Tires & inner tubes	14.6	2.3	6.5	2.5	4.4	79.3	−0.6	0.3	3.0	4.3

Iron & steel foundries	18.2	3.9	6.5	2.0	4.0	122.8	−1.1	0.2	2.6	3.9
Engines & turbines	30.8	5.5	6.4	3.5	3.6	85.1	−0.6	−0.2	4.1	3.7
Construction-related machinery	56.5	6.8	6.4	4.5	3.9	240.5	0.6	1.7	3.8	2.1
Search & navigation equipment	38.5	1.0	6.2	−0.5	4.2	154.6	−5.8	−1.0	5.8	5.0
Miscellaneous fabricated textiles	24.0	4.2	6.2	2.6	4.7	222.7	0.5	0.0	2.0	4.6
Misc. fabricated metal products	52.8	6.0	6.2	4.6	3.7	280.5	1.4	1.6	3.0	1.8
Medical equip., instruments, supplies	62.9	8.4	6.0	6.9	3.4	290.4	1.7	1.6	5.1	1.6
Cutlery, handtools, & hardware	22.0	3.8	6.0	1.7	3.6	134.4	−0.1	−1.0	1.6	4.5
Nonferrous rolling & drawing	59.7	3.4	5.8	3.2	3.1	176.2	0.0	−0.2	3.1	2.9
Metal cans & shipping containers	12.4	−0.3	5.8	0.0	3.7	35.9	−3.5	−3.3	3.2	7.7
Paints & allied products	21.3	4.3	5.8	1.6	3.8	51.7	−1.7	0.7	3.2	2.9
Miscellaneous chemical products	27.6	3.9	5.8	1.8	3.5	93.3	−0.6	0.2	2.2	3.1
Soap, cleaners, & toilet goods	65.6	4.5	5.8	3.1	3.6	155.9	−0.3	0.6	3.4	2.8
Books	25.6	3.4	5.6	−0.2	2.9	136.4	0.3	0.8	−0.6	2.1
Metalworking machinery, equipment	39.5	4.3	5.6	2.0	3.0	330.9	−0.3	0.0	2.6	2.7
Electric lighting & wiring equipment	32.5	4.8	5.5	3.6	2.6	183.8	−0.6	0.6	4.0	1.8
Glass & glass products	25.0	3.4	5.5	2.6	2.9	150.2	−0.8	−0.6	3.5	3.3
Nonferrous foundries	14.3	6.3	5.4	5.2	2.9	94.1	0.7	0.5	4.0	2.2
Logging	14.8	−1.1	5.4	−4.0	1.7	119.6	−0.6	−0.1	−3.6	2.0
Sawmills & planing mills	33.7	4.6	5.4	1.9	2.6	189.1	−0.9	0.0	2.6	2.3
General industrial machinery	44.1	4.6	5.3	2.0	2.9	255.9	0.1	0.3	2.0	2.2
Rubber products, hose, footwear	26.4	4.9	5.3	3.1	2.8	188.7	0.4	−0.2	2.6	2.7
Hydraulic cement	8.3	6.3	5.3	2.7	3.7	17.7	−0.6	−1.0	2.7	4.8
Refrigeration, service machinery	48.6	5.3	5.2	3.8	3.2	216.5	0.9	1.3	2.7	1.5
Miscellaneous electrical equipment	32.4	3.3	5.2	2.4	3.8	146.5	−1.3	0.9	4.0	2.7
Metal forgings & stampings	52.6	4.9	5.1	4.4	2.9	254.7	0.7	0.0	3.4	2.8
Fabricated structural metal products	80.1	5.6	5.0	4.0	2.9	498.4	1.1	0.8	2.5	2.1
Other converted paper products	65.1	3.9	5.0	2.3	2.2	240.9	0.0	0.0	2.4	1.9
Grain mill products, fats, & oils	69.7	1.9	4.9	2.3	1.0	151.7	−0.3	−0.1	2.6	0.9
Electronic components, accessories	184.7	11.0	4.9	27.2	7.0	684.7	1.0	1.6	25.7	5.2
Misc. transportation equipment	17.3	8.6	4.8	6.9	3.1	85.8	3.2	1.7	3.4	1.3
Primary nonferrous smelting, refining	16.1	−0.1	4.6	2.5	1.3	36.5	−2.0	−0.3	4.4	1.6

Table 3-5 (*continued*)

Industry	Current-dollar output			Inflation-adjusted output		Total jobs			Inflation-adjusted output per man-hour	
	Billions of dollars	*Annual percentage growth*		*Annual percentage growth*		*Thousands of jobs*	*Annual percentage growth*		*Annual percentage growth*	
	2000	1989–2000	2000–2010	1989–2000	2000–2010	2000	1989–2000	2000–2010	1989–2000	2000–2010
Millwork, plywood, structural members	37.7	4.1	4.4	1.2	2.1	343.7	1.9	0.7	−1.1	1.4
Jewelry, silverware, & plated ware	8.3	2.5	4.4	1.6	1.3	62.3	−1.3	−0.4	3.0	1.6
Household audio & video equipment	11.4	1.4	4.3	2.6	4.0	79.6	−0.9	−0.3	3.8	3.8
Manufactured products, nec	28.8	3.9	4.3	2.0	2.1	261.5	0.4	−0.3	1.8	2.1
Wood containers, misc. wood products	20.2	4.7	4.2	1.8	1.9	153.6	0.3	0.6	1.3	1.3
Miscellaneous petroleum, coal products	23.0	5.5	4.2	3.4	2.5	42.9	0.9	1.0	2.6	1.2
Electric distribution equipment	16.4	4.7	4.2	2.8	2.0	85.3	−1.8	−1.0	4.7	2.8
Aerospace	141.6	1.4	4.1	−0.2	1.7	553.0	−4.4	1.7	4.3	−0.1
Ophthalmic goods	3.8	7.6	4.0	6.9	2.1	33.3	−1.7	0.2	8.3	2.3
Miscellaneous textile goods	10.0	2.6	3.9	1.9	2.0	53.7	0.2	0.8	1.8	0.9
Periodicals	43.5	7.3	3.9	3.4	1.5	155.5	1.2	0.9	2.2	0.8
Household furniture	33.9	4.5	3.7	2.4	1.8	304.8	−0.1	−0.5	2.4	2.3
Concrete, gypsum, plaster products	47.7	6.0	3.7	3.0	2.4	248.3	1.3	0.6	1.4	1.8
Sugar & confectionery products	27.4	2.7	3.6	1.7	1.3	93.2	−0.7	−0.8	2.2	2.3
Plumbing, nonelectric heating equipment	11.9	6.4	3.6	3.7	0.9	59.5	−0.5	−0.8	4.1	1.5
Knitting mills	14.5	0.0	3.6	−0.5	1.7	127.5	−4.7	−0.4	4.6	1.7
Ordnance & ammunition	5.9	−2.2	3.6	−3.9	2.1	39.1	−6.0	−0.6	2.2	2.6
Bakery products	34.3	3.6	3.5	0.9	1.0	208.5	−0.6	−0.6	1.4	1.4
Meat products	112.6	2.9	3.5	2.5	2.1	508.3	1.9	0.7	0.5	1.5

Pulp, paper, & paperboard mills	61.2	0.5	3.4	−0.7	0.9	198.8	−1.9	−1.2	1.5	1.9
Partitions & fixtures	15.4	8.7	3.4	6.4	1.2	94.4	1.2	2.4	5.1	−1.3
Newspapers	50.1	3.5	3.1	−1.3	−0.2	461.2	−0.5	−0.3	−1.0	0.2
Blankbooks & bookbinding	6.7	4.4	3.1	1.5	0.3	62.7	−2.1	−0.8	3.4	1.2
Paperboard containers & boxes	50.2	4.7	3.1	2.0	1.2	218.8	0.3	−0.4	1.6	1.5
Stone, clay, mineral products	30.8	5.2	3.0	3.1	1.0	186.0	0.1	−0.6	3.2	1.3
Apparel	45.3	0.1	3.0	−0.9	1.3	429.0	−6.4	−2.7	5.8	3.9
Dairy products	61.3	2.8	3.0	1.1	1.2	146.4	−1.0	−1.8	1.8	3.0
Commercial printing, business forms	79.9	2.9	2.7	0.8	0.4	631.6	−0.1	−0.1	0.9	0.3
Household appliances	23.6	3.3	2.5	3.0	0.5	116.2	−1.2	−1.8	4.3	1.9
Weaving, finishing, yarn, thread mills	37.9	1.1	2.5	0.8	0.4	289.3	−2.8	−1.3	3.6	1.7
Carpets & rugs	14.0	1.9	2.5	1.0	1.2	65.5	0.3	1.2	0.4	0.4
Industrial chemicals	105.2	1.5	2.4	−1.0	−0.7	218.3	−2.4	−1.4	1.5	0.3
Miscellaneous foods, kindred products	41.4	3.1	2.3	1.4	0.7	179.6	0.3	0.4	1.2	−0.2
Beverages	91.5	4.4	2.1	2.5	0.4	188.3	−0.2	−1.3	2.2	1.8
Blast furnaces, basic steel products	73.7	1.1	2.1	1.5	−0.7	225.4	−2.0	−2.4	3.1	1.9
Greeting cards	4.6	4.6	2.0	0.5	−0.3	26.5	0.4	0.5	0.2	−1.3
Ship & boat building & repairing	19.0	1.4	1.8	−0.9	−0.4	168.1	−1.7	0.3	1.1	−1.3
Special industry machinery	46.2	7.8	1.7	5.6	−0.9	174.8	0.4	−0.8	5.1	−0.2
Footwear, except rubber & plastic	2.5	−4.8	0.8	−6.3	−1.5	31.0	−8.7	−7.5	2.4	6.7
Service industries for the printing trade	5.3	1.5	0.7	0.6	−0.9	50.0	−2.8	−1.6	3.4	0.6
Computer & office equipment	142.6	6.1	0.7	27.5	14.8	363.3	−2.1	−0.3	30.4	14.9
Tobacco products	59.8	7.2	0.5	0.5	0.8	33.9	−3.5	−1.6	3.7	2.5
Petroleum refining	220.7	4.5	0.1	0.7	0.7	84.6	−2.9	−2.6	4.0	3.0
Preserved fruits & vegetables	57.9	3.0	0.0	1.7	−2.3	220.7	−0.9	−1.1	2.4	−1.3
Photographic equipment & supplies	25.1	1.6	−3.1	1.9	−5.6	70.2	−3.6	−2.4	5.8	−3.5
Luggage, handbags, leather products	7.9	3.4	−4.0	2.4	−6.4	46.0	−2.1	−3.6	4.9	−3.5
Watches, clocks, & parts	0.7	−6.8	−13.4	−7.8	−14.7	5.3	−6.7	−7.2	−0.4	−9.1

Source: U.S. Department of Labor, Bureau of Labor Statistics, November 2001.

Using the growth rates for output expressed in current dollars rather than in inflation-adjusted dollars has an effect on the order of industries in table 3–5. Nevertheless, among the 27 fast-growth industries measured on a current-dollar basis, 22 of these industries would still be in a list of fast-growth industries measured in inflation-adjusted dollars. The exceptions are agricultural chemicals; engines and turbines; miscellaneous fabricated metal products; medical equipment, instruments and supplies; and cutlery, hand tools, and hardware. These are fast output growth industries when measured in current dollars, but not when measured in inflation-adjusted dollars.

The two large industries that are at the top of the list of fast inflation-adjusted output growth are electronic components and computers. These two industries, however, rank quite low on a list of industries where growth is measured in current dollars. Computers rank first in terms of growth on an inflation-adjusted basis; the industry is expected to post inflation-adjusted growth of 15 percent a year from 2000 to 2010. Because of the increasing speed of semiconductors and other continuing advances in electronic technology, the prices of computers will drop at nearly the same annual rate as output. The current-dollar value of the computer industry's output is expected to increase only at a rate of less than 1 percent a year in this decade. This slow rate of growth places the computer industry in 92nd place out of 98 manufacturing industries in terms of growth in current-dollar output. Similarly, electronic components rank fourth in terms of inflation-adjusted output growth in the 2000–2010 period, but only 49th out of 98 manufacturing industries when projected growth is measured in current-dollar revenue.

Manufacturing industries with the slowest expected current-dollar output growth over the 2000 to 2010 period and which had a combined one-third of total manufacturing output in 2000 are shown in the lower third portion of table 3–5. The combined 31 slow-growth industries have a projected annual growth rate of only 1.9 percent from 2000 to 2010. Individually, they are expected to grow from 3.5 percent to negative 13.4 percent a year. The slow-growth industries accounted for about one-third of manufacturing output in 2000. Because of their relatively slow rate of growth, these industries' share of manufacturing is falling over time. The 31 slow-growth industries accounted for 38 percent of manufacturing output in 1989, but they are expected to comprise only 26 percent of total manufacturing output in 2010.

Structural changes resulting from technology and changing consumer preferences explain why some industries have low or declining output. Several food industry products—preserved fruits and vegetables, beverages, miscellaneous foods and products, dairy products, meat products, and bakery products—are slow-growing industries because consumer preference has shifted, for example, to dining out rather than preparing meals at home. There are also physical limits on food consumption that are imposed by population

Table 3-6
Comparison of Fast-, Middle-, and Slow-Growing Manufacturing Industries

	Fast-Growing	Middle-Growing	Slow-Growing
Output growth (current dollars) 1989–2000 (annual rate of growth)	6.0	4.4	3.3
Import as a percent of consumption 2000 (percent)	21.8	17.9	21.7
Export as a percent of consumption 2000 (percent)	11.5	12.7	8.7

Source: U.S. Department of Labor, Bureau of Labor Statistics, November 2001.

growth. Another industry change that is structural in nature is the movement from print media to television, the Internet, and other electronic media. The shift away from print media accounts for the decline in photographic equipment and supplies and slow growth in service industries for the printing trade; greeting cards; commercial printing and business forms; newspapers; and pulp, paper, and paperboard mills. Furthermore, innovations such as plastic shrink and bubble wrap, containerized shipping, and other packaging technology are competing for the market for paperboard containers and boxes.

In other industries, foreign competition, foreign outsourcing, and changing customer preferences combine to hurt an industry. Clothing and apparel products are a prime example. Domestic production of watches, clocks, and parts; luggage, handbags, and leather products; footwear; and apparel is small compared to consumption. In 2000, imports accounted for 85 percent of watch, clock, and parts consumption; 46 percent of luggage, handbags, and leather products consumption; 84 percent of footwear; and 62 percent of apparel.

Trade by itself cannot explain the differences in growth prospects for manufacturing industries. As shown in table 3-6, both the fast-growing and slow-growing manufacturing industries have the same high import penetration in 2000. Exposure to foreign competition by itself does not seem to be the difference between fast- and slow-growing industries. Many fast-growing industries seem to thrive amid intense foreign competition, while other industries often languish. One reason for the success of the fast-growth industries is that they have countered the import competition with a higher rate of exports.

Another explanation for the role of trade in the success of an industry is the nature of the import competition. In general, slow-growth industries have high labor costs relative to their total costs, so their production is often being moved offshore for economic reasons. Imports are replacing domestic production. Fast-growth industries, on the other hand, attract foreign competition because demand for the product is so strong in the United States. Imports are viewed as another competitor to domestic manufacturers, and the competition spurs innovation in the industry. Both domestic and foreign manufacturers are attempting to get a larger share of the fast-growing market.

Productivity Affects Employment in Manufacturing Industries

A main theme for the manufacturing outlook is that the sector will not generate many net additional jobs. Total manufacturing jobs declined at a 0.5 percent annual rate from 1989 to 2000, and jobs are expected to rise at only a 0.3 percent annual rate through 2010. The exposure to intense foreign competition, continuing waves of innovative products and production methods, outsourcing, and downsizing will lead to strong productivity growth through 2010. Overall manufacturing labor productivity grew at a 4.3 percent annual rate in the 1989–2000 period and is forecast to expand at a 2.7 percent annual rate in the current decade.

Fast-growth and moderate-growth manufacturing industries, in general, will generate a modest number of jobs over the current decade, while slow-growth industries will eliminate jobs. In the 27 fast-growth manufacturing industries which made up one-third of total manufacturing output in 2000, jobs grew at a 0.6 percent annual rate from 1989 to 2000, and are expected to increase at a 1.0 percent annual rate from 2000 to 2010. The 41 moderate-growth industries posted a 0.4 percent per year decline in jobs in the 1989 to 2000 period, but they are forecast to increase jobs by 0.5 percent annually through 2010. It is the 30 slow-growing manufacturing industries that collectively are eliminating jobs. Total jobs at slow-growth industries fell at a 1.5 percent annual rate from 1989 to 2000, and are expected to continue to fall at a 0.7 percent annual rate through 2010.

Table 3-7 ranks the 98 manufacturing industries on each of five criteria. Industries are ranked 1 to 98 based on their expected current-dollar output growth rate, inflation-adjusted output growth rate, job growth rate, productivity growth rate, and size of the trade balance relative to consumption for the product. The rankings show that several fast-growth manufacturing industries were able to generate superior labor productivity growth and moderate job growth. Toys and sporting goods; industrial machinery nec; metal coating, engraving, and allied services; drugs; farm and garden machinery; motor vehicles and equipment; and screw machine products, bolts, and rivets all are in the top 27 industries for both productivity growth and job growth. Growth in output in these industries is relatively strong, and even with above-average productivity growth, more workers are needed.

In general, there is a trade-off between productivity and job growth. After all, productivity (output per man-hour) is the alternative to adding workers. If firms can enable their existing workforce to produce more per hour of work, this directly impacts the demand for labor. Four of the fast-growth industries are in the top 27 in productivity growth, but in the slowest 30 industries in terms of expected job growth. The electrical industrial apparatus industry ranks 4th in productivity growth but 87th in job growth; plastic materials and synthetics ranks 7th in productivity but 88th in job growth; search and navigation equipment ranks 9th in productivity growth but 77th in job growth; and cutlery, hand tools, and hardware ranks 14th in productivity but 76th in job growth. The top two industries for job growth rates have fast output growth, but their expected productivity growth ranks in the bottom third of manufacturing industries. Wood buildings and mobile homes ranks 1st out of 98 industries in job growth rate but 83rd in productivity growth, and office and miscellaneous furniture and fixtures is 2nd in job growth rate but only 76th in productivity growth.

Among the slow-growth industries, a few also have stark trade-offs between employment growth and productivity growth. The partitions and fixtures industry ranks 4th in terms of its employment growth rate but 94th in productivity growth. The carpets and rugs industry ranks 14th in employment growth but only 85th in productivity. On the other side of the equation, the apparel, footwear, and computer and office equipment industries have strong productivity growth rates and also are projected to eliminate jobs through 2010. The apparel industry ranks 18th among 98 industries in its growth rate for productivity but 94th in job growth. The footwear industry is 5th in terms of productivity growth but ranks last (98th) in job growth. Computers and office equipment ranks 1st in productivity but 61st in job growth.

CHANGING OCCUPATIONAL STRUCTURE OF MANUFACTURING

For many people, the word "manufacturing" evokes an image of products made by workers on an assembly line. Actually, production occupations accounted for slightly over 50 percent (51.7 percent, or 9.5 million jobs) of the 18.5 million manufacturing jobs in 2000. White-collar employees and those blue-collar workers who provide services to the production line and logistic activities, but are not involved in assembly, hold the remainder of manufacturing jobs. As shown in column 3 of table 3-8, in 2000 8.5 percent of manufacturing jobs were in management, business, and financial occupations; 9.5 percent were professional and related occupations like computer specialists, engineers, scientists, and designers; 10.5 percent were office and administrative support occupations; 8.9 percent were in transportation and material moving occupations; 4.7 percent were in installation, maintenance, and repair occupations; 2.9 percent were in sales and related occupations;

Table 3-7
Output, Jobs, Productivity, and Trade Rank by Detailed Manufacturing Industry

	Numerical ranking 1 to 98 for each industry				
	Current-dollar output growth	*Inflation-adjusted dollar output growth*	*Jobs growth*	*Output per man-hour growth*	*Trade balance as a percent of consumption*
Industry	2000–2010	2000–2010	2000–2010	2000–2010	2000–2010
Toys & sporting goods	1	2	26	3	94
Industrial machinery, nec	2	3	17	6	19
Metal coating, engraving, allied service	3	5	3	23	26
Railroad equipment	4	11	30	17	65
Drugs	5	6	5	25	79
Farm & garden machinery	6	7	16	20	22
Electrical industrial apparatus	7	8	87	4	81
Agricultural chemicals	8	29	21	42	3
Wood buildings & mobile homes	9	9	1	83	25
Motor vehicles & equipment	10	16	24	26	67
Measuring & controlling devices	11	13	53	10	30
Plastic materials & synthetics	12	24	88	7	5
Screw machine products, bolts, rivets	13	10	18	24	36
Communication equipment	14	12	36	16	75
Office & misc furniture & fixtures	15	19	2	76	60
Miscellaneous publishing	16	18	19	29	37
All other primary metals	17	17	60	12	29
Tires & inner tubes	18	15	42	15	68
Miscellaneous plastic products, nec	19	20	6	49	40
Iron & steel foundries	20	23	45	19	33
Engines & turbines	21	34	57	22	2
Construction, related machinery	22	25	9	50	41

Search & navigation equipment	23	21	77	9	11
Miscellaneous fabricated textiles	24	14	49	13	78
Misc. fabricated metal products	25	28	10	59	48
Medical equip., instruments, supplies	26	36	11	67	24
Cutlery, handtools, & hardware	27	32	76	14	70
Nonferrous rolling & drawing	28	38	56	32	47
Metal cans & shipping containers	29	31	95	2	17
Paints & allied products	30	27	29	33	23
Miscellaneous chemical products	31	35	44	28	13
Soap, cleaners, & toilet goods	32	33	33	35	42
Books	33	45	23	52	54
Metalworking machinery, equipment	34	40	47	37	82
Electric lighting & wiring equipment	35	49	35	60	58
Glass & glass products	36	43	69	27	61
Nonferrous foundries	37	44	37	48	32
Logging	38	64	52	54	6
Sawmills & planing mills	39	48	48	46	56
General industrial machinery	40	46	40	47	69
Rubber products, hose, footwear	41	47	55	39	85
Hydraulic cement	42	30	78	11	52
Refrigeration, service machinery	43	37	13	68	20
Miscellaneous electrical equipment	44	26	22	38	77
Metal forgings & stampings	45	41	50	36	15
Fabricated structural metal products	46	42	25	51	31
Other converted paper products	47	52	46	56	43
Grain mill products, fats & oils	48	74	54	80	4
Electronic components, accessories	49	4	12	8	45
Misc. transportation equipment	50	39	8	77	51
Primary nonferrous smelting, refining	51	68	59	65	80
Millwork, plywood, structural members	52	55	31	72	59

Table 3-7 *(continued)*

	Numerical ranking 1 to 98 for each industry				
	Current-dollar output growth	*Inflation-adjusted dollar output growth*	*Jobs growth*	*Output per man-hour growth*	*Trade balance as a percent of consumption*
Industry	2000–2010	2000–2010	2000–2010	2000–2010	2000–2010
Jewelry, silverware, & plated ware	53	69	65	66	93
Household audio & video equipment	54	22	63	21	95
Manufactured products, nec	55	54	62	53	90
Wood containers, misc. wood products	56	60	34	74	74
Miscellaneous petroleum, coal products	57	50	15	78	12
Electric distribution equipment	58	58	79	34	66
Aerospace	59	62	7	89	1
Ophthalmic goods	60	57	43	44	87
Miscellaneous textile goods	61	59	27	81	76
Periodicals	62	65	20	82	16
Household furniture	63	61	67	45	89
Concrete, gypsum, plaster products	64	51	32	61	34
Sugar & confectionery products	65	67	73	43	39
Plumbing, nonelectric heating equipment	66	78	74	69	63
Knitting mills	67	63	66	64	84
Ordnance & ammunition	68	56	68	40	14
Bakery products	69	76	70	73	28
Meat products	70	53	28	70	8
Pulp, paper, & paperboard mills	71	77	81	58	72
Partitions & fixtures	72	71	4	94	55

Newspapers	73	87	58	88	21
Blankbooks & bookbinding	74	86	72	79	86
Paperboard containers & boxes	75	73	64	71	9
Stone, clay, mineral products	76	75	71	75	83
Apparel	77	66	94	18	92
Dairy products	78	72	89	30	35
Commercial printing, business forms	79	84	51	87	27
Household appliances	80	82	90	57	88
Weaving, finishing, yarn, thread mills	81	83	83	63	18
Carpets & rugs	82	70	14	85	73
Industrial chemicals	83	90	84	86	53
Miscellaneous foods, kindred products	84	80	39	91	44
Beverages	85	85	82	62	46
Blast furnaces, basic steel products	86	91	92	55	64
Greeting cards	87	88	38	95	50
Ship & boat building & repairing	88	89	41	93	49
Special industry machinery	89	93	75	90	62
Footwear except rubber & plastic	90	94	98	5	98
Service industries for the printing trade	91	92	86	84	10
Computer & office equipment	92	1	61	1	57
Tobacco products	93	79	85	41	7
Petroleum refining	94	81	93	31	71
Preserved fruits & vegetables	95	95	80	92	38
Photographic equipment & supplies	96	96	91	97	91
Luggage, handbags, leather products	97	97	96	96	96
Watches, clocks, & parts	98	98	97	98	97

Source: U.S. Department of Labor, Bureau of Labor Statistics, November 2001.

Table 3.8
Manufacturing Employment by Occupation, 2000 and Projected 2010

	2000		2010		2000–2010
Occupation	Jobs (000s)	Percent of industry	Jobs (000s)	Percent of industry	Annual percent change
Total, all occupations	18,469.4	100.0	19,046.8	100.0	0.3
Management, business, and financial occupations	1,578.2	8.5	1,681.8	8.8	0.6
Management occupations	1,135.9	6.2	1,202.0	6.3	0.6
Business and financial operations occupations	442.3	2.4	479.8	2.5	0.8
Professional and related occupations	1,745.2	9.5	1,920.7	10.1	1.0
Computer and mathematical occupations	325.1	1.8	420.0	2.2	2.6
Architecture and engineering occupations	968.7	5.3	1,003.4	5.3	0.4
Life, physical, and social science occupations	184.6	1.0	201.2	1.1	0.9
Arts, design, entertainment, sports, and media occupations	245.7	1.3	273.2	1.4	1.1
Service occupations	199.6	1.1	211.3	1.1	0.6
Protective service occupations	28.8	0.2	27.5	0.1	−0.5
Building and grounds cleaning and maintenance occupations	148.8	0.8	163.1	0.9	0.9
Sales and related occupations	532.4	2.9	543.6	2.9	0.2
Advertising sales agents	53.1	0.3	60.6	0.3	1.3
Sales representatives, wholesale and manufacturing	291.8	1.6	290.3	1.5	−0.1
Supervisors, sales workers	46.9	0.3	46.4	0.2	−0.1
All other sales and related workers	140.6	0.8	146.4	0.8	0.4
Office and administrative support occupations	1,934.7	10.5	1,930.8	10.1	0.0
First-line supervisors/managers of office and administrative support workers	102.8	0.6	108.2	0.6	0.5
Financial, information, and record clerks	651.8	3.5	629.6	3.3	−0.3

Table 3.8 (*continued*)

Occupation	2000 Jobs (000s)	2000 Percent of industry	2010 Jobs (000s)	2010 Percent of industry	2000–2010 Annual percent change
Material recording, scheduling, dispatching, and distributing occupations	610.7	3.3	640.4	3.4	0.5
Secretaries, administrative assistants, and other office support occupations	546.0	3.0	535.5	2.8	−0.2
Farming, fishing, and forestry occupations	87.0	0.5	87.4	0.5	0.0
Construction and extraction occupations	333.1	1.8	382.2	2.0	1.4
Installation, maintenance, and repair occupations	863.0	4.7	877.8	4.6	0.2
First-line supervisors/managers of mechanics, installers, and repairers	63.5	0.3	67.9	0.4	0.7
Electrical and electronic equipment mechanics, installers, and repairers	68.6	0.4	70.9	0.4	0.3
Vehicle and mobile equipment mechanics, installers, and repairers	68.0	0.4	74.9	0.4	1.0
Other installation, maintenance, and repair occupations	663.0	3.6	664.0	3.5	0.0
Production occupations	9,547.1	51.7	9,748.3	51.2	0.2
First-line supervisors/managers of production and operating workers	617.5	3.3	616.4	3.2	0.0
Assemblers and fabricators	2,169.4	11.8	2,228.2	11.7	0.3
Food processing occupations	419.5	2.3	423.7	2.2	0.1
Metal workers and plastic workers	2,479.2	13.4	2,636.3	13.8	0.6
Plant and system operators	141.3	0.8	135.0	0.7	−0.5
Printing occupations	437.1	2.4	430.4	2.3	−0.2

Table 3.8 (*continued*)

Occupation	2000 Jobs (000s)	2000 Percent of industry	2010 Jobs (000s)	2010 Percent of industry	2000–2010 Annual percent change
Textile, apparel, and furnishings occupations	765.0	4.1	686.3	3.6	−1.1
Woodworkers	294.2	1.6	324.9	1.7	1.0
Other production occupations	2,223.8	12.0	2,267.0	11.9	0.2
Transportation and material moving occupations	1,649.1	8.9	1,663.0	8.7	0.1
Supervisors, transportation and material moving workers	53.7	0.3	56.6	0.3	0.5
Motor vehicle operators	322.5	1.8	338.1	1.8	0.5
Material moving occupations	1,266.7	6.9	1,262.2	6.6	0.0

Source: U.S. Department of Labor, Bureau of Labor Statistics, November 2001.

and the remaining 3.4 percent of manufacturing jobs were in occupations related to services, construction and extraction, and farming, fishing, and forestry (lumber industry).

When the manufacturing sector is viewed as a collection of occupations, rather than simply as industry employees, it is easy to conceptualize opportunities for outsourcing. Nortel, Cisco, and Nike, for example, have outsourced production activities to contract manufacturers; that is, they continue to manage, market, research, and design products, but they contract the actual production, process services, and logistics to outside specialists. Many other manufacturing firms view production as a core competency, but outsource nonproduction services. Some of the most popular nonproduction occupations outsourced include accounts payable, receivables, and other transaction-oriented finance functions; information systems and computer management; and facilities maintenance and protective services. In addition, firms contract for advertising development and marketing campaigns; engineering and design activities; and sales, distribution, and logistic services. These are just a few examples; many other functions can be and are being outsourced. The growing use of outsourcing has contributed to the decline in manufacturing employment in the past and will contribute to the projected slow growth in the future because firms classified in the service sector increasingly are suppliers to the manufacturing sector.

The occupational mix within manufacturing is expected to change in favor of professional and technical workers. Management and professional occupations are expected to grow faster than average manufacturing employment over the next ten years. The additional jobs created in management are a result of the need to manage more complex organizations requiring greater coordination of activities with suppliers and customers. In addition, all types of professional occupations are expected to have faster-than-average growth, but computer and mathematical occupations should experience the fastest growth among all the major occupations. Rapid advances in computer technology and continuing demand for new computer applications, like the Internet and company intranets, should drive the demand for computer-related occupations. Computer and mathematical occupations in manufacturing are expected to increase 29 percent by 2010.

Those holding professional jobs will increasingly face competition from professionals in other countries. Firms are hiring engineers and computer programmers in India, for example, to work on projects when it is nighttime in the United States. Technology is making more white-collar occupations compete as tradable services.

Improved business information systems have the side effect of reducing the need for sales and office administration occupations in manufacturing. The rising use of automated sales systems, including electronic order entry, should reduce the number of sales representatives and sales supervisors. Also, continued office automation and the growing use of temporary office workers supplied by personnel firms are expected to reduce the number of financial, information, and recordkeeping clerks, secretaries, and administrative assistants employed by manufacturing firms. Workers in foreign countries will take on more administrative jobs dealing with call centers, data entry, and administrative services for U.S. companies.

Production worker occupations are expected to decline as a share of all manufacturing occupations. In the year 2000, 51.7 percent of all manufacturing jobs were production worker occupations. By 2010, production worker occupations are forecast to account for 51.2 percent of all manufacturing jobs. Advances in technology, like faster machines, more automated processes, and better designs that simplify assembly, will improve blue-collar productivity. The changing industrial composition of manufacturing also affects the occupational mix of production workers. The decline in the U.S. textile and apparel industries means there are now far fewer textile, apparel, and furnishings production workers. This decline is partially offset by a large numeric gain expected for the metalworkers and plastic workers occupations.

Increased Education Required for Manufacturing Jobs

Manufacturing workers have about the same educational profile as the total workforce. In 2000, 1.0 percent of manufacturing jobs were filled by a person with a professional or doctoral degree, 4.2 percent had a master's degree, 7.8 percent had an associate's degree, 15.9 percent had a bachelor's degree, and the remaining 71.1 percent did not have a degree.

The U.S. Department of Labor projects that in the current decade the educational requirement for jobs will rise. More workers are expected to have bachelor's and associate's degrees in 2010. In addition, a small increase is expected in the proportion of jobs requiring a professional or doctoral degree.

While there are no official forecasts for educational requirements in the manufacturing industry, manufacturing is likely to move even more toward higher education. Low-skill (low educational requirement) jobs are the ones that are most vulnerable to being moved offshore. Manufactured products that require a high labor content of low-skilled workers will be increasingly difficult to justify producing in the United States when there are so many countries like Mexico, China, and India that have a huge supply of low-skilled, low-wage workers. In addition, manufacturing firms will continue to outsource noncore, nonproduction jobs to the service sector. The overall result should be an increase in the skill and educational mix of the manufacturing sector in the United States. This is consistent with the overall conclusion of this book that U.S. manufacturing will move toward higher value-added services, with rapid innovation and high productivity, as it competes in the global marketplace.

Chapter 4

The Central Role of New Technology Development and Application

by Jeremy A. Leonard

INTRODUCTION

Innovation and application of new technologies have become the central pillar of economic growth in the manufacturing sector. In the 1970s and early 1980s, productivity gains were led by increasing capital intensity, allowing manufacturers to increase output while reducing overall employment. As a result, labor productivity in manufacturing grew at about 2.5 percent per year on average. The flip side of this coin was that capital productivity declined (continuing trends dating from the 1950s and 1960s) and aggregate innovation (proxied by multifactor productivity) ground to a halt.

The late 1980s and 1990s saw very different trends in productivity measures. Labor productivity accelerated and, more surprisingly, capital productivity began to drift upward, reversing a 40-year trend of declines. Multifactor productivity (MFP) also returned to levels seen in the 1950s and 1960s.

What caused this broad-based acceleration in productivity measures? This chapter argues that an acceleration in innovative activity in the U.S. manufacturing sector, driven by global competition, is largely responsible. Because the labor content of manufacturing output is so low, innovations that improve capital productivity and/or the management of the labor-capital mix will take center stage in the 21st century. Manufacturers of automation equipment and systems are key players in these developments. In addition to bringing U.S. manufacturing back to a leadership position, they and other manufacturing innovators have pushed (and will continue to push) benefits out to other sectors of the domestic and global economies.

Table 4-1
Sources of U.S. Economic Growth Since 1959
(average annual rates of growth)

	1959–1973	1973–1990	1990–1995	1995–1999
Real GDP growth	4.33	3.13	2.74	4.76
		Percentage points		
MFP (innovation)	**1.01**	**0.33**	**0.36**	**0.99**
Capital inputs	1.44	1.16	0.91	1.73
Labor inputs	1.25	1.17	1.18	1.44
Consumer durables	0.63	0.47	0.29	0.61
		Percent of total real GDP growth		
MFP (innovation)	**23.3**	**10.6**	**13.1**	**20.8**
Capital inputs	33.2	37.0	33.1	36.3
Labor inputs	28.9	37.6	43.1	30.2
Consumer durables	14.6	14.9	10.7	12.8

Source: Dale W. Jorgenson and Kevin J. Stiroh, "Raising the Speed Limit: U.S. Economic Growth in the Information Age," in *Brookings Papers on Economic Activity*, vol. 2 (Washington, DC: Brookings Institution, 2000), Table 2, p. 143.

THE ORIGINS AND MEASURE OF INNOVATION

Innovation in its most general formulation had become an increasingly important source of U.S. economic growth in the 1990s, after having reached a postwar low in the period 1973–1990, as shown in table 4-1. Multifactor productivity, which acts as a proxy for innovation, contributed an average of 0.99 percentage point to annual gross domestic product (GDP) growth from 1995 to 1999 (see text box 1 for a discussion of the link between multifactor productivity and innovation). This represents a dramatic increase in both absolute and percentage terms in rates last seen in the 1960s. Relative to the 1973–1990 period, MFP doubled its percentage contribution to economic growth in 1995–1999, at the expense of all other major sources of growth. Accumulation of consumer durable goods added a small amount to output growth by providing a value stream to consumers over an extended period. The contribution of consumer durables to growth shows trends similar to MFP, but of a smaller magnitude. This in part reflects the impact of innovation on their quality and functionality.

Table 4-2 shows clearly that, by any measure of productivity, manufacturing industries have consistently outperformed the rest of the business sector since 1973, after having lagged somewhat in the prior quarter-century. Average rates of innovation (again proxied by multifactor productivity) were roughly the same from 1973 to 1990, but accelerated nearly fivefold in manufacturing industries by the end of the 1990s.

Table 4-2
Growth in Selected Productivity Indexes, 1950–1999
(average annual rates of growth)

	1950–1973	1973–1990	1990–1995	1995–1999
Multifactor productivity				
Manufacturing	1.4	0.5	1.2	2.4
Nonmanufacturing	2.3	0.5	0.5	1.0
Labor productivity				
Manufacturing	2.6	2.4	3.2	4.3
Nonmanufacturing	3.1	1.1	1.1	2.2
Capital productivity				
Manufacturing	−0.3	−1.2	0.7	0.1
Nonmanufacturing	0.5	−0.8	−0.1	−0.5

Sources: U.S. Department of Labor, Bureau of Labor Statistics, and author's calculations.

Innovation results from the nexus of research, product development, and the business decisions that put that research and development (R&D) to work. It is a key component of productivity growth and competitive advantage, since it allows companies to:

- Increase the level of output for a given amount of labor, capital, and raw material inputs, thus reducing unit costs of production.
- Improve the value of output, because of either introduction of a new product or improvements to an existing product.

Figure 4-1 shows the schematic relationships between innovation, capital deepening, and productivity growth. Innovation is the more important of the two major supports of productivity growth and competitive advantage, because it boosts them both directly and via capital deepening. Obviously a new or improved product increases competitive advantage by providing additional value to the consumer with minimal changes in production structure. Process improvements, in contrast, are generally dependent on complementary changes in management and investment. For instance, a decision to automate storage and retrieval of parts requires a heavy investment in the relevant machinery and guidance systems, training for the operators charged with overseeing their operation, and possible reorganization of the layout of storage facilities. Such process improvement decisions are driven by the capability of capital goods.

Without continuous improvement in the quality and efficiency of capital equipment via the embodiment of innovation, the capital side of the pro-

The Link Between Multifactor Productivity and Innovation

Multifactor productivity (MFP) measures growth in economic output that cannot be quantitatively attributed to growth in inputs. In principle, growth in gross domestic product can be expressed as a weighted average of growth in labor, capital, and raw material inputs.* However, this calculation invariably leaves a "residual" portion of actual GDP growth that cannot be accounted for by measured increases in inputs. In essence, MFP is this residual. This residual was labeled "technical change" when first described in the 1950s, on the presumption that the extra growth must be due to management improvements, innovation, and other factors that boost output without commensurate increases in inputs.** It has been closely identified with innovation ever since.

Because it is a residual, MFP may in practice be affected by factors unrelated to true "technical change." For instance, if inputs are mismeasured, residual growth captured by MFP will be either overstated or understated, depending on the direction of the mismeasurement. However, if this mismeasurement is reasonably consistent over time, then overstatements and understatements of MFP are consistent as well, implying that ***changes in the growth rate*** of MFP will reflect true acceleration or deceleration in technical change.

Another potential problem is correctly modeling the interaction of labor, capital, and raw materials when calculating "predicted" output. The Bureau of Labor Statistics (BLS) uses a fairly simple functional form which includes limited flexibility for reflecting changes in the structure of inputs. However, private-sector productivity analysts have calculated alternative measures of MFP using more flexible production models, and they behave very similarly to the official figures published by the BLS.

* A detailed discussion of the methodology for calculating multifactor productivity is beyond the scope of this chapter. For further information on multifactor productivity, see Bureau of Labor Statistics, *BLS Handbook of Methods* (Washington, DC: BLS, April 1997), Chapter 10.

** Robert Solow, "Technical Change and the Aggregate Production Function," *Review of Economics and Statistics*, 39 (August 1957): 312–320.

ductivity equation would be much less important than it actually is. This "embodiment" effect of innovation on output growth is nearly as large as the effect due to quantitative increases in the capital stock with respect to output growth.[1]

While innovation is commonly conceived as product improvement, it is in fact a much broader concept, comprising any action taken by a company to increase the cost-effectiveness of its production process—including improved management of the input mix, flexibility of production lines, and other organizational factors. Because of the link between innovation and capital goods, the companies that develop and manufacture new technologies with wide applicability (such as supply chain automation systems, machine

Figure 4-1
Schematic Relationships Between Innovation, Capital Deepening, and Competitive Advantage

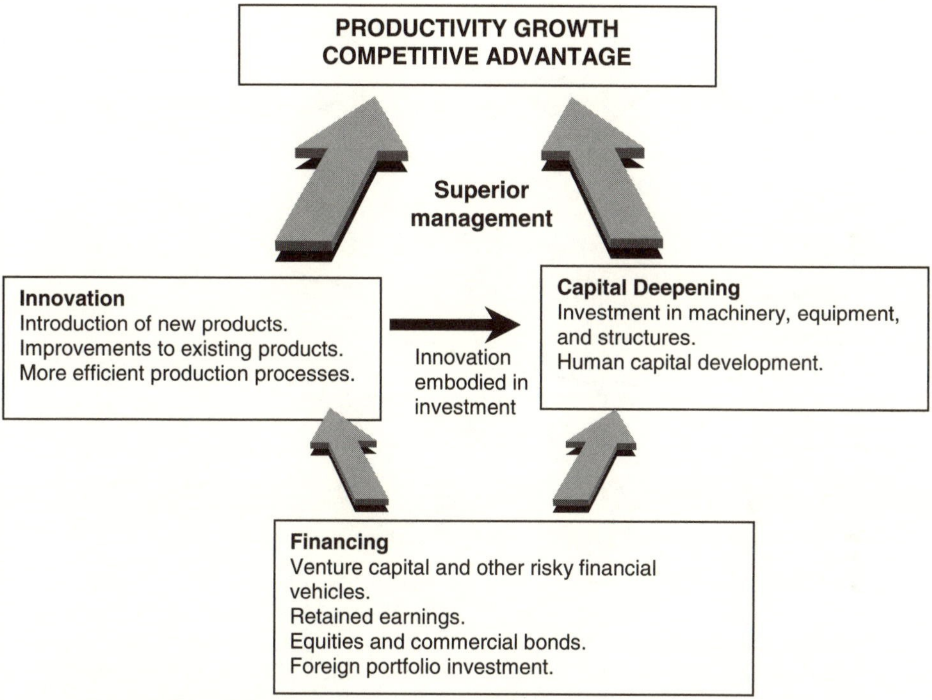

Source: Manufacturers Alliance/MAPI.

tools with embedded information technology [IT] linked to computer-aided design systems, and others) will spread innovation across the manufacturing sector and, for the more generic innovations, throughout the entire economy. In this way, the sector that dominates innovation will be the engine of future economic growth. Such knowledge spillovers are large, and will be analyzed at length in the third section of this chapter.

While they are not the primary subjects of this chapter, it is important to acknowledge that all innovative and capital-deepening activities require financial resources. The United States benefits from a flexible and diverse financial market structure with strong incentives to move resources to their most productive uses. This fact has in itself been quantitatively linked to superior U.S. economic performance in the 1990s relative to other large industrial economies.[2]

As the nature of manufacturing changes, so must the nature of innovation and the sources of productivity growth. U.S. manufacturing competitiveness has in the past been driven by meteoric rises in labor productivity, as in-

Figure 4-2
U.S. Inflation-Adjusted R&D Funding, 1960–2000
(millions of 1996 dollars and percent of GDP)

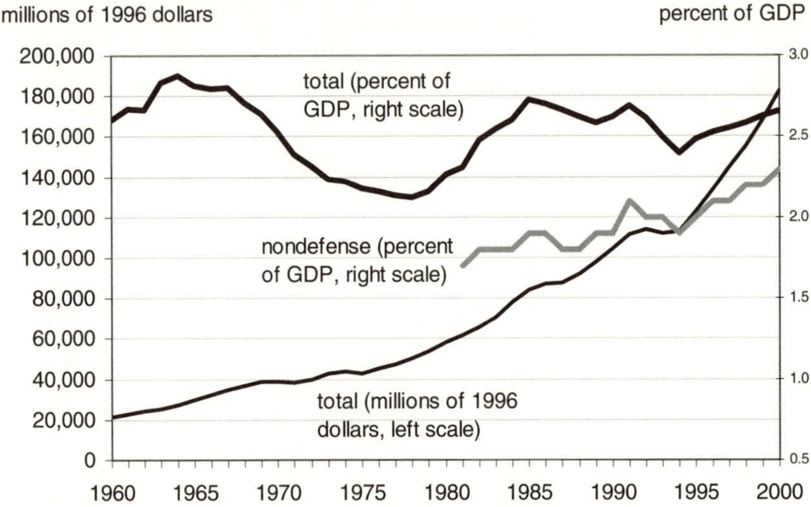

Note: Data for nondefense R&D spending are not available prior to 1981.

Source: National Science Foundation.

vestment in machinery and equipment vastly increased output relative to employment. However, the labor content of value added in manufacturing declined steadily from nearly 40 percent in 1950 to about 18 percent in 2000, diminishing the impact of increases in labor productivity on profitability. The key to future manufacturing strength will thus turn to innovations that improve the productivity of capital and optimize production processes.

MANUFACTURING'S DOMINANCE OF R&D, PATENTS, AND INVESTMENT

Research and Development

Total U.S. current-dollar R&D spending reached nearly $265 billion in 2000, or 2.7 percent of GDP. Figure 4-2 shows historical trends in U.S. R&D spending expressed in inflation-adjusted 1996 dollars and as a percent of GDP. Inflation-adjusted R&D spending has increased ninefold since 1960, reflecting strong long-run increases in economic growth. As a percentage of GDP, R&D spending bottomed out in the 1970s as the large expenditures associated with the space program wound down. It rebounded during the defense buildup of the 1980s and dipped again immediately following the 1990–1991 recession. Since 1994, however, U.S. R&D's spend-

Figure 4-3
U.S. R&D Funding by Business and the Federal Government, 1960–2000

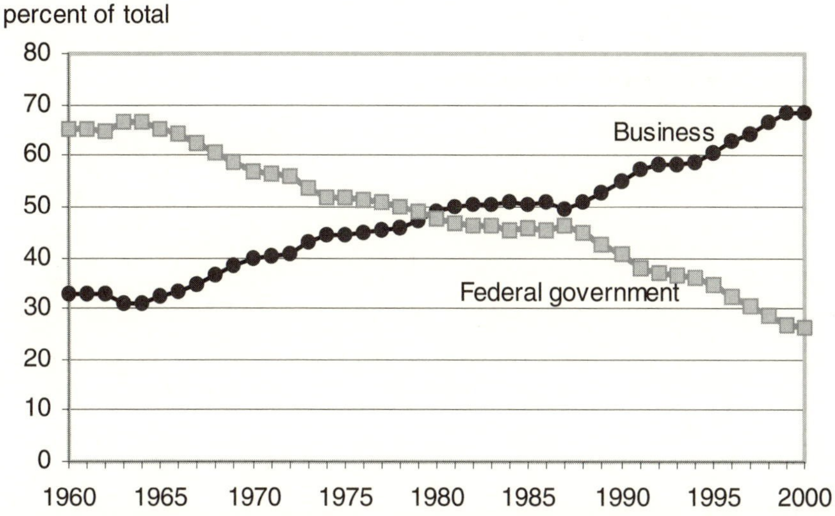

Note: Chart excludes R&D funded by universities, state governments, and nonprofit organizations, which together accounted for 5.3 percent of total R&D funding in 2000.

Source: National Science Foundation.

ing share of GDP has risen strongly, driven entirely by the nondefense component.

The sources of R&D funding have changed dramatically since 1960, as shown in figure 4-3. The business sector's share of R&D funding has steadily increased from 32.9 percent of total R&D in 1960 to 68.4 percent in 2000, the most recent year for which data are available. This proportion increased most rapidly in the 1990s, due to large increases in industry R&D efforts and to sluggish growth in federal funding. From 1988 to 1994, federal R&D funding fluctuated in a narrow band between $60 billion and $62 billion, before resuming modest growth. For all of the 1990s, federal R&D funding increased by only 0.7 percent per year in current-dollar terms. Industry-funded R&D took up the slack of weak federal spending and then some, increasing an average of 7.9 percent per year in the 1990s.

Manufacturing has long dominated business-sector R&D performance. Data are provided in figure 4-4. Through the late 1980s, manufacturing industries accounted for over 90 percent of total business R&D performance. However, the rapid expansion of R&D efforts in nonmanufacturing industries reduced this share to just over 60 percent by 2000.

Within manufacturing, just four industry groups (computers and electronic products, transportation equipment, chemicals, and machinery) ac-

Figure 4-4
U.S. Business Sector R&D Funded by Manufacturing Firms, 1970–2000

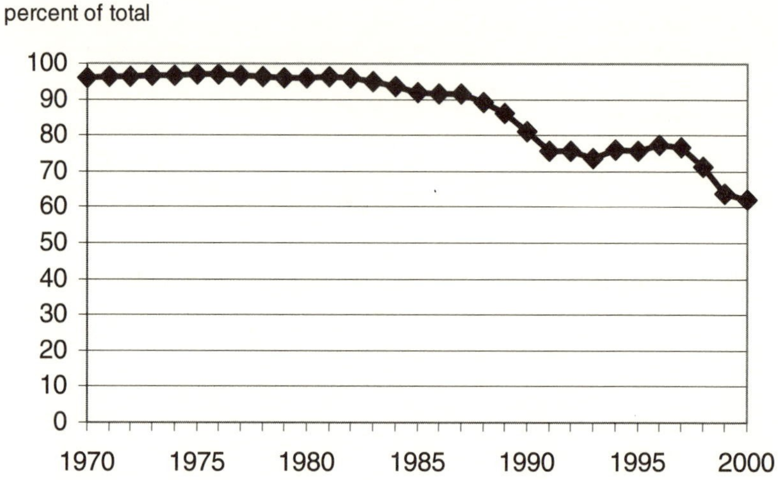

Source: National Science Foundation.

counted for 82.7 percent of all manufacturing R&D in 2000. The remaining 17.3 percent was spread across the other 13 groups included. Notable trends within dominant industries are as follows.

Computer and electronic products.—This group's share of total manufacturing R&D has been climbing steadily, from 28.1 percent in 1997 to 36.3 percent in 2000, and it performs more R&D ($45.1 billion) than the transportation equipment group ($30.1 billion), compared to an equal amount in 1997. In 2000, the largest subgroups were navigational, measuring, electromedical and other control instruments ($15.1 billion), semiconductors and other electronic components ($12.9 billion), and communications equipment ($11.6 billion).

Transportation equipment.—This group's share of manufacturing R&D fell steadily from 40 percent in 1987 to 24 percent in 2000, but remained essentially constant in dollar terms ($30-$34 billion per year). Aerospace accounts for approximately one-third of this amount. Of the remainder, the vast majority is performed by the automotive industry, although the exact amount is unknown due to data confidentiality. In 1993, the most recent year of publicly available data, the total for transportation equipment was $27.3 billion, including $15.1 billion for aircraft and missiles and $11.7 billion for motor vehicles and equipment.

Chemicals.—There is very little disaggregation of the $20.9 billion in chemical industry R&D performed in 2000, due to data confidentiality issues. However, the pharmaceutical subsector is the dominant R&D player in this industry; it accounted for nearly 60 percent of the industry total in

1995, compared to 52 percent in 1992. The other major R&D performer is the industrial chemical subgroup.

Machinery.—R&D performed by industrial machinery manufacturers reached $6.6 billion in 2000, or 5.3 percent of total manufacturing R&D. Perhaps reflecting the increasing sophistication of machinery with respect to automation and precision, R&D spending in this industry has nearly doubled since 1993, making it one of the fastest-growing components of manufacturing R&D.

The sharp decline in manufacturing's share of industrial R&D since the late 1980s merits closer attention. Nonmanufacturing firms performed $75.5 billion worth of R&D in 2000, over seven times more than a decade earlier. This R&D was heavily concentrated in three sectors: wholesale trade in durable goods ($25.0 billion), computer software publishing and system design ($17.8 billion), and engineering and scientific services ($16.3 billion).

All of these sectors perform R&D whose major impact is on manufacturing industries. Wholesale trade in durables is essentially the distribution network for manufacturers, and it is likely that the rapid recent increase in R&D in this industry has been directed toward inventory and supply chain management innovations.[3] For example, W.W. Grainger and other distributors of manufactured products have invested heavily in Web-based systems that allow real-time coordination of ordering, shipping, and inventory adjustment. While the IT infrastructure that drives such systems is often developed in other industries, the underlying system design results from internal R&D efforts. Computer software and system design are responsible for, among other things, delivery of integrated systems such as computer-aided design and computer-aided manufacturing (CAD/CAM) and enterprise resource planning, which are widely (and, in the case of CAD/CAM, almost exclusively) used in the manufacturing sector. Finally, engineering and scientific services cater in large part to manufacturers seeking outside expertise with regard to product design and development.

Most of the decline in manufacturing's share of total R&D reflects a transfer of innovative activities to closely allied service industries. This is no accident. With changes in the economy, the boundaries of manufacturing are expanding, as manufacturing enterprises add related service components such as distribution, logistics, and after-sale maintenance and technical support to their traditional goods production. This trend, described in more detail in chapters 3, 5, and 6, implies that manufacturing's "footprint" in the economy is larger than measures of employment and output suggest.

Intellectual Property and Patents

The United States is a net exporter of technological capital transferred as intellectual property. Data compiled by the Bureau of Economic Analysis reveal that gross royalties and license fees received by U.S. companies and

Table 4-3
Distribution of U.S. Patent Approvals by Major Industrial Sectors, 1963–1995 and 1996–2000
(percent of total)

	SIC code	1963–1995	1996–2000
All manufacturing industries	**N/A**	**91.8**	**92.1**
Electrical and electronic machinery	36	19.6	26.1
Machinery, except electrical	35	23.5	22.1
Professional and scientific instruments	38	11.9	13.7
Chemical and allied products	28	14.4	13.6
Other manufacturing industries	N/A	22.4	16.6
All nonmanufacturing industries	**N/A**	**8.2**	**7.9**

Source: U.S. Patent and Trademark Office.

individuals amounted to $38 billion in 2000, while U.S. companies paid $16.1 billion to foreign entities. Of the fees received, $26.6 billion reflected payments within multinational companies, while the remaining $11.4 billion consisted of payments among unaffiliated companies. Geographic distribution of incoming royalties includes Europe, $18.5 billion, largely from France, Germany, the Netherlands, Switzerland, and the United Kingdom; the Asia-Pacific region, $11.9 billion, largely from Japan, Korea, Singapore, and Australia; and Canada and Mexico, $2.1 billion and $949 million, respectively. On a net basis, manufacturing industries account for roughly 50 percent of such royalties and license fees.

A detailed study of the more than 400 U.S. patent classes is beyond the scope of this chapter. Nevertheless, the U.S. Patent and Trademark Office has developed a concordance algorithm between patent classes and 55 product fields based on Standard Industrial Classification (SIC) codes, allowing us to gauge the dominance of manufacturing in the patenting arena. Table 4-3 shows a summary of patent distribution by major industrial group for two periods from 1963 to 2000. Consistent with their R&D intensity, manufacturing industries account for over 90 percent of all U.S. patent approvals, a share which, unlike R&D, did not diminish in the 1990s. The bulk of these patents are held in machinery industries of all kinds, scientific instruments, and chemical products. Consistent with the rapid expansion in IT-related industries, the share of patent approvals granted to electrical and electronic machinery manufacturers rose from 19.6 percent in the 1963–1995 period to 26.1 percent in the next four years.

Of course, patenting activity is a very crude proxy for innovation, for two major reasons. First, many companies find it is in their interest (and feasible) to protect their intellectual property via trade secrets rather than by patenting. Vivid examples are recipes for soft drinks. Their manufacturers, seeing the capacity for imitation after the 20-year exclusivity of a patent expires, have generally chosen not to patent their recipes. To the extent that trade secrecy is used as a substitute for patenting, innovative activity may be understated by patent statistics. While no reliable data on trade secrets exist, for obvious reasons, it is not unreasonable to believe that manufacturers hold them in approximately the same proportion as patents.

At the other end of the spectrum, some companies find it in their interest to engage in "defensive patenting" that is, patenting of processes with no known commercial value simply to prevent others from capitalizing on the patented knowledge in unexpected ways. Anecdotal evidence suggests that this has become more prevalent in recent years as companies acknowledge the growing general importance of intellectual property. However, if defensive patents are not exploited, they tend to overstate growth-enhancing innovative activity.

Capital Accumulation

Manufacturing accounts for 17.5 percent of total non-real estate investment, roughly in line with its share of GDP. This share is the same for both structures and equipment/software. However, its share of non-real estate capital stock is 19.4 percent, and it is 26.1 percent for equipment and software. This is the type of capital that is, obviously, most directly associated with innovation and productivity growth. In the fourth section of this chapter, I show that capital goods manufacturing, while not dominant in quantitative terms, drives much innovation in industries outside manufacturing.

THE IMPACT OF INNOVATION ON OUTPUT

There is a large economic literature on the effect of a manufacturing firm's innovative activity on its value added. A priori, the theoretical basis for believing that R&D and other innovative activity boost output and profitability is strong: R&D projects are funded based on a risk-adjusted rate of return, and innovations can be at least partially protected from competitors via patents and trade secrecy. Numerous empirical studies since the mid-1970s have demonstrated a strong positive relationship between R&D intensity, innovation, and various measures of corporate performance.[4]

Of particular importance in the context of this book is the ***application*** of new technologies. Creating innovation capital is only the first step. In the late 1970s and early 1980s, U.S. manufacturers were struggling to maintain their competitive edge against Japan and other countries whose manufacturers seemed more adept at integrating new technologies into their production processes. As observers pointed out at the time, many of those technologies were developed in the United States, whose R&D intensity

Table 4-4
Technical Change Embodied in Installed Base of Capital Equipment by Major Asset Class and Selected Subclasses, 1970–2000
(average annual rates of growth)

Asset class	1970–1979	1980–1989	1990–2000
Total equipment and software	**3.6**	**4.6**	**6.3**
Information-processing equipment and software	**11.7**	**9.4**	**10.6**
Computers and peripheral equipment	26.5	18.2	22.5
Communications equipment	7.3	8.5	12.9
Prepackaged software	18.1	15.8	9.9
Industrial equipment	**1.3**	**2.1**	**3.6**
Engines and turbines	1.7	3.4	5.9
Special industry machinery	2.7	3.6	5.2
Fabricated metal products	1.2	4.4	4.7
Transportation equipment	**2.0**	**3.0**	**4.3**
Aircraft	3.5	9.1	10.6
Trucks, buses, and truck trailers	1.5	3.3	4.0
Ships and boats	0.3	3.0	3.4
Other equipment	**0.5**	**2.0**	**2.5**
Service industry machinery	3.6	4.6	5.1
Electrical equipment	1.1	2.4	3.0
Construction machinery	0.5	1.6	2.6

Source: Jason G. Cummins and Gianluca L. Violante, "Investment-Specific Technical Change in the U.S. (1947–2000): Measurement and Macroeconomic Consequences," *Review of Economic Dynamics*, 5, no. 2 (2002): Table 2, p. 259.

remained well above that of other countries. New technologies had been developed, but simply were not reaching U.S. factory floors.

There are several conduits by which innovations are put into practice, but the most important is capital investment. High rates of investment increase the quantity of physical capital, and they also increase its quality as worn-out equipment is replaced with newer, more productive counterparts.

The quality of the U.S. capital stock increased throughout the post-World War II period, but the rate of that increase accelerated in the 1980s and 1990s. Cummins and Violante[5] have constructed indexes of technical change embodied in the installed base of capital equipment by type, and the highlights of that work are reproduced in table 4-4. Text box 2 briefly describes the methodology for estimating trends in capital quality.

The rapid growth in the quality of IT-related investment comes as no surprise, given the combination of meteoric technological change, sharp price declines, and rapid obsolescence. What *is* surprising about the table is

Measuring the "Quality" of the Aggregate Capital Stock

Measuring the change in quality of a capital stock as large and diverse as exists in the U.S. economy perforce requires some simplifying assumptions. Economists generally use quality-adjusted price indexes as the starting point of their analysis. Just as their name suggests, these indexes track the price of goods whose capacity or functionality does not change over time. In reality, the functionality of most goods changes over time, meaning that quality-adjusted price indexes will differ from sticker price changes.

Computers provide a striking example. The price of a fully equipped, entry-level desktop home computer today is on the order of $1,000, not much different than it was several years ago. However, the capability and functionality of such computers are much greater than several years ago, meaning that quality-adjusted prices have fallen substantially even as retail prices that buyers pay have held fairly steady. In fact, the U.S. Department of Labor reports that quality-adjusted prices of computer and peripheral equipment have fallen by an average of 34 percent per year since 1997.

The opportunity cost of innovating—whether it is computing equipment or any other innovation—is foregone consumption. Economic intuition, therefore, suggests that a comparison of quality-adjusted investment prices with a quality-adjusted consumption price is an informative measure of technical change, and that is the technique used by Cummins and Violante, as well as previous analyses of capital equipment quality.* In simpler terms, if quality-adjusted prices for any given class of capital equipment grow more slowly than quality-adjusted prices for other goods, then their relative quality must be increasing. For each class of capital equipment, a quality-adjusted price index is compared with the quality-adjusted price index of consumption goods. The difference between the two is capital quality improvement.

* A formal derivation of the definition of quality change can be found in Cummins and Violante, "Investment-Specific Technical Change in the U.S. (1947–2000): Measurement and Macroeconomic Consequences," *Review of Economic Dynamics*, Volume 5, Issue 2, pp. 247–248.

that all major classes of investment have experienced a significant increase in embodied innovation. Table 4-4 also shows the three subclasses with the largest rate of change in the 1990–2000 period. The aggregate quality of several classes of industrial equipment (including special industry machinery and service industry machinery) increased by over 5 percent per year in the 1990s, up sharply from the 1970s. This reflects the widespread adoption of IT-embedded machine tools and other technologies that support automated fabrication and assembly processes.

As a result, innovation-led growth is significant and broad-based. Cummins and Violante find that increasing capital quality accounted for 30 percent of economic growth in the 1990s, significantly higher than in prior

Figure 4-5

Investment-Embodied Innovation Gap in Major U.S. Industrial Groups, 1970–2000
(percent difference between best technology and average technology)

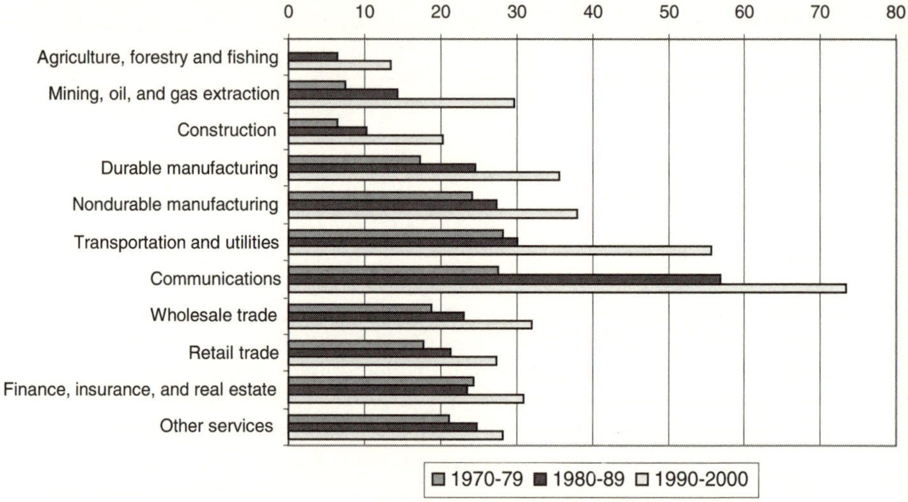

Note: The technology gap in agriculture, forestry, and fishing was negligible in the 1970s.

Source: Reprinted from *Review of Economic Dynamics*, Vol. 5, No. 2, Jason Cummins and Gianluca Violante, "Investment-Specific Technical Change in the U.S. (1947–2000)," Table 7, p. 275, Copyright 2002, with permission from Elsevier.

decades. More important, rising capital quality (both IT and non-IT) has accounted for over 40 percent of the acceleration in labor productivity since 1995.

Of course, there is a difference between average industry practice and the investment leaders. When rates of innovation are low, this embodied technology gap can be safely ignored. However, a corollary of the acceleration in capital-embodied innovation shown in table 4-3 is a wider innovation gap. Figure 4-5 shows the innovation gap (expressed as the percentage difference between the quality of new investment and the average quality of the existing capital stock) for the major industrial groups of the economy.

The innovation gap widened in all major industry groups in the 1990s, particularly in manufacturing, transportation and utilities, and communications. Further disaggregation of the data is not available. This trend is all the more remarkable given the heavy investment intensity during that decade. As has been noted by the Manufacturers Alliance/MAPI in the past, the 1990s saw an unprecedented expansion in business investment in equipment of all kinds as well as in computer software.[6]

Two related factors have conspired to widen the innovation gap. First, rapid technological change, particularly in IT-related capital equipment, has rapidly pushed out the innovation frontier in sectors that use such equipment heavily. Second, if only a small minority of industry players invests in next-generation equipment, the innovation gap will remain large, even if the innovation frontier stabilizes. The technology frontier is moving so rapidly that even the robust investment in the 1990s did not succeed in narrowing the innovation gap.

These technology gaps in many cases represent future business opportunities for companies that manufacture innovation capital. Take durable manufacturing as an example, where the difference between the quality of new equipment and that of the total installed equipment base was on the order of 35 percent in the 1990s, up sharply from prior decades. Equipment investment was strong in the 1990s, yet the innovation embodied in state-of-the-art equipment outpaced this investment. To the extent that technology laggards have strong incentives to narrow the gap in order to remain competitive, high-tech capital goods suppliers are poised to enjoy strong demand for their products. Similar opportunities will present themselves in other sectors for which the technology gap is large and increasing, such as nondurable manufacturing, transportation services, utilities, and wholesale trade. The large technology gap in telecom services likely overstates future business opportunities, since much of it can be explained by the massive new investment in the late 1990s, much of which has been idled in the severe sectoral slowdown that began in 2000.

Table 4-5 shows a further breakout of the average technology gap in manufacturing industries for various periods since 1970, sorted in descending order based on the 1996–2000 gap. While these data are less reliable than those in figure 4-6 (due to smaller sampling universes), they do provide a more precise lens on potential markets for innovation products.

Compared to the average for all manufacturing industries, five industries (leather, textiles, printing and publishing, aircraft, and tobacco) had large technology gaps in the late 1990s. Three of these industries (leather, textiles, and tobacco) are relatively small and have experienced declining output in recent years. The large technology gaps are indicative of a small number of firms seeking to carve out high-end niche markets and, in the case of tobacco, the fact that cigarette manufacturers are generally more automated than raw tobacco producers.

The large gap in the aircraft industry, in contrast, is a new phenomenon. Prior to 1990, its technology gap was lower than for overall manufacturing, but widened rapidly thereafter. This dramatic change could be indicative of a market opportunity for innovation providers. Other industries that have experienced a substantial widening of their technology gap include instruments and related products, printing and publishing, and electrical equipment and components.

An interesting point is that several industries commonly thought to be experiencing rapid technological change (such as motor vehicles and fabricated metal products) in fact have relatively small technology gaps. This

Table 4-5

Investment-Embodied Innovation Gap in Major U.S. Industrial Groups, 1970–2000
(percent difference between best technology and average technology)

Industry	1970–1979	1980–1989	1990–1995	1996–2000
Leather and leather products	34.1	42.9	58.3	55.6
Textile mill products	27.5	33.5	45.0	52.8
Printing and publishing	23.8	27.5	40.1	51.0
Aircraft and parts	17.5	23.0	40.7	50.8
Tobacco manufacturing	22.5	20.1	38.3	50.0
Apparel and other textile products	23.0	30.6	38.3	44.6
Chemicals and allied products	24.4	29.1	38.6	43.3
Instruments and related products	11.6	19.3	31.0	42.1
Paper and allied products	20.8	20.5	31.7	41.1
Electrical equipment and components	15.9	26.0	37.3	40.1
Lumber and wood products	17.9	22.0	36.5	40.0
Average for all Manufacturing	**19.7**	**24.5**	**35.0**	**39.8**
Industrial machinery and computer equipment	25.2	29.4	37.6	39.6
Food and kindred products	29.3	28.3	35.8	39.0
Petroleum and coal products	21.2	24.2	32.6	38.7
Primary metal industries	17.8	24.0	33.7	36.8
Furniture and fixtures	15.8	22.1	29.9	33.7
Stone, clay, glass, and concrete products	17.3	26.7	36.8	33.5
Miscellaneous manufacturing industries	17.2	21.2	28.6	31.5
Fabricated metal products	10.3	13.6	23.2	27.6
Rubber and miscellaneous plastic products	12.6	18.0	21.6	22.4
Motor vehicles and parts	7.8	11.9	19.5	22.1

Source: Jason Cummins and Gianluca Violante, "Investment-Specific Technical Change in the U.S. (1947–2000)," *Review of Economic Dynamics*, 5, no. 2 (2002), and author's calculations.

undoubtedly reflects the fact that companies in these industries cannot remain profitable without continuous investment in cutting-edge equipment, thus keeping the laggards relatively close to the leaders.

What does all this mean for manufacturers? First, the importance of capital investment has never been greater. Manufacturers that embrace and apply new technologies by investing in next-generation equipment and systems will reap additional competitive advantages, while laggards will at best muddle through or at worst regress to bankruptcy. Second, as noted in the discussion of figure 4–1, good management is a necessary complement to effective implementation of new technologies. Third, and perhaps most important, the companies that push out the technology frontier via development of next-generation innovation capital will take leadership positions in the global economy. It is well understood that the large manufacturers of computers, telecommunication equipment, and software are in this club (notwithstanding the sectorial slowdown of the early 21st century). What is less appreciated is that manufacturers of industrial machinery, automation tools, and other non-IT factory-floor equipment have joined the club as well.

INNOVATION CAPITAL: PUSHING MANUFACTURING INNOVATION OUT TO THE REST OF THE ECONOMY VIA SPILLOVERS

It is often—and correctly—noted that manufacturing is "fundamental" to the larger economy in the sense that it is a necessary condition for the existence of most service industries. One only needs to look at the importance of, for example, manufactured goods such as bats, balls, uniforms, hot dogs, and beer for the added value of baseball game services. Rapid productivity growth in manufacturing has freed up resources to provide the wide variety of services that we enjoy today; without that productivity growth, today's service sector would not exist.

An equally important dimension of the fundamental importance of manufacturing is its role as the source of virtually all innovation capital in the economy, and that is the focus here. Although manufacturing does not dominate capital accumulation quantitatively speaking, the innovation embodied in that investment makes it much more potent at pushing innovation out to nonmanufacturing industries, for several reasons.

First and most obvious, the origin of all physical capital accumulation in nonmanufacturing industries is capital goods manufacturers. Thus, the appropriate metric for measuring U.S. manufacturing's impact on investment is economywide investment in equipment and software, which amounted to $916 billion in 2001 after a cyclical peak of $980 billion in 2000. U.S. capital goods production accounted for about 80 percent of this amount and for an additional $300 billion worth of equipment exported annually. This is one clear indication that the U.S. capital goods sector is not being "hollowed out" by foreign competition.

As manufacturers and nonmanufacturers alike enlarge and modernize their capital stocks, they benefit from the embedded innovation capital. A striking example of this is the semiconductor industry. Exponential increases in the raw productivity of semiconductors and microprocessors have now begun to filter through the economy as firms across numerous industries learn to use their computing power effectively. As late as 1999, some economists asserted that little, if any, meaningful increase in productivity outside computer manufacturing could be attributable to noncyclical factors.[7] However, subsequent research strongly suggests that the productivity of noncomputer manufacturing is accelerating due to the innovation capital embedded in IT investment.[8] Since information technologies are a general purpose technology that has potential applications throughout the economy, this ripple effect has already had an impact on the financial services sector and is almost certain to reach other service industries as well.

Second, many innovation-laden manufactured goods are directly used to provide services. Health care provides a telling example. A surprising fact is that the health services sector performs very little R&D—$1.2 billion in 1998. The innovation in health services in fact comes from the manufacturers of pharmaceutical products and medical equipment, which poured nearly $30 billion into R&D activities that same year.

The Importance of Innovation Spillovers

The most important characteristic that distinguishes manufacturing as the dominant engine of economic growth is that other manufacturing firms (as well as nonmanufacturing firms) learn and benefit from their innovative activities more generally. R&D spillovers—benefits of R&D that accrue to entities other than the company performing the research—are large and span industries.[9] Figure 4-6 shows a schematic diagram of how R&D activities by a single firm result in benefits that are much larger than the direct corporate profits that result from the innovation. Useful knowledge leaks from companies that perform R&D, through employee migration and market intelligence during the R&D phase as well as through reverse engineering and product analysis during the marketing phase, allowing other companies to improve their own products. The result is total economic returns that are much larger than the profits reaped by the firm undertaking R&D.

Numerous empirical studies since the mid-1970s suggest that, at an aggregate level, spillover benefits represent 40 percent to 50 percent of the total long-run return on R&D investment.[10] This leads to positive feedback, as R&D performers earn sufficient return to justify investments while simultaneously permitting other companies across the industrial spectrum to learn from the original innovation.

The traditional approach to analyzing the impact of innovation spillovers on productivity is to link value added in a specific industry to a measure of external R&D stocks available to that industry. Since the fruits of R&D most commonly flow across industries via capital goods purchases, the external R&D measure for any given industry is generally a weighted sum of R&D spending in capital goods-producing industries, where the weights correspond to the share of capital goods purchased by the industry under study.

A recent empirical study[11] of spillovers in U.S. manufacturing based on a

Figure 4-6
Schematic Representation of the Link Between R&D Investment and Spillover Benefits

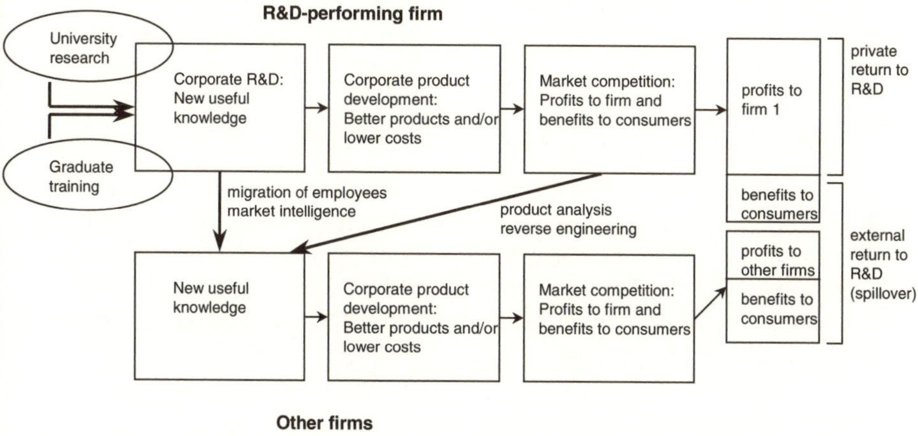

Source: Jeremy A. Leonard, "Assessing the Adequacy of Public Funding of ICT-Related R&D in Canada," report prepared for the Canadian Institute for Telecommunications Research, January 2001.

sample of approximately 7,000 U.S. firms suggests that the impact of R&D obtained from other industries is much more important to productivity growth than R&D performed in-house. It is only in high-tech industries (which, for the purposes of the Los-Verspagen study,[12] include pharmaceutical products, computers and office machines, electronic products, aerospace, and instruments) that in-house R&D has an appreciable effect on a firm's productivity. For the others, their innovation-led growth originates in the capital goods industries that provide the products for their investment.

A more recent study of spillovers by William J. Baumol, an eminent scholar of innovation, indicates that their economic benefits are much larger than previous studies suggested.[13] The basic reason for this assertion is that innovation allows increases in economic output without commensurate increases in input, thus liberating resources for capital spending, investment in education and training, and other activities that themselves further increase output and economic welfare. By this interpretation, the tremendous growth in capital spending and human capital investment that began early in the 20th century and continues to this day would not have been possible without innovative activities, including innovation spillovers.

Using this theoretical framework, Baumol crudely estimates that the "spillover ratio" (the ratio of economywide benefits to corporate profits attributable to innovation) is 80 percent, much larger than earlier studies. Significantly, this figure agrees with more careful recent studies of the question.[14]

The inescapable conclusion is that companies which successfully exploit the innovation directions noted in the third section of this chapter not only will grow to dominate their industries, they will strengthen the entire U.S. economy by setting the example for organization, management of the input mix, and productivity for other industries as well.

Technology Sharing as an Intended Spillover

To this point the analysis has focused primarily on "unintended spillovers" culled from reverse engineering, simple observation of a product's design, and other activities that manufacturers cannot prevent. However, there is another dimension to the importance of spillovers that at first blush appears to contradict basic economic and business principles. It is in fact often in companies' self-interest to share strategic information regarding innovations, even if they can be protected by trade secrecy or patents.

Prima facie evidence of this assertion can be found in figure 4-7, which shows the average time between the initial introduction of 46 major product innovations and competitive market entry for 20-year periods since 1887. Despite patent laws that have maintained 20-year protection of innovations, their diffusion has declined steadily over the last century. At the same time, R&D expenditures have continued to grow. Referring to figure 4-2, R&D expenditures have substantially increased in inflation-adjusted terms and have held steady as a percentage of GDP since 1960. This confirms that the acceleration of innovation diffusion has not diminished the incentive to innovate in recent years.

The growing prevalence of technology licensing explains the trends apparent in figure 4-7. As with any other proprietary input, it is often in a firm's best interest to license the use of innovations to other companies—even their competitors. If an external firm can use a given innovation more profitably than its owner and is willing to pay for that privilege, then the owner of the innovation has a profit incentive to license it. For example, other firms may be able to produce and/or market a product more efficiently than the product inventor. Companies such as QUALCOMM have prospered by inventing new products and encouraging their adoption through broad licensing. Licensing is common in most industries, and many Manufacturers Alliance/MAPI companies engage in the practice.

In this way manufacturers can create intellectual property profit centers to complement traditional production. As another example, IBM's licensing revenue reached \$1.7 billion in 2000, or more than 20 percent of total profits. In addition to reaping these profits, IBM has pushed out its knowledge to countless other manufacturing and service companies alike, thus helping drive further innovation and growth elsewhere in the economy.

Another example of intended spillovers is technology alliances. Under such arrangements, a group of related firms agrees to undertake related research

Figure 4-7
Average Interval Between Introduction of an Innovation and Competitive Entry

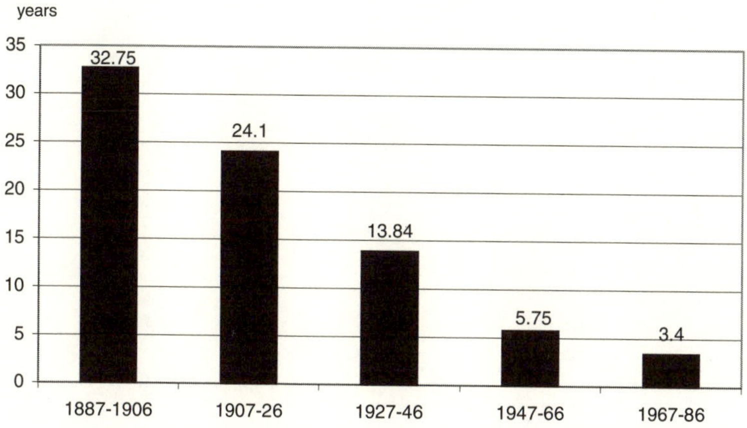

Source: Rajshree Agarwal and Michael Gort, "First Mover Advantage and the Speed of Competitive Entry, 1887–1986," *Journal of Law and Economics* (April 2001): 161–177.

with the understanding that results will be shared with all partners. This eliminates the duplicative R&D that might otherwise occur in a purely competitive environment. Perhaps the best-known example of a technology alliance is SEMATECH, a group of 12 semiconductor manufacturers created in 1986 (with the aid of federal funding) to reinvigorate the U.S. semiconductor industry. However, the majority of alliances are formed without government involvement, and exist in nearly all industries that engage in R&D, although the most prevalent are information-technology and biotechnology ventures.[15] Table 4-6 shows the number of research alliances created from 1990 to 2000, broken down by region. U.S. firms were involved in 80 percent of all alliances formed during the 1990s, and half of these were with other U.S. companies.

It is thus incorrect to characterize the typical manufacturing firm as a zealous protector of its innovations. There is often a legitimate profit incentive to explicitly disseminate technology to other firms, even to competitors under certain circumstances. This incentive encourages selective cooperation and—as the next section demonstrates—geographic proximity.

Geographic Clusters and Intentional Spillovers

A second manifestation of intentional spillovers is "clusters," which are defined as a group of geographically proximate and interrelated industries. The best-known examples of clusters in the United States include Silicon Valley (information technology), Boston (biotechnology), and Wichita (aerospace), but there are many other examples.[16] They embody the fact that

Table 4-6
Number of Research Alliances Created by Geographic Region, 1990–2000

Region	Number	Percent of total
U.S.-U.S.	2,658	41.0
U.S.-Europe	1,654	25.5
U.S.-Japan	511	7.9
U.S.-others	364	5.6
Europe-Europe	657	10.1
Europe-Japan	239	3.7
Europe-others	234	3.6
Japan-Japan	104	1.6
Japan-others	56	0.9
TOTAL	**6,477**	**100.0**

Note: Because research alliances are generally limited in term and scope, the total overstates the number of alliances actually in existence at the end of the period.

Source: National Science Foundation.

having access to a skilled and specialized local labor force, as well as to high-quality postsecondary academic institutions, is a critical element to innovation. More important, being geographically close to suppliers (and even competitors) facilitates the kinds of R&D knowledge-sharing and cooperation described in the previous section.

These dynamics provide a strong reason to believe that high-value-added manufacturing activities will remain an important and growing part of the U.S. economy, even as some activities such as assembly move offshore to take advantage of lower labor costs.[17] The reason is simple, and returns to a recurring theme of this book: the labor content of manufactured goods is small and declining. The new sources of value are found in the knowledge and innovation contained in products, and the United States provides a superior business environment to develop and exploit this value.

FUTURE DIRECTIONS FOR TECHNOLOGY AND INNOVATION IN MANUFACTURING

To assess future directions, it is helpful to see where we are currently with regard to technology use in manufacturing. Unfortunately, the last large-scale survey of technology use among U.S. manufacturers was completed in 1993 by the U.S. Bureau of the Census, and is thus too dated to be of relevance here. However, in 1998 the Manufacturers Alliance/MAPI conducted a similar survey of technology officers at 107 of its member companies. Table 4-7 summarizes the key results of that survey.

Table 4-7

Use of Advanced Manufacturing Technologies in the United States, 1998

(percent of respondents)

		Not currently used in operations				
		Plan to use:		*No plans to use because:*		
	Used in operations	Within 2 years	In 2 to 5 years	Does not apply to operations	Not cost-effective	Other
Design and Engineering						
Computer-aided design (CAD) and/or computer-aided engineering (CAE)	98	0	0	2	0	0
CAD output used to control manufacturing machines (CAD/CAM)	71	8	9	10	0	2
Digital representation of CAD output used in procurement	56	19	6	9	1	9
Fabrication, Machining, and Assembly						
Flexible manufacturing systems	78	5	4	9	2	2
Numerical-controlled machines	90	0	0	7	0	3
Materials working lasers	42	7	8	30	7	6
Pick and place robots	51	1	7	19	11	12
Other robots	50	1		19	11	12
Automated Materials Handling						
Automatic storage and retrieval systems	37	3	7	14	31	8
Automatic guided vehicle systems	24	3	4	19	37	13
Automated Sensor-Based Inspection and Testing						
Performed on incoming or in-process materials	50	6	9	15	8	12
Performed on final products	62	5	8	10	7	8
Communication and Control						
Local area network for technical data	91	9	0	0	0	0
Local area network for factory use	89	6	3	0	0	2
Intercompany computer networks or Extranets	71	17	10	1	0	1
Programmable controllers	94	3	0	1	0	1
Computers used for control on factory floor	85	4	6	2	0	3

Source: Richard R. MacNabb, *Manufacturing Technologies in U.S. Industry: A Manufacturers Alliance Survey on the Use of Advanced Technologies and R&D in Manufacturing*, Economic Report 460 (Washington, DC: Manufacturers Alliance/MAPI, November 1998).

Table 4-8
Prevalence of Advanced Manufacturing Initiatives in Selected G-7 Nations, 1998
(percent of surveyed manufacturing plants)

	United States	Japan	Germany	United Kingdom	Italy
Flexible automation	95	94	95	75	86
Computer-aided design	98	95	98	98	99
Just-in-time production	90	83	78	88	80
Manufacturing resource planning	87	68	75	86	84
Simultaneous engineering	70	55	70	86	68

Source: Roger B. Schroeder and Barbara B. Flynn, eds., *High Performance Manufacturing: Global Perspectives* (New York: John Wiley and Sons, 2001), Chapter 2.

Some advanced technologies, such as computer-aided design/computer-aided engineering (CAD/CAE) and corporate data networks, are nearly universally used. However, there are other technologies whose implementation is several years away, and in some cases is burdened at present by excessive cost. Many of these involve linking several elements of production via automated information flow, such as CAD connections to manufacturing machines, flexible manufacturing, and automated materials handling.

The global opportunities for innovation capital providers are larger than table 4-7 implies. Comparable international data on manufacturing technologies are scarce, but table 4-8 shows the prevalence of selected advanced manufacturing initiatives (which often entail the use of multiple new technologies) in 164 plants across five industrialized countries. The United States is the leader in all areas except computer-aided design (which is almost universally used) and simultaneous engineering. The United Kingdom appears to have room for growth in terms of flexible automation, while Japan and Italy lag by differing degrees in just-in-time (JIT) production, manufacturing resource planning (MRP), and simultaneous engineering. Germany is equal to the United States in terms of technology penetration with the exception of JIT production and MRP.

Synthesizing the trends in tables 4–7 and 4–8 with general innovation trends discussed earlier in the chapter, it is apparent that new directions for innovation are likely to be in three general categories: (1) technologies to improve the productivity of capital; (2) technologies to improve the flexibility of production lines and supply chains to adapt to rapidly changing demand; and (3) improving resource management via outsourcing. Because the labor content of U.S. manufacturing production is so small, and still declining, the winners in the innovation battles of the 21st century will be those who work to improve the cost-effectiveness of nonlabor elements of production.

Improving the Productivity of Capital

Computer numerical controls (CNCs).—Descendants of numerical controls that first appeared in the 1950s, CNCs allow machine tooling instructions to be stored digitally so they can be reused by other workers. This results in more uniformity and better quality of machined parts, and decreases downtime as machine tools are reconfigured for new products. This is an example of a technology that enhances the productivity of capital. More recent innovations in CNCs involve linking machines directly to CAD model specifications to regulate their movements, thus obviating the need for manual programming of machine tools based on hard-copy blueprints. Since 1983, the percentage of the installed base of machine tools using CNCs (as opposed to prior-generation numerical controls) has risen from 5 percent to 32 percent, leaving plenty of room for future productivity gains.

A specific example of CNC-based benefits can be found in the McDonnell-Douglas manufacture redesign of the C-17 landing gear bulkheads, as described in Popkin.[18] Improved digital control of machine tools allowed the company to reduce the number of bulkhead parts from 72 to 2 and the number of fasteners from 1,720 to 35, accelerating the manufacturing process for this part fifteenfold. High-speed complex machining also has been widely used in the automotive industry.

Automation.—Starting in 1998, Motorola implemented an automated design-to-manufacturing system, the details of which are described in Tirpak.[19] Essentially, it allows product design data created via CAD/CAE systems to be communicated in real time to the machines that will ultimately fabricate and assemble the product. Though there were substantial up-front costs incurred to build the information database that drove the system, benefits have been sufficient to justify the initial investment. Those benefits consist of reduction in design times for circuit boards, as well as modest gains in throughput attributable to setup and program optimization.

In addition to this example taken from the business case study literature, Manufacturers Alliance/MAPI member companies have been at the forefront of automation. A further discussion of these efforts is presented in chapter 6.

Improving the Flexibility of Production Lines and Supply Chains

As described in Fulkerson,[20] Deere & Company uses assembly-line sequencing software to optimize the trade-off between production and controlling cost. Assembly-line sequences are generated daily as a function of the constraints on machines, materials, labor, and logistics. Customers placing orders can thus request a delivery date and, if it is feasible, Deere's production schedule will automatically be adjusted to meet that request at the lowest cost. Such pinpoint prioritization of factory scheduling based on real-time receipt of orders would have been unthinkable without the IT and software infrastructure to support complex scheduling decision-making.

Improving Resources Management via Outsourcing

A key to productive efficiency is making sure that capital and labor inputs are sufficiently flexible to accommodate swings in supply and demand. As described previously, enhanced flexibility of machine tools combined with optimized production schedules can accomplish this on the shop floor. However, there is a second dimension to the issue of resource management, and that is outsourcing of corporate functions. Large numbers of manufacturers have experimented with outsourcing since the 1990s, particularly with regard to the human resources, accounting, IT, and legal functions. According to the Outsourcing Institute, U.S. companies spent $340 billion on outsourced services in 2000, up from about $125 billion in 1996.[21] By purchasing certain services on a contract basis, a firm can theoretically adjust its overhead costs in response to changes in business conditions more easily than if it provided the functional service internally. Indeed, cost control is the primary reason cited by most companies when contemplating outsourcing.

Empirical research supports the hypothesis that outsourcing improves productive performance. Raa and Wolff[22] compare productivity trends in the service components performed internally by manufacturers with the productivity of equivalent service sectors outside manufacturing. If there is a large productivity advantage outside manufacturing, then it pays to outsource. Their analysis shows that the payoff from outsourcing was particularly high in the 1980s and persisted into the 1990s. Furthermore, across 29 manufacturing industries there is a strong negative correlation between that industry's productivity growth and productivity growth of sectors from which services are purchased. This suggests that manufacturers have succeeded to some extent in pushing low-productivity activities to external providers, thus improving their bottom line.

CONCLUSION

U.S. manufacturing firms have taken the lead in embracing the 21st-century economy, which is increasingly driven by ideas, intellectual capital, and innovation. They are, and will remain, the leaders in R&D, patenting, technology licensing, and other measures of innovation. The fruits of these efforts have manifested themselves in an unprecedented acceleration of innovation capital that has already brought about a stunning renaissance of U.S. manufacturing and related benefits that is beginning to fan out to the entire economy.

Future directions for innovation will be governed by the interaction of information technologies, industrial machinery, and operations management. As labor's share of manufacturing inputs becomes ever smaller, improving the productivity of capital and increasing the flexibility of supply chains and production lines will take center stage in terms of productivity. The companies that ***develop*** and produce products and services that accomplish these goals will become the global innovation leaders, while the companies that ***implement*** them will become the business leaders in their respective industry groups.

Chapter 5

Broadening Value Added to Include "Solutions," Customized Products, and Related Services

by Joseph V. Kennedy

Modern economies generate significantly more wealth than the traditional iron-and-steel economies of the immediate post-World War II era. They also exhibit significantly more complexity. The neat distinctions between different industries, and between manufacturing and services, become less useful as new markets evolve and as companies concentrate on using their core competencies to increase returns on investment rather than on simply selling as much of their traditional products as possible.

This chapter looks at how manufacturing companies have increasingly altered the conception of the product that they sell to the market. It examines how demand in a wealthy society differs from demand in earlier ages, creating a role for products that deliver unique value to the individual customer. Increased disposable income allows consumers to pursue a better lifestyle, placing greater value on the less tangible attributes of a product. By concentrating on these intangibles, companies have often succeeded in obtaining higher margins, even as they build a closer relationship with the customer. Simultaneously, advances in computer and telecommunications technology allow manufacturers to increase the information content of their products and to rearrange their internal operations in ways that allow them to lower costs and concentrate on the things they do best. To take advantage of these trends, companies must increase the flexibility of their manufacturing operations and improve the flow of information within the company. This creates new opportunities for their suppliers to step forward and assume greater responsibility for their role in the supply chain.

The trends examined in this chapter are not new. They are well established among many firms in different markets. Nor is there any one formula for future success; as complexity increases, so will the number of viable strategies and market niches. The following pages show a number of distinct but non-exclusive strategies that companies have pursued to remain competitive. Rather than pointing to any single solution, they indicate that in the future, opportunities for profitable manufacturing will expand rather than contract, although profitable markets will undoubtedly be less stable and more competitive.

UNDERLYING FORCES CAUSING COMPANIES TO CHANGE STRATEGIES

Since the 1980s, four dominant forces have changed the economic and political environment in which companies operate. Each of these trends has reinforced the others (figure 5-1). While it is possible that one or two aspects of each trend might stall or even reverse themselves, it is extremely unlikely that their general thrust will diminish much. As a result, the competitive pressure to improve company performance will continue to grow.

The first trend is the increased globalization of the markets. This trend is the main topic of chapter 7. Decreased transportation costs, falling trade barriers, increased cross-border communication, and other changes have reduced barriers between national markets. Goods, services, and even labor now flow more freely, forcing companies to adopt a global strategy for sourcing and marketing their products.

Second, domestic economies have shown a similar trend. Deregulation of major sectors such as transportation, finance, and communications has increased the role of private enterprise. Continued market innovation has blurred the division between previously separate markets and opened up new opportunities for companies to distinguish their products. At the same time, trends such as greater capital liquidity and a looser antitrust policy have increased the pressure on corporate boards to increase shareholder value.

Third, governments have shown a much greater appreciation of the importance of market forces and the limits of government planning. Most economists recognize that strong economic growth can be more effective than income redistribution in lifting the living standards of the poor and middle classes. Nations have competed with each other to attract new investment. Privatization has opened up new opportunities for companies, and increased liberalization has made new markets available.

Finally, rapid technological progress has broadened the range of products companies can offer. Computers and telecommunications have had a major impact on society by reducing the cost of communication and increasing the ability to perform the complex calculations underlying financial transactions and business optimization models. Rapid advances also have occurred in material sciences, biotechnology, and nanotechnology. In fact, a caveat is needed here. There is a distinct chance that within the near future one or more of these technologies could cause a disruptive change in the basic na-

Figure 5-1
Sources of Competitive Change

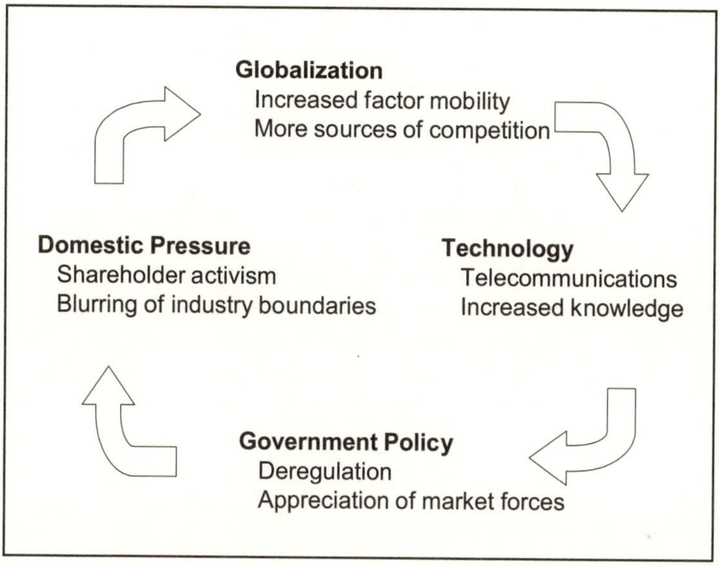

Source: Manufacturers Alliance/MAPI.

ture of manufacturing. This chapter assumes that such an event will not occur before 2010.

As long as these forces continue in their basic direction, the competitive pressure on manufacturing companies will increase. This will force companies to continue to adapt both the products they offer and the strategies they pursue in getting those products to market. Given these forces, certain other trends follow.

EVOLUTION OF DEMAND IN A MODERN SOCIETY

People often base their forecasts of the future on a linear interpretation of past events. Because it is hard to imagine discontinuous leaps in technology, many forecasters discount their possibility. Some observers have expressed pessimism about the future of manufacturing in a technology-intensive economy. The argument is that we have already discovered how to make cars, washers, milling machines, and other standard products. Since everyone has this knowledge and globalization allows anyone to enter our markets, companies making these products will be forced to compete largely on cost, thereby reducing profit margins. In fact, if companies are stuck with heavy sunk costs (as in the steel industry), they may even be forced to run large

Figure 5-2
Maslow's Hierarchy of Needs

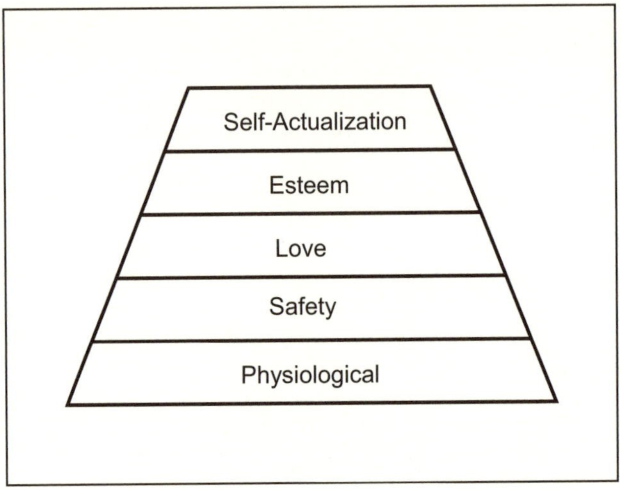

Source: Manufacturers Alliance/MAPI.

operating losses, putting further pressure on the industry. Investment and talent will increasingly be drawn to the more profitable high-tech fields such as computing, telecommunications, and biotechnology, or into expanding service industries such as education and health care.

Other chapters in this volume provide many arguments against this outlook. Here we focus on how companies can change the mix of activities they perform to increase the value they provide to their customers. History shows that, given a supportive environment, the economy generates more and more opportunities to add value. There is every reason to think that this progress will continue far into the future. Companies will inevitably recognize and take advantage of these opportunities.

The structure of future demand is closely tied to consumer psychology. Psychologist Abraham Maslow theorized that individual development ascends along different levels of needs. These needs are arranged along a prepotent hierarchy, meaning that each level begins to emerge only after the previous levels have achieved a sufficient level of satisfaction (figure 5-2). At the bottom level are the purely physiological constraints needed to survive. People experiencing a famine simply want food; its nature and even its quality are of secondary importance. They also usually lack the income to pay for much more value added. At the next level are safety needs. Here the individual is primarily concerned with physical security and is relatively risk-averse. Life is uncertain enough that individuals are reluctant to risk the little they have in order to try and get more. Even when disposable income exists, it is likely to be saved rather than spent.

But when basic physiological and safety needs are assured, individuals begin to express higher needs, including the need for love, self-esteem, and, at the apex, self-actualization. In developed countries most people have begun to pursue these highest needs. But even in the developing world, including many of the largest markets, such as China, India, Brazil, Poland, and South Africa, a large middle class is emerging whose basic needs are sufficiently assured and who increasingly have the disposable income to pursue better lifestyles.

Several traits of these higher values are relevant in determining the nature of future demand. First, these needs, especially self-actualization, are unlimited. Few individuals reach the point where their wants are totally satisfied. There are always unmet desires, matched by a greater ability to pay for their satisfaction. As long as companies can provide better products, they will find a market.

Second, these needs are extremely subjective and individual. Each consumer has her own idea of the perfect lifestyle to express her unique personality. As a result, the market becomes much more diverse. Consumers are no longer satisfied with the basic, standard product. They are increasingly willing and able to pay for one that suits their own tastes. This is one of the motivations behind customized production; creating at least the illusion that each product has been manufactured specifically to meet the individual's needs. This places large demands on the supply chain of manufacturers, opening up new opportunities for them and their suppliers.

Third, these desires are not determined in a vacuum; they are influenced by the opinions of other individuals and by advertising. They also can change periodically, leading the individual to purchase an entire new set of products more in line with his new personality. It is, therefore, important for the seller to establish an ongoing relationship with customers and project a consistent image. In fact, the relationship itself may provide the customer with subjective value, giving assurance that he will be satisfied with the purchase.

Fourth, demand for these products is often relatively price-insensitive, provided that close substitutes do not exist. Once a consumer decides that a product would make him happier, he is likely to buy it as long as the price lies within a broad range that he regards as fair. This price range will depend more on its subjective value to the consumer than on the actual cost of manufacture.

Finally, products that are purchased with discretionary income increasingly compete with other products in different industries. A worker with $5,000 in disposable income might choose between the down payment on a new car, an expensive vacation, or having the floors redone in his house. Assuming that the disposable income will allow him to purchase only one of these, he must decide which purchase would give him the greatest satisfaction. Companies will increasingly compete indirectly with other industries for the consumer's disposable income. In doing so, they must appeal to the customer's subjective desires and tastes.

Designer clothing provides a glimpse into future markets. Individuals with high incomes are persuaded to purchase a new wardrobe every season at exorbitant prices. The money spent is no longer related to their need for clothing; they already have full wardrobes. Nor is it related to the new clothing's functionality. Buyers could satisfy their need for warmth and covering by purchasing regular brands for a fraction of the price. Instead, they are essentially buying exclusivity, status, and self-expression. The value added is no longer in the wool or the sewing. It is in the design, custom fabrication, and individual attention that the industry affords the customer. And margins are high.

It is not likely that everyone will purchase haute couture in the future. But it is likely that a greater portion of the population will have the financial means to pursue the general type of desires that drive high fashion, and that these desires will extend into markets other than clothing. It is conceivable that if cars were designed accordingly, drivers would pay a thousand dollars every year for a new body, leaving the internal machinery the same. Similarly, they might purchase new furniture every five years to reflect a closer match to their evolving personality.

The possibilities for future product markets should not be underestimated. Tom Peters points out that at one time virtually every product started out as a frivol that only the rich could buy.[1] Successful ones then become necessities that everyone wants. This process also applies to existing products that demonstrate significant improvements in quality or style. At first television was considered a novelty. By the 1960s almost every home had a television, but its picture was in black and white. Eventually people replaced their televisions with ones that offered color. Then they purchased a larger screen. As the price of televisions came down, they purchased more than one. Over the next few years, many consumers will switch to high-definition televisions and home entertainment systems.

The last point is worth emphasizing. Cost pressure need not be seen as an impediment to profits. If the pressure results in costs being taken out of the system, lower prices can increase sales even as margins and the return on capital increase, allowing a small market to blossom. Centuries ago most people had only one or two sets of clothes. Fabric was expensive and its manufacture was highly labor-intensive. When labor-saving machines were introduced, workers often fiercely resisted them. Yet the steady fall in the price of clothing allowed individuals to own more than one suit. Eventually it allowed most people to own a full wardrobe that they changed quarterly with the seasons and yearly with the fashion. The new technology allowed the industry to increase demand for its products. Swatch has managed a similar transformation in the watch industry, combining low cost with fashion to encourage people to purchase more than one watch.

As shown above, the clothing industry of today is dramatically bigger and contains many high value-added opportunities that the old market could never have afforded. And there are still opportunities. For example, besides offering fashion advice, as Nordstrom does, for a fixed fee retailers could design a customer's wardrobe, guarantee his satisfaction with it, and update it annually, taking the old clothes back. The consumer would benefit by making fewer unwise purchases, saving time, and getting greater overall satisfaction from his wardrobe. In addition to a steady fee, the company would gain better access to the customer, opening up the opportunity for related sales, more information about fashion demand, and greater control over the supply chain. The last advantage reduces the need for inventory and opens up opportunities for reverse logistics, such as using last year's clothing as a resource for other markets.

Although these trends are directly relevant to most consumer goods, they also apply to industrial markets. Increased complexity and customer pressure in the consumer market will place greater demands on retail companies. These firms in turn will have to maximize the efficiency of their supply chains by handing more responsibility to their suppliers.

However, the value proposition is slightly different for companies that do not sell directly to consumers. For the most part, their demand is derivative: it exists only because somewhere a consumer purchases a final product. But whereas individual consumers are likely to value intangible benefits and evaluate price according to a subjective concept of fairness, companies will evaluate their suppliers strictly on profit considerations. The main motivation behind company purchases is the desire to reduce costs, raise revenues, and increase return on investment, a much more objective test. Producers who, for example, sell machine tools, warehouse systems, and seat assemblies to original equipment manufacturers (OEMs) in the automobile sector must therefore understand not only the driver who ultimately buys the end product, but also the economics of how their products increase the OEM's profits. The common imperative is to add value. As John Kay stated, "The added-value corporation . . . may or may not build the products sold under its name. Some do, some do not. For all of them, success lies not so much in the efficiency of the process of manufacture, but in their control of a key element of it—the syrup (Coke), the standard (Nintendo), the patent (Glaxo), the coordinating function (Benetton)."[2]

EVOLUTION OF PRODUCTS IN A MODERN SOCIETY

Modern economies are not just bigger than traditional economies, they are also much more complex. Simple distinctions between different industries or different products no longer hold. Nor does the neat distinction between manufacturing and services. The latter distinction was never exact. To begin with, manufacturing always required a variety of complementary

Figure 5-3
Complementary Goods and Services Associated with an Automobile

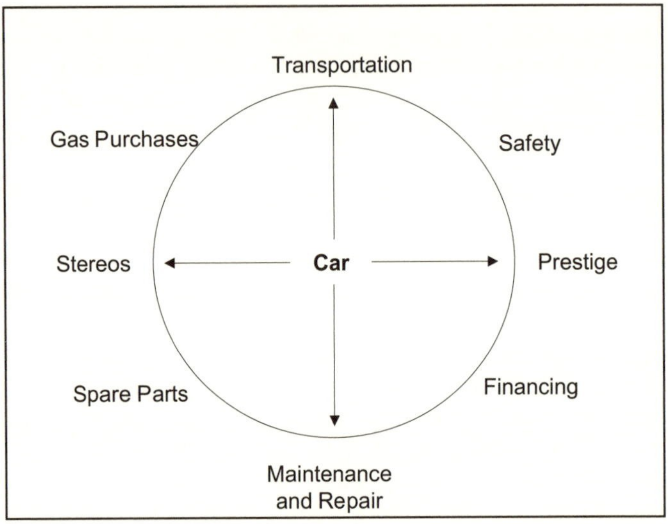

Source: Manufacturers Alliance/MAPI.

services, such as office cleaning, accounting, secretarial help, and legal advice. At the same time that many firms are increasingly outsourcing these services in order to concentrate on their core competencies, they are adding services such as financing, engineering, design, and after-sale service to their core products. The typical laborer of the early industrial era worked on the assembly line, putting things together in a preassigned way. Today's worker increasingly works behind the factory floor, concentrating on how to make products better, faster, and cheaper. To take a step further away from the factory line and have the worker concentrate on design, brand marketing, or customer consultation merely continues the evolution of manufacturing away from standard products delivering fixed attributes, and toward individualized solutions that meet the customer's specific needs.

In an early industrial society, most products are purchased purely for their functionality. Individual industries remain more or less separate. In modern economies, products often satisfy a variety of needs and are accompanied by a web of related services. For example, an automobile does not simply provide transportation for a fixed price paid up front (figure 5-3). Automobiles often provide the buyer with status and a sense of safety. They can offer telephone service, assistance with directions, access to E-mail, increased comfort, and high-fidelity sound systems. The purchase itself often comes with financing and insurance. Leasing and occasional rentals may be offered as alternatives. And whether it is part of the package or not, each purchase implies the need for periodic servicing. Automobile manufacturers can increasingly choose to offer some or all of these related products and services. They may tailor their offerings to the individual customer, and even build a car exclusively for that customer. Not every activity will offer high margins, but the manufacturer's ability to find activities that do are much greater today than ever before. And return on investment is likely to be higher if the company can present customers with a package of products and services that meets their individual needs.

MARKET STRATEGIES FOR SUCCESS

A modern economy offers an increasing diversity of choices within each product category. The makers of Crest now give the consumer no fewer than 12 different options for toothpaste. Less noted is the fact that modern economies offer a much wider range of successful business strategies that companies can pursue to achieve higher returns. Not only do markets expand into finer and finer submarkets, but the gaps between markets close, providing opportunities for firms to bridge them by offering complementary products, financing, and servicing. Companies within the same industry may pursue radically different tactics and still experience success. On the other hand, simply copying the approximate strategy of a successful competitor is unlikely to produce profits; precise execution is also critical.

This chapter reviews several strategies that successful companies have followed to broaden their product base and achieve high margins. These strategies are not exclusive. In fact, most successful companies have pursued several of them simultaneously. To a large extent, success in one strategy that can increase the profitability of others. One important caveat is needed, however. Modern economies are much more competitive than their predecessors. For this reason, past success is even less of a guarantee of future profitability than it was before. Even companies that have pursued a strategy with great success can quickly fall behind as the result of mismanagement, misjudgments, or complacency. Companies like Lucent, Enron, and Polaroid pursued successful strategies in the past but, for one reason or another, failed to sustain those strategies in the face of change. Some, like Harley-Davidson and IBM, managed to recover. Others did not.

GENERIC MANUFACTURING STRATEGIES

Low-Cost Producer

Many of the most dismal projections regarding the future of manufacturing revolve around the fear of commodification. The thought is that if producers compete mainly on price, their margins will be squeezed to the point where they have great difficulty remaining profitable. This is especially true if the main competitors all have huge sunk costs already invested in the industry. Yet overall cost leadership was one of three generic strategies that Michael Porter originally identified as potentially successful approaches to outperforming other firms in an industry.[3] The components that Porter mentioned as part of this strategy are construction of efficient factories, tight cost and overhead control, and avoidance of marginal accounts. As successful examples of this type of strategy, Porter cited Briggs & Stratton in small horsepower gasoline engines and Lincoln Electric's arc welding equipment and supplies. Solectron's ability to offer companies efficient manufacturing facilities is another example of low-cost competition, as is the ability of Dell and Wal-Mart to advertise their lower costs while still achieving high profitability and improved service.

Companies that pursue this strategy often concentrate on maximizing the efficiency of their supply chain, both to eliminate costs and to distinguish their product from others. No product is purely a commodity. Service, quality, and add-ons such as financing can give the manufacturer a marketing advantage capable of commanding either a higher price or, in Wal-Mart's case, greater market share. The key is to be able to take costs out of the supply chain so that lower prices do not harm returns on investment.

Differentiation and Focus

The other two generic strategies mentioned by Porter are differentiation and market focus. The goal of differentiation is to establish the firm's product as unique so that it cannot be compared to others on the basis of price only. Products can be differentiated according to many criteria, including brand image, technology, and service. The more the product is differentiated, the more difficult it is to find an adequate substitute. To differentiate, a company needs to have a good understanding of its customers and how they perceive the product.

The goal of a focus strategy is to select an economic niche where the company has a strategic advantage over its competitors. In an increasingly complex economy, there will be more and more possible niches for individual companies to fill. The dependence on focus may put a limit on the firm's ability to grow, but as long as it stays focused, larger companies will have a difficult time displacing it. Large companies can take advantage of these opportunities through spin-offs and joint ventures.

SPECIFIC MANUFACTURING STRATEGIES

Modern technology has increased the number of specific strategies that firms can use to pursue one of the generic strategies listed by Porter. Unlike the generic strategies, specific strategies are not exclusive. A successful firm is likely to pursue more than one at a time. Each strategy creates additional opportunities to increase returns. These strategies rely heavily on new technology in computers and telecommunications. Each also requires a significant amount of organizational change if the company is to take full advantage of the technology.

Supply Chain Optimization

The first strategy is threefold. First, it involves outsourcing certain activities that the firm has traditionally performed to companies that can do them better. Second, it requires the firm to expand the scope of its core competencies by offering them to other companies both within its existing supply chain and in other industries. Third, it involves increasing the efficiency of company practices by making better use of information already in the supply chain.

Increased competition will force companies to continue taking cost out of the supply chain by making the movement of products, information, and money as efficient as possible. One of the traditional justifications of the firm is the need to reduce transaction costs. In a hierarchical organization, top executives can simply issue commands to their subordinates, rather than engage in lengthy negotiations with separate entities. In theory, internalizing operations also reduces strategic behavior, such as hoarding information, that benefits one part of the company at the expense of overall efficiency.

Delivering a product to a customer requires a large number of diverse activities, including product development, manufacturing, human resources, transportation, warehousing, marketing, and service. Michael Porter divides these activities into five major functions, each of which contains a large number of discrete activities (figure 5-4). Few firms are equally proficient at all of these activities.

Each company's value chain forms part of a broader supply chain that stretches from the initial producer of raw materials to the final seller of consumer products. Most industrial companies have several firms ahead of and behind them in the supply chain. A number of factors, including deregulation, globalization, and mass communication, have increased the competitive pressure firms face. Increasingly, supply chains compete against other supply chains to deliver the most value to the customer. A company's viability is determined not only by its own competitiveness but also by that of firms in its supply chain.

In the past, factors such as high transaction costs, industry segmentation, and regulated financial markets limited both the competition that companies faced and their ability to collaborate with each other. As a result, companies performed most of the activities within their value chain, including those they were not particularly good at. But supply chains can no longer afford to have certain functions performed poorly. At the same time, advances in telecommunications and computing power, combined with better manage-

Figure 5-4
The Internal Value Chain

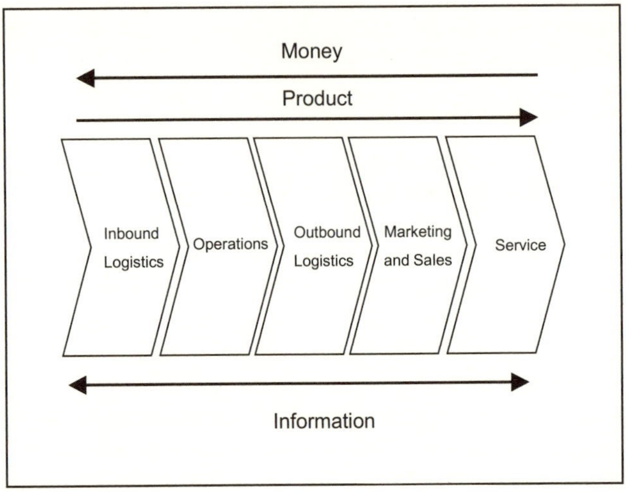

Source: Manufacturers Alliance/MAPI.

ment techniques, have made it easier to collaborate with other companies. Poorly performed activities can increasingly be turned over to companies that can do them better.

By making the flow of information, money, and product more visible to everyone, enterprise resource planning and other information systems allow companies to increase the efficiency of their operations. This efficiency can take many forms, such as the elimination of excess inventory among suppliers and customers, fewer errors in ordering and invoicing for parts, and better communication with customers.

Ultimately, these information systems allow companies to move toward demand-pull systems in which the company produces a product only after it has been sold, produces it right the first time, and delivers it as efficiently as possible. By allowing companies to reduce mistakes due to miscommunication, to react to market changes much faster, and to lower inventories, supply chain optimization increases profit margins by lowering costs even as prices remain constant.

Linking information systems across firms' boundaries makes it easier for them to partner with each other. This gives companies the option of outsourcing functions that they are not particularly good at. Outsourcing also allows companies to focus harder on their core competencies: those activities where they have a defensible strategic advantage over their competitors. Finally, supply chain optimization allows companies to extend their core competencies into other industries, without having to master all of the other activities involved in the new industry's supply chain. Rather than perform all of the activities within a simple supply chain, a fully optimized company might perform only those in which it has a core competency, but perform them for other companies as well, extending fewer discrete activities into a greater number of industries.

With supply chain optimization, management has more time to focus on the key strategic issues facing the business. By smoothing the regular production process, executives can manage by exception, getting involved only when a problem is detected.

One of the outstanding examples of this new type of firm is Dell. A customer ordering a computer on Dell's Web site may view the transaction as being no different from his dealings with any other company. Yet behind the scenes, Dell has optimized the process so that production begins only after the order is received and payment is booked. Almost all of the physical activity normally associated with manufacturing, including the final assembly, is outsourced to other companies. Because suppliers have access to the orders coming into Dell, they can see exactly what they have to produce and when they have to deliver it. This allows them to reduce their inventory of rapidly depreciating parts.

Dell has exerted heavy pressure on its suppliers to hold their costs down, and its business model makes it easier for them to do so. The visibility of orders reduces the need for costly inventories, and Dell's payment model allows it to pay its suppliers quickly, reducing their accounts receivable. Although competition will ensure that most of the gains from supply chain optimization eventually are passed down to customers, manufacturers that are ahead of the curve and continually increase efficiency should be able to capture higher margins for many years.

Adding a Service Component to the Products

Very few products are purchased in isolation and then consumed immediately. Usually products deliver value as part of a package of goods and services. By entering into related activities that create additional value, companies can capture more of the total value received by the customer. In fact, by understanding the broader need that the customer is trying to satisfy, companies can deliver better overall solutions that increase the total value they deliver.

Kenichi Ohmae describes the process of building a better coffeemaker for one of McKinsey & Company's clients.[4] By conducting research on coffee and why people drink it, the company discovered several related factors associated with producing a better cup of coffee. Using this knowledge, the company produced a coffee machine that ground the coffee and filtered the water in addition to brewing the coffee. The result was a machine that increased the value received by the customer and allowed McKinsey's client to increase its profit margins.

In some cases the services that a firm offers can become totally divorced from its original products. Both General Electric and General Motors have realized large profits by entering into financial services. Originally this activity was limited to their own products. By providing customers with the financing needed to purchase their product, these companies were able to capture a greater share of the total cost paid by the consumer. In time, GE developed a core competency in financing, which it then extended to other markets.

The degree to which companies should wander from their original markets is one of the most important decisions managers face. In general, most companies endeavor to develop a core competency in those activities that deliver the highest value to their customers. This is made more difficult by the fact that the sources of value are likely to change over time and that it is often more efficient to perform activities in a package. It is easier to develop a core competency in markets with which the company is already familiar. Thus most companies will find it easier to confine the delivery of new services to existing customers. Occasionally, however, a company will find it worthwhile to develop a new activity as a separate core competency that it can extend outside of its traditional markets.

It is true that manufacturing firms have increasingly outsourced many services, from litigation to janitorial service, in which they do not have a competitive advantage. The trend has not been universal, however. Some companies, such as John Deere in health care costs and Caterpillar in logistics, have transformed service activities into one of their core competencies and now offer these services to other companies as well. At some point both companies may decide to spin these activities off into separate corporations, thus officially divorcing them from the manufacturing sector. Even if they do, similar opportunities for the profitable extension of services will remain. Decisions on outsourcing and core competencies should not depend on whether the activity involves manufacturing or services. Two factors are important. First, does the company perform this activity significantly better or worse than its competitors (alternatively, does the activity deliver a high or low return on investment?) Second, is the activity important to the overall competitive advantage of the supply chain? Companies should consider getting out of activities that they do not do particularly well or that are not especially important to their overall success. They should try to expand their role in activities that they perform significantly better than the industry average or that are a critical part of the supply chain.

One of the most common activities is the need for after-sales service. GE has long enjoyed much higher margins from servicing its airplane motors than it has from the original sale of the motors. The business has become so profitable that GE has decided to extend its service to the repair of its competitors' engines. The major car companies have begun to look at replicating this strategy by offering service work directly rather than leaving this to dealers or independent repair shops.

Some companies have expanded the concept of service even further. By focusing on the underlying service that their product delivers to the customer, they have re-formed their business model around the provision of a service rather than the selling of a product. Shaw Industries has transformed its business and its relationship with the customer from the one-time sale of carpeting by offering the ongoing service of providing cleaning and repair. The company regularly cleans the carpeting of its customers and automatically replaces worn or faded areas. This gives it a closer relationship with its customers and a steady stream of revenue.

The automotive industry has adapted this model by leasing cars and providing rentals. Although these service industries tend not to be owned by the OEMs, there is no reason why they could not be in the future. Similarly, Trane has gone from selling air-conditioning units to providing the service of air-conditioning in which it designs, installs, services, and eventually replaces the equipment needed to deliver the service. By expanding their points of contact with the customer, these companies leverage their core competencies and make it more difficult for buyers both to compare competing products solely on the basis of price and to switch suppliers. By expanding their presence in the industry, they gain greater control over their product and ensure that an increase in efficiency or performance anywhere in the supply chain increases their profit margin. These improvements can come through more efficient products, better recycling of replaced products, or better maintenance during the life of the product.

Even firms that have outsourced many of the indirect service activities associated with the past model of manufacturing have at the same time increased the direct service component of the products they offer customers. Modern products contain far more software, design features, and specialized knowledge regarding proper use and servicing than their predecessors. For many goods, the costs of the physical components and direct production labor constitute only a fraction of the total price. Associated services—such as financing, design, user training, software development, and marketing—make up most of the value. Because these service activities directly impact on the total value delivered by a product, manufacturers tend to keep them in-house.

The result is that many traditional manufacturers increasingly look more like service companies. McKinsey & Company is definitely in a service industry. But IBM offers many of the same services. IBM used its knowledge of computer design to create a new business: assisting other companies in the design of computer systems, including helping these companies expand into e-commerce. Xerox tried a similar strategy when it described itself as the document company. Kodak is following the same idea when it enables its customers to place their pictures on the Internet and mail them to family members and friends.

This often leads manufacturing companies to expand the total value they offer by selling a package of products rather than individual components. For other companies, the switch has been from offering individual products that customers need to solve a problem to taking direct responsibility for solving the customer's problem, allowing the customer to focus on other activities.

One of the keys to the success of Johnson Controls has been its decision to offer assembled seating modules rather than traditional parts. This involves the company in several high-value service activities, such as engineering and design. It also forces greater collaboration between the company and its customers. Dana Corporation has pursued the same strategy by focusing on the undercarriage of the automobile, participating in the design and delivery of entire modules to all of its customers' worldwide locations.[5]

A final component of adding service content is the move to just-in-time production. As companies move away from large stockpiles of product, they depend more on the ability of their suppliers to deliver products of the specified quality at the specified time. More and more suppliers are finding that, with the right customer, vendor-managed inventory and even consignment selling can offer increased returns. Without reserve inventories, failure by a supplier can mean shutting down production. To avoid these large costs, companies increasingly value consistency and reliability as well as price when making their purchasing decisions.

Perhaps the epitome of the subjective nature of many value-added services lies in brand image. In many cases a brand provides useful assurance of quality and consistency. But it can be much more. Harley-Davidson's brand is one of its most important strategic assets. The brand does much more than help the company command higher prices for its motorcycles. Through cross-licensing its brand with other products ranging from mechanics' tools to clothing, the company has turned its brand into an independent source of revenue. Brand image is not limited to consumer items. Caterpillar has become the third leading brand image, with branded products such as hats and boots producing over $1 billion in annual revenues. The downside of branding can be seen from the fallout that Arthur Andersen is experiencing from the mistakes it made auditing Enron.

The distinction between manufacturing and services is becoming increasingly strained. Major manufacturing names like IBM, GE, and Caterpillar already derive a large portion of their revenues from activities that would normally be classified as services. Manufacturers will also benefit from the growth in spending on service industries such as health care and education. Much of the future value added in these industries is likely to come from better products, such as computed axial tomography machines that allow hospitals to provide better care at lower prices. Similarly, in education, new products, especially software, will make it easier to give each student individualized attention and feedback.

Technology Leader

This strategy comes closest to Porter's differentiation strategy; in this case, the company differentiates its products as being functionally better than those of its competitors. Strictly speaking, the source of improvement need not be due solely to technology. Black & Decker realized large sales by redesigning its sander to make it more functional to the average user. Apple has always tried to differentiate its computers partly by their style. This strategy requires constant improvement, however, since rivals can readily copy many market innovations. A company pursuing this strategy must continually develop new products to keep itself one step ahead of its rivals. For this reason, 3M and Emerson both require every business to derive a certain percentage of its revenue from new products every year.

This strategy is likely to be most successful when the improvements occur in those features that customers are most dissatisfied with.[6] These features place the greatest constraints on the product's overall value, making customers willing to pay more for products that push the constraints back. In the early age of computers, memory was one of the largest constraints limiting their functionality. Hence large returns went to those companies that delivered expanded memory. Presently, lack of memory seldom constrains users, so they are unwilling to pay much for additional units. Instead, transmission speeds, especially when accessing the Internet, have become a major constraint. We can expect companies that deliver faster transmission capacity to earn higher margins until their competitors catch up.

Intel has pursued this strategy aggressively. By continually introducing new computer chips that extend the boundaries of processing power, a key constraint on computer power, it captures large margins. Because processing power is a significant constraint for computer uses such as video games and Webcasts, users are willing to pay more for faster chips, and even to purchase new computers just to get the higher capacity. These margins quickly erode, however, making continuous improvement a necessity. Intel also pays attention to its brand image, making sure customers associate it with the latest technology.

Enormous scope exists for better products. At present the most efficient engines convert only 30 percent of the available energy in gasoline. Almost one-third of all electrical generation is lost in transmission. We are just beginning to use biotechnology to produce better crops. Research in miniaturization and nanotechnology has yet to be applied in a significant way to manufacturing. And materials science still shows great promise for delivering stronger and lighter machinery.

Stanford economist Paul Roemer has pointed out that the activities involved in manufacturing consist of thousands of variables; these can be used in millions of combinations, only a small fraction of which have been explored. By continuing to experiment with different combinations, researchers will produce incremental improvement in almost every field. Roemer's words are the best expression of why innovative companies will continue to deliver new value.[7]

In a world characterized by more possibilities than the mind can comprehend, we will never arrive at the best possible design or the best sequence for any complicated set of actions. In even moderately complicated systems, a small change in how things are done can have effects that are so hard to forecast that there is often no substitute for trial and error and experimentation. Workers engaged in the process of assembly may be best positioned to experiment and ask questions if they are given the freedom and incentive to do so.

The essence of flexible production or continuous improvement is a set of arrangements and physical imperatives that push everyone in an organization to look for small improvements in how things are done.

There is no reason why this trend should not continue. Those companies on the leading edge should be able to turn their innovations into higher margins, especially where the improvements push back the most pressing constraints on customer value.

Integrating Products into the Information Web

One of the most exciting options open to manufacturers involves the design of products that take full advantage of the information network, especially the Internet. Advances in computers, telecommunications, and miniaturization will create new opportunities for products to capture, transmit, and act on information. By providing more information on demand, manufacturers can create new markets to meet needs that customers previously could not express.

Any information network consists of six basic parts (figure 5-5). Input devices sense information and often transform it into digital form. This information is usually transmitted elsewhere, allowing a wide variety of other individuals to use it. Software programs often process the data to put it in a number of possible forms that are more valuable to the users. The information is often stored for later use. Eventually the information is transmitted to a final user or mechanical device for action. Finally, a source of power is needed to operate each part of the mechanism.

The central fact of modern communications is that each component of this system is experiencing rapid increases in capability and rapid decreases in the price of a given technology. The most widely known example of this is Moore's Law, by which processing power doubles every 18 months. But similar gains have been made in the accuracy and size of sensors, memory

Figure 5-5
The Information Network

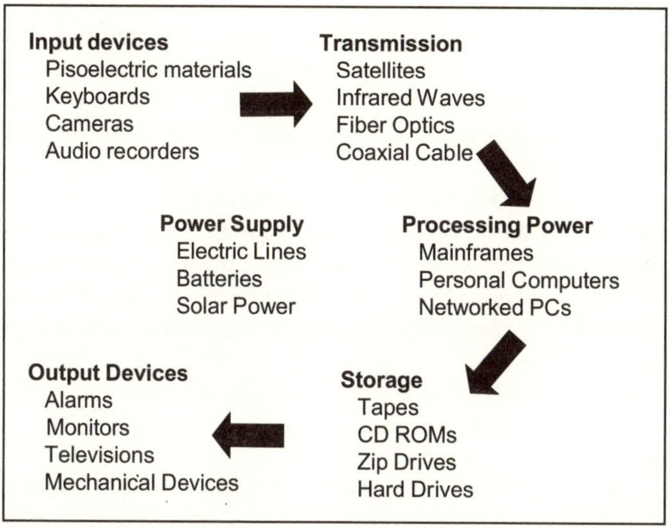

Source: Manufacturers Alliance/MAPI.

capacity, transmission speed, microelectromechanical devices, and battery capacity. The Internet represents a quantum leap in the power of information networks, primarily because of its open standards and global reach. Once information is entered into the Internet, it can be sent almost anywhere and used without having to build a separate system. These trends ensure that it will become both easier and more affordable to collect, transmit, and use information of any type.

The trend is already under way. Bar-coding equipment allows warehouses, shippers, and retailers to keep better track of their inventory and change prices quickly, with little effort. FMC has created a new service which tracks the location of railroad cars by placing small global positioning satellite (GPS) transmitters on each car. This allows railroads to pinpoint the location of each car at any time. SKF has placed vibration sensors in strategic positions in its machinery, allowing it to predict when a bearing will fail, thus minimizing downtime and giving both SKF and its customers greater flexibility in scheduling repairs. John Deere has inserted similar sensors into its combines, protecting farmers against expensive failures during harvest time.

The scope for adding value through the information network is virtually endless. As explained at the outset of this chapter, human desires do not face many natural limits. These desires stem from problems that individuals want solved. Any problem can be classified as either solvable or unsolvable. A problem is solvable if information exists somewhere that, if known and understood, would make the problem disappear. The actual solution then becomes a technical problem of obtaining, processing, and delivering the information where it is needed.

Future advances will ensure two things. First, an increasing number of problems will move from being unsolvable to solvable as scientific understanding of causal relationships advances. Second, progress in computers and telecommunications will make it increasingly affordable to collect and use the necessary information.

A patient with AIDS currently faces an incurable problem. We do not know how to defeat the virus and return the patient to full health. However, future scientific progress may transform this into a solvable problem by giving us the knowledge to kill the virus without serious side effects. A patient with an undiscovered tumor containing 100 cells faces a solvable problem. Unfortunately, he is unlikely to discover the tumor until it has grown much larger, by which time his problem may be unsolvable. Medical products that detect smaller tumors while they are still easily treatable can therefore deliver tremendous value.

Applied Digital Solutions has developed an implantable computer chip that automatically transmits personal information to a nearby scanner.[8] Similar technology could be used to locate lost persons, to provide doctors with precise measurements of blood content, and to verify personal identity. Chips outside the body can help airports increase security and reduce lost baggage. Chips can also be used to reduce theft in libraries and homes by allowing the owner to track the location of property anywhere it goes.

Information products already allow diabetics to send data from their blood glucose monitors to their physicians. By giving the doctor a history of periodic readings, they deliver far more information about the patient's condition without requiring a visit. Doctors can track more patients more frequently and devote more of their time to the cases that are most in need. A recent trial in Florida showed that the product could reduce hospitalization, clinic, and prescription drug costs by 74 percent, while increasing patient health.[9]

Information products have played a major role in making supply chains more efficient. GPS monitors placed on trucks allow shippers to monitor the location of each driver, thus helping companies sell unused hauling capacity more effectively and reducing theft. The combination of pricing software and location monitoring allowed one company to increase the amount of hauling each driver does by 15 percent since 1990.[10]

The main lesson is that integrating information technology into products adds value both by reducing the cost of performing standard activities and by making it possible to solve more of the problems that face society. In most industries, the proportion of a product's total value that is represented by its software is likely to continue to increase. The scope for products taking advantage of this technology is virtually endless, limited only by the imagination of product designers and the needs and income of customers.

Customization

High-income consumers are increasingly willing to pay a premium for products that appeal to their unique self-image. Firms that are able to deliver a unique product to match each customer's individual tastes can therefore command higher margins. Under the traditional model of manufacturing, longer production runs lowered average costs. This created an incentive to standardize products whenever possible. Standardization is still important in fostering competition, but it no longer guarantees lower costs and increasingly does not deliver the highest value to the consumer.

Virtually every consumer product line has exhibited increased diversity over the past several years. I noted earlier in this chapter that Crest offers at least 12 identifiable types of toothpaste. While this gives the customer greater choice, real customization lets the consumer design the product himself and delays final production until the product has been ordered. According to a report in the *New York Times Magazine*, General Mills is planning to open a new Web site, www.mycereal.com, that will allow consumers to order a personalized cereal mix and have it delivered to their homes for about $1 per serving.[11]

More significantly, modern technology allows companies to produce products that exactly meet the customer's needs. Several clothing companies, including Brooks Brothers, use laser scanners to take the customers' exact measurements and electronically send them to the factory for clothing tailored to his body. At www.customatix.com, a buyer can design his own athletic shoe, picking not only the size, but the style and colors, all for $70. Tailoring like this can increase profit margins in two ways. First, the buyer in many cases is willing to pay more for a product that exactly meets his needs and provides him with an individual avenue of self-expression. Second, by eliminating the guesswork involved in producing for future demand and obtaining payment sooner, companies can reduce their costs by avoiding unsold inventory and shortening their cash cycles. This increases returns on investment.

In most cases, the full realization of mass customization requires a dramatic change in industry structure. This has been one of the primary reasons why the automotive industry has made so little progress toward realizing the tremendous advances customization can deliver in terms of increasing the value to the customer and reducing the cost to the producer. The technology for ordering a custom car in three days already exists, but institutional obstacles limit its use. The existing dealership system has a strong vested interest in preventing customers from buying directly from automakers. But even without this hurdle, the manufacturers must make significant changes in automotive design, factory layout, and delivery infrastructure before they can take full advantage of the technology's promise. Customers will have to accept changes in the way they interact with both dealers and the manufacturers. These institutional changes take time to accomplish and often cost a great deal of money over the short term.

Similar trends exist in industrial markets. Increased competition and complexity will force companies to pursue different strategies based on their individual core competencies and to devote more of their attention to the care and expansion of these competencies. This encourages them to turn more activities over to their suppliers, but because each company's strategy is different, these suppliers will face pressure to deliver a unique solution tailored to each customer's existing strategy and markets. Rather than deliver a standard machine that the customer must then set up, service, and integrate into existing operations, suppliers will be asked to take on the entire problem associated with the particular function that the machine is asked to perform.

CHANGES IN ORGANIZATIONAL DESIGN

Chapter 8 in this volume examines the changing nature of the firm in great depth. In order to take full advantage of the strategies listed above, most companies must undergo significant organizational change. A company that outsources major activities while extending its own core competencies into other industries, that produces to individual order rather than to stock, and that takes full advantage of the services and information content typically associated with its products must operate very differently than the standard model. The natural resistance of human institutions to rapid organizational change may present a more serious barrier to profitability than either the economic or the technical challenges.

The specific organizational structure will depend on a variety of factors, including industry, technology, and the firm's strategic intent. However, a study of successful companies demonstrates certain common themes. Firms will have to increase their flexibility so that they can respond quickly to market opportunities. One way to do this is to reduce the amount of fixed costs, so that companies can remain profitable even if demand shifts or drops. In 1998, temporary help services constituted 2.7 percent of the private economy, up from 0.6 percent in 1982.[12] The Bureau of Labor Statistics estimated that over 30 percent of all temporary workers are placed in manufacturing companies, a figure far higher than their proportion of the total workforce.[13] In addition, firms have increasingly outsourced many overhead functions to firms that are better able to diversify the risk of business trends, in the process transforming them into variable costs.[14] Finally, modern finance has allowed companies to sell off specific risks and to hedge against a greater number of uncontrollable factors.

Companies will have to decentralize decision-making. The traditional corporation relied heavily on information passing up and down functional silos. This worked well when information was hard to transmit and market conditions remained relatively stable. Modern manufacturing increasingly relies on information flowing across functions and requires that those closest to the information have the authority to respond to it quickly. This in turn has forced a number of organizational changes. Important decisions are increasingly made by cross-functional teams working collaboratively. Power has been decentralized by giving lower levels the authority to act on customer requests. At the same time, responsibility has been decentralized by giving lower-level managers individual profit-and-loss responsibility and linking pay to performance through stock options, profit-sharing plans, and placing company stock in employee pension plans.

Information technology has become the backbone around which the new company is organized. Information systems increasingly capture information only once, to eliminate duplication and errors. They also share the information more broadly, so that the entire supply chain can get the information it needs. Successful companies in the future will have to make the capture and use of knowledge relevant to their markets a strategic asset.

Finally, a company's top management must be realigned. Information systems and ISO 9000 standards have helped create common procedures so that more time can be devoted to exception-based management: focusing on the relatively small percentage of problems, customers, and projects that have a disproportionate influence on the company's profitability. Companies must become capable of launching a large number of small trials to test new products and markets. Just as important, they must be prepared to stop work on project failures and quickly add resources to trial successes in order to take full advantage of the relatively small number of blockbuster opportunities.

In order to implement these changes, companies must rely heavily on suppliers of all types. As complexity increases, no company will possess a competitive advantage in all of the skills that it needs. Specifically, opportunities will exist for industrial firms to step closer to the consumer end of the supply chain by delivering products like machine tools and controllers that automate much of the production process. In order to respond quickly to changes in consumer markets, companies such as Wal-Mart, Nike, and Ford will need flexible factories capable of changing runs quickly and at low cost, taking and tracking consumer orders, and self-diagnosing problems to avoid downtime. Information and expanded capability increasingly will be contained in the machines that companies use to manufacture their product. As manufacturing systems become a competitive differentiator, more opportunities will exist for the companies that design, install, and run them.

Many of these opportunities may come outside the company's traditional markets, making the ability to collaborate with other companies another key skill. Strategic alliances and other forms of cross-company collaboration have a number of advantages. They lower the cost of entering new markets or offering new products. They allow a company to leverage its brand name, the way that Harley-Davidson has done with tool sets and clothing. They reduce the risk of new ventures. And they allow companies to spread fixed costs over a wider and more stable base; for example, SKF shares warehousing facilities with two of its major competitors. Management will have to acquire the ability to manage these collaborations well and ensure that they remain consistent with the firm's overall strategy.

In the late 1970s and early 1980s, many policymakers worried about the future of U.S. manufacturing. At the time the worry was mainly focused on the relative competitiveness of American companies and, unlike today, it had a great deal of basis in fact. American firms had lost competitiveness to international companies, especially the Japanese and Germans. Although the call for a national industrial strategy was misplaced, restructuring was urgently needed.

Today much of that restructuring has occurred. As a result, American firms are far better placed than their competitors to take advantage of the opportunities before them. Although the wave of downsizing, reengineering, and corporate restructuring has often been painful, it has helped companies reduce their cost structures and concentrate on core competencies. Deregulation and a looser antitrust policy exposed new industries to competition. Strong anti-collusion enforcement and low trade barriers created strongly competitive markets. Shareholder activism and the growth of defined contribution pension plans increased pressure on management to show financial results, while financial deregulation made it easier to achieve changes in management.

As we enter the new millennium, America leads the world in the development of those technologies, such as biotechnology, nanotechnology, and computers, that are seen as crucial to the future. Using this base of knowledge and their hard-won competitive positions, American manufacturers should continue to find profitable opportunities to leverage their core skills.

CONCLUSIONS FOR MANUFACTURERS

Although many of the examples discussed above are taken from consumer markets, these trends hold direct relevance for all manufacturing companies.

First, the demand for the products produced by many manufacturing firms is derivative. It depends on the ability of their customers to offer products that consumers will buy. The continuous pursuit of higher values in a richer society means that consumer markets should continue to grow and that demand for new and innovative products should be high over the long run. It also means that the ability to deliver customized products quickly and at a competitive cost is likely to be one of the key strategic differentiators in many industries. Companies will increasingly turn to their suppliers for solutions that help them increase the competitiveness of their production processes.

Each company's needs are likely to be different, requiring the supplier to gain a deeper appreciation of the customer's specific problem and forcing it to offer a tailored solution rather than a standardized product. The trade-off is that customers are likely to find it more profitable to pay suppliers to deliver a total solution rather than to purchase individual products and figure out the solution themselves. Unlike the consumer market, industrial firms will have to sell products based on the ability to increase the return on investment that their customers receive in their own markets.

All manufacturers will have to look carefully at each of the major activities they perform, asking two questions: Do we perform this activity particularly well? Is this activity vital to the broader supply chain we find ourselves in? If the answer to both questions is "no," the activity should be outsourced to a company that can do it better or cheaper. If the answer to the first question is "yes," then the company should consider transforming the activity into a core competency that it can use as a platform to expand its business. Expansion is likely to be most successful if the activity is strategically important to the supply chain and is closely related to the company's existing markets. Companies also must deal with any activities that are important to their strategic success but are not core competencies. These represent potential areas of weakness where the firm should either increase its ability or outsource the activity to a trusted partner that will perform it well.

Manufacturers have many opportunities to add services to the line of products they offer. Opportunities in information technology will be discussed in more depth in chapter 6, but obvious examples are consulting, financing, servicing, installation and training, leasing, and even operation. The decision to engage in any of these activities should depend on whether it helps distinguish the company's products from those of its competitors and on the returns it offers to investment. In many cases, it will make sense for customers to use more of a manufacturer's overall expertise. Companies that allow suppliers to take over more of the services associated with the supplier's products can free up resources to concentrate on the things they do well. To move into these areas, suppliers will have to consider expanding their scope of authority, perhaps to the point of retaining ownership and even control of the products they place in customers' plants.

Continued advances in technology are also critical to manufacturing's success. Pressure to produce faster, better, and cheaper will maintain the demand for advanced production facilities. The new generation of machine tools has played a leading role in the recent increases in productivity.[15] Each supplier must continue to develop new technologies built around its core competencies. The marketing function will have to switch from trying to find markets for the company's existing products to working with engineers to identify future market opportunities. Product developers must match the technology push of new discoveries with the market pull of customers. The most difficult task will not be finding new technologies to employ. The challenge will come in choosing the right technologies and then integrating them into profitable products that customers want to buy. Like other components of a successful strategy, this of course entails a deep understanding of the customers' needs and operations.

Information technology offers a unique opportunity to add value. Products increasingly need to be tied into the information that flows through customers' value chains. Integrating the plant floor into the rest of the company may be the most profitable market opportunity available to a supplier. Computers have played a major role in making products more productive since the 1990s. Modern software allows for remote diagnostics, real-time inventories, and smaller footprints. These in turn help companies increase productivity, add flexibility, and improve return on investment.

For many companies, total manufacturing cost is likely to remain a key component of success. These companies will continue to demand products that allow them to reduce their costs. By offering solutions that help their customers produce faster and more precisely at lower costs, suppliers provide them with value. They are likely to add the most value to customers in end markets that are growing and in which flexible and efficient manufacturing is a key component of profitability.

To take advantage of these opportunities, companies need a process of continued organizational changes. These changes will require both less and more leadership. Managers must let go of many business details, giving those closest to the customer more authority to act on the information they get. At the same time, top executives should consider the value of spending more time planning the company's structure and future. A recent survey in *The Economist* magazine listed three virtues of successful management: honesty, frugality, and preparedness.[16] It might have added a fourth: the willingness to make decisions and commit resources on limited information. There is no substitute for bold leadership. For while there is no single solution that offers guaranteed success, there are a large number of promising opportunities.

Chapter 6

New Paradigms for 21st Century Manufacturing and Their Impacts on Automation

by Jeffrey F. Werling

INTRODUCTION AND CONCLUSION

This chapter examines the forces driving the technology of productive processes in the 21st-century economy and assesses the implications of these trends for firms that provide automation technologies. Perhaps the most important driver pushing firms to apply production innovations over time is competition. Most (though certainly not all) important changes in products, processes, and markets can ultimately be traced to competitive pressures. Because the global community is rapidly integrating, deregulating, and innovating all at the same time, competition is intensifying, especially in manufacturing.

The increasingly competitive environment in business today is forcing global manufacturers to focus, more strongly than ever, on customer value. Firms today are maximizing customer value by delivering goods and services optimized across the following objectives: low cost, quality, fast delivery, rapid innovation, flexibility, and feasibility. To execute these strategies, firms are looking to their capital goods suppliers for help. For example, manufacturers want new production systems that drastically reduce total product costs, slash lead times, operate in a build-to-order environment, eliminate variations, and support rapid product innovation. ***Therefore, capital equipment manufacturers and automation providers can no longer be organized and manned just to make and sell equipment. Specifically, and in addition to their traditional technical skills, they will have to bring to the table capabilities in financial analysis, lean manufacturing, Six Sigma, information technology, asset management, software development, and supply chain integration. These skills will be needed to design, install, and***

maintain production systems that directly support their clients' business objectives.

Automation providers must also assist their customers in meeting another of their most pressing challenges: automating the flow and the use of information. With the dawn of the Internet, its common standards, and the new supply chain methodologies that it makes possible, the automation of and reliance on global communication will continue to expand dramatically. Starting from the customer, back up the value stream through to the raw material provider, and back up the other stream to the original designer, seamless product and information flow is binding operations together, not only within firms but among them as well. Organizing and controlling data flows involves great complexity, and turning enormous quantities of data into useful information requires great insight. To cope in this environment, manufacturers need well-designed and well-implemented automated information systems that ***get the right information to the right person (or machine) at the right time.***

Most companies are still far from this standard, and the ideal model itself is changing constantly. Implementing this dynamic vision will be the main battleground for information and communications technology over the next decade. ***More specifically, it is software development that provides the most important challenges for improving the smooth coordination and functioning of the supply chain.*** Integrated and open software systems are needed to connect design, strategy, planning, control, maintenance, and collaboration from the customer to the factory floor and to the corner office. Precisely because of this need to integrate and standardize, the field is going to become increasingly competitive. ***It may not be enough to defend current market positions through constant upgrades of existing products. Rather, these systems will have to be retooled to fight for automated control of the customer value chain.***

Finally, manufacturers sell in a global market, produce in a global environment, and must meet global standards. Yet most companies still have much change and work ahead in their quest to become truly global. ***For automation providers, the globalization process means that they must be ready to supply customers with world-class, standardized equipment and services anywhere across the globe. By successfully meeting this challenge early, they will be provided the lucrative opportunity to help their customers prosper in the global environment.***

We argue that these propositions will continue to greatly influence the manufacturing community for at least another ten years. To be sure, the modern conceptions of customer focus, lean manufacturing, the "information revolution," and globalization have been around for almost a decade. But talks with manufacturing engineers, executives, and other experts reveal that the radical changes that these developments portend have only begun to be played out. Core competencies will continue to change. The lean enterprise concept is in the infant stage for most companies. Experts have no more than a fuzzy idea of the ultimate outcome of the information revolution. Moreover, much of the rest of the world currently lags only slightly behind the United States in experiencing some of these trends. Globalization will ensure that they catch up, whether or not they want to. Therefore, it is worth considering these concepts in a new context to see what they might imply for capital goods suppliers in general and automation solution providers in particular.[1]

COMPETITION AND THE NEW CUSTOMER FOCUS

As the 21st century dawns, globalization, deregulation, and new information technologies are greatly increasing competition, especially within most manufacturing industries. While competition has advanced steadily in the post-World War II period, competitive challenges have become particularly intense since 1990, sparking great technological progress, important management innovations, and a period of rapid progress in global manufacturing. The real prices of most manufactured goods have fallen significantly since 1990, a testament to the fact that productivity has skyrocketed. There is a countless array of new products, most of which were only vague ideas ten years ago. Manufacturing processes are cleaner, less wasteful, and safer.

While the increasingly competitive setting in business today greatly benefits consumers, to remain profitable, global manufacturers need to constantly reinvent and restructure their product offerings, operational processes, and business organizations. Some companies are attempting to expand economies of scale and strengthen their global market position by buying complementary product lines, competitors, and/or strategic partners. Others focus on "core competencies," divesting and/or outsourcing other activities. Most important, successful firms sustain profit margins by delivering a bundle of goods and services designed to maximize customer value. The important parameters of customer satisfaction vary greatly across customers, products, and markets. Moreover, because supply chain performance is integral to the survival of their business, intermediate customers often demand even greater performance than do final consumers. A summary of the mission might be the following: Firms must provide their customers with what they want, when they want it, and at the price they want to pay for it.

Objectives of Automation

Modern manufacturers derive value from capital equipment and automation systems only when they enable them to better accomplish their missions of customer satisfaction and profitability. In the commercial setting, automation is the application of automatic control technology to production and ancillary processes. In general, firms apply automation technology to optimize their manufacturing operations, in order to boost profitability and maximize customer value, through one or more of the following ***objectives***:

- reduce production costs
- enhance product quality
- increase the speed of production to reduce delivery lead times
- improve the pace and scope of innovation
- expand process and product flexibility
- make feasible the production of goods or services that could not otherwise be created.[2]

Each of these purposes requires some elaboration.

Costs.—Costs have a direct impact on the profitability of firms in competitive as well as noncompetitive environments, and therefore cost reduction has always been, and always will be, the most important driver of changes in production processes. The focus in this chapter will be most often concerned with the total cost of delivering a product to a customer, including design and start-up costs, direct labor and material costs, indirect costs such as administration and marketing, and capital costs such as machine expenditures and inventory maintenance. Evaluations of capital expenditures, including those for automation, are increasingly being made in this "total cost" framework.

Quality.—In this context, quality can be defined as the extent to which the final product meets customers' specifications. Standards will vary from product to product and consumer to consumer, of course, but purchasers commonly express expectations for characteristics such as performance, durability, dependability, and attractiveness. Automation most often contributes to tighter tolerances of product quality by enhancing the control, reliability, and consistency of production processes.

Speed.—An important element of business practice in today's impatient world is speed. There is one measure of speed that is becoming increasingly important to manufacturers: the lead time between intention to purchase and delivery. For most final consumer products, delivery is usually instantaneous, but the inventory cost of this feature is high. Therefore, lead time compression remains a major objective all along the supply chain, not only for manufacturing firms but for transportation, wholesalers, and retailers as well. When possible, build-to-order systems are seen as ideal. Automation often fills an important role in speeding processes.

Innovation.—Innovation is the important process by which products change through time. To accommodate the dramatic shortening of product cycles, firms must enhance their ability to innovate year after year, while simultaneously slashing the cost of new product development, engineering, and marketing. To compress product-cycle times, manufacturers have come to rely on highly automated design and engineering tools that are tied into marketing and manufacturing systems. Because of the necessity of integration, the borders between research, design, engineering, manufacturing, distribution, and even marketing are becoming increasingly blurred.

Flexibility.—Flexibility is the ability to vary a product's characteristics in line with customer specifications. Futurists insist that the age of mass customization is just around the corner for a vast range of products. Perhaps. But many manufacturing firms are still struggling with the logistics of relatively basic variations and the often irritatingly high costs of routine machine setups. Flexibility can also refer to an ancillary package of goods and services delivered with the primary product, such as customized and attractive packaging or the bundling of associated services such as installation, warranties, and financing. Perhaps the biggest role that technology is currently playing in increasing product and process flexibility is through the automation of information flow; that is, by getting the right information to the right person at the right time.

Feasibility.—This concerns automation's capability to create the goods or services that simply could not be produced using manual dexterity and/or human control. Manual production could be impractical for reasons of physics, economics, or complexity. There are countless examples, but perhaps the most outstanding example of a family of products that would be almost impossible to envision without automation is microelectronics. The smaller electronic components become, the more unworkable it would be to design and fabricate them by hand. Other items produced through automation that are readily taken for granted include hazardous chemicals, a large proportion of processed food products, and statistical modeling.

Collectively referred to here as ***CQSIFF***, the automation objectives of ***cost, quality, speed, innovation, flexibility, and feasibility*** flow directly from competitive pressure and the modern firm's focus on providing value and satisfaction to customers. The following sections describe the most important forces driving the application of automation technology for the next decade. In these descriptions, the discussion will be consistently framed around the definition of automation and its six main purposes.

AUTOMATION SUPPLIERS MUST BECOME INTEGRATED SOLUTION PROVIDERS

The current competitive environment and manufacturers' focus on customer value create great opportunities and important new challenges for automation providers and capital goods suppliers. These companies must do much more than ensure that their own products are delivered at lowest cost, on time, and to rigorous specifications. Automation providers must be prepared to work more closely with their customers than ever before, in order to design and implement optimized and integrated manufacturing solutions. This role goes well beyond the traditional model for producing and selling capital goods. It will require organizations that can leverage knowledge about the new business strategies and operating tactics that manufacturers are using to maximize customer value and profitability. More specifically, four important trends are becoming important among manufacturers:

1. Greater focus on core competencies
2. New approaches toward measuring and managing costs
3. Increasing importance of noncost objectives
4. Optimizing automation for the new operating strategies.

The following sections outline each of these trends and discuss its implication for automation technology.

Focusing on Core Competencies

The objectives of CQSIFF are not mutually exclusive. For instance, there is often a great overlap between quality and feasibility. Some products would not exist without the precision (quality) made possible only through automation. The best of new production techniques can simultaneously improve cost, quality, speed, and flexibility. But just as frequently, pursuit of the primary objectives can entail clear and important trade-offs. Higher quality, faster delivery, and greater flexibility most often come at a higher cost. Compromises between speed and customization are made all the time. Therefore, in formulating their competitive strategy, firms must usually strike an explicit balance among the core objectives of CQSIFF.

Myriad strategic and tactical implications fall out from this need to identify a "competitive space" among CQSIFF that a firm wants to occupy in the attempt to maximize customer value. One of the most important implications of customercentric behavior is that firms are increasingly interested in pursuing only the activities that support their vision and only within what they regard as their core competencies. Given the struggle to provide customer value better than any competitors, there is less business motivation for doing something secondary to a firm's business strategy, especially when that function can be done better by someone else. Therefore, outsourcing of noncore activities is becoming widespread.

In the extreme case, the "virtual company" concentrates on narrow functions such as design and marketing. It then hires partners and coordinates the supply chain logistics, manufacturing, and distribution in concert with them. Dell Computer and Cisco Systems are two of the prominent examples of this model. Other companies regard manufacturing as a core activity and might outsource maintenance, repair, and operations purchasing, marketing, and distribution. Flextronics and Solectron represent successful companies in this niche. While specialization varies in all sorts of combinations, one trend is emerging: the management of capital equipment assets is increasingly designated as a "noncore" activity. Who will fill this space?

The focus on customer value and core competency is opening up vast new possibilities for capital equipment manufacturers and automation providers as manufacturers look to outsource capital asset management functions such as production equipment and system design ownership, installation, monitoring, maintenance, repair, and even operation. Capital equipment providers have the knowledge and experience, the facilities and personnel, and now, through modern information and communications technology, the means to expand their customer value proposition by bundling capital asset management services with equipment purchases.

Installation services and maintenance contracts were the first of these services and have been around for a long time. Equipment leasing was next. Now, capital goods providers are offering entire suites of asset management services, including preventive maintenance facilitated through remote monitoring and diagnostics over the Internet. The "customized solutions" division has been formed in more than a few capital goods companies. For example, Cincinnati Machine recently inaugurated CINCINNATI PLUS℠, a service package that provides comprehensive "life-of-the-machine" support, serving customers' needs before, during, and after the installation of their machine tool. Provided to maximize customers' return on capital investment, the program is designed to optimize machine performance, availability, and life at a lower maintenance cost.

Providers of more integrated systems are finding that to provide such comprehensive services, they need to develop cross-platform capabilities and, in some cases, partnerships with other manufacturers, including competitors. Of course, a primary motivation of customers looking to outsource functions is the constant pressure to cut total supply costs. Drilling down to this next level reveals further implications.

New Approaches Toward Measuring and Managing Costs

Over the years, automation has played a leading role in cost reduction, especially of direct labor costs. Some argue that the industrial revolution was born when manual processes such as spinning and weaving were transferred to "automated" machines in the late 18th century. Whatever its origins, the most important economic aspect of this 200-year-old revolution was the dramatic spreading of laborsaving technologies across virtually every productive activity. In manufacturing, the automatic control of processes accelerated greatly after World War II through the new electric and electronic devices, especially the programmable logic controller invented in the late 1960s.

The emphasis on increasing labor productivity was a logical progression when labor was a significant portion of total costs, the potential for economies of scale was great, and consumer demand for homogeneous, mass-produced goods was growing briskly. More recently, however, advocates of "world-class" manufacturing techniques are reevaluating this traditional role of automation and its focus on direct labor costs. In fact, there are several stories of automation gone awry in U.S. manufacturing, including ill-fated forays into robotics and automated assembly lines that turned out to be uneconomic.

Frequently, traditional investments in automation and other technologies were locally focused on improving the efficiency and effectiveness of individual production processes. But the total benefits attributable to these investments were often disappointing because they were made without regard to the productivity and cycle time of related processes and to conditions in the broader supply chain. For example, because machine utilization was often the primary measure for justifying an investment, and setups tended to be complicated and costly, machine time per unit was reduced in many automation solutions by producing large batches. But increasing the throughput of a process without equivalent enhancements in downstream processes results only in increased queue time and work-in-process (WIP) at the next steps. Moreover, large batch production tends to hide quality problems. When "islands of automation" coexisted in the supply chain with less efficient processes, other unintentional costs were created which at least partly offset the benefits of installing the machinery.

Many observers trace the origin of these problems to traditional cost accounting (TCA) systems. TCA often allocated indirect costs to products based on some relatively arbitrary volume measure, such as labor time or machine usage. In the former case, TCA would exaggerate the cost savings of increasing labor productivity. In the latter it might exaggerate the benefits of buying a faster machine.

Paradoxically, because direct labor outlays have fallen so much over the years because of automation, indirect costs now loom much larger in the cost equation. Activity-based costing (ABC) was developed in the 1980s to change the thinking surrounding indirect cost structures.[3] ABC attempts to take a closer look at indirect costs and to allocate them as closely as possible to the "activity" or product with which they were most closely associated. This focus necessitated, perhaps for the first time, cost analysis across the entire supply chain for individual products. It also began to shed light on the cost categories that seemed to be growing just as direct labor costs were falling: machine setup and maintenance, inventory, and quality.

Manufacturers are now embracing even newer accounting structures and other metrics designed to improve incentive systems and management decision-making. Especially relevant in regard to capital purchases is economic value added (EVA). EVA subtracts from after-tax profits the cost of the capital invested in the business. At the very least, EVA establishes an explicitly computed cost of capital statistic as the return on the investment hurdle rate. More important, it places capital costs, including those for inventory, on the same level as labor, material, or office supplies. In practice, EVA makes managers take a second look at capital expenditures, such as those on automation, to ensure that investments will deliver economic returns.

Moreover, the "lean enterprise" philosophy delves even further into value chain analysis to enhance bottom-line results by emphasizing the elimination of "waste" such as machine setup time, unnecessary product or human movement, and other nonvalue-added activity. Like EVA, lean implementations concentrate on reducing the costs of inventory and capital, and are designed to enhance customer value through measured quality improvement, lead time reduction, and increased flexibility. Six Sigma works to meet the same objectives by focusing first on quality in general, and variability reduction in particular. It is also a very rigorously metrics-driven program. There will be more to say about lean manufacturing and Six Sigma later in this chapter, but in the current context it is important to note that a whole new array of performance metrics is springing from these philosophies: customer satisfaction, on-time delivery, inventory turns, cycle time, defects per million opportunities, and the cost of quality, to name a few. Such metrics tend to be very specific and focused on the objectives at hand, which sometimes do not include cost at all.

At any rate, the cost-saving propositions for capital investment will be increasingly evaluated in the framework of total value chain cost, using modern financial computations such as ABC, EVA, and the performance metrics evolving from lean manufacturing and Six Sigma. These approaches stress that return on investment computations must include cost-and-benefit impacts across the entire supply chain, including the financing cost of any innovations. ***Automation providers will need to be prepared to participate in these computations, providing specific and precise information on the bottom-line effects of their goods and services. This preparation will require applications engineers, distributors, and other personnel equipped with capabilities for computing and communicating the financial benefits of applying new production infrastructure and processes.***

The Increasing Importance of Noncost Objectives

In a preceding chapter, it was pointed out that the increase in incomes and the evolution of society's values mean that product characteristics besides cost are becoming, if not more important than cost in absolute terms, then more important than cost in relative terms. For example, consumers have consistently demonstrated a willingness to pay a premium for reliability, on-time delivery, customization, and technological sophistication. In fact, the objectives of quality, speed, innovation, flexibility, and feasibility (QSIFF), which might once have been thought of as secondary targets for manufacturing technology, are becoming much more important in the 21st century. Indeed, some combination and/or variation of these goals is well established in most manufacturing strategic plans. Moreover, with the great emphasis today on supply chain excellence, the objectives are at least as important in industrial markets as they are in consumer markets.

The increasing importance of QSIFF is having an accelerated impact on manufacturing technology. The earliest programmable logic controllers, the grandfathers of modern automation technology, enhanced the speed and flexibility of automated production. Numerical control and computer numerical control machines improved many aspects of manufacturing, but because they ushered in a new era of process consistency, their biggest impact may have been on quality. Computer and network technologies have helped to streamline production and the associated information flow in order to enhance speed and flexibility.

Several new technologies are coming on stream to meet new standards for QSIFF. Sensor technologies have long been used for control and quality enhancement. Now, firms are using the information they collect from the sensors to create complementary products. In the food processing industry, for instance, producers are able to obtain increasingly better information concerning the quality and integrity of the ingredients and the process. In turn, this information can be used to better safeguard the food supply. Intelligent manufacturing systems promise to further automate the forecasting, coordination, execution, and maintenance of production.

Furthermore, automation technologies will help make feasible an ever-broader array of new product concepts. Biotechnology will help create the customization of food crops, advanced organic materials with myriad applications, and new medical procedures. In each case, equipment manufacturers will be called on to develop the equipment to bring these inventions to fruition. Scientists and entrepreneurs are only now beginning to contemplate the commercial implications of nanotechnology, where microscopic machines will make possible a whole new era for manufacturing and a whole new type of capital equipment.

In the current highly competitive environment, cost remains critical. ***But customers' demands for QSIFF are gaining ground in importance, and new advancements in manufacturing and automation technology will continue to reflect this fact. Moreover, manufacturing firms, with the help of their capital equipment providers, will need to optimize the use of these technologies through an explicit identification and consideration of the relative importance of these objectives.***

However, competition, customer value, and the increasing importance of QSIFF have had the largest impact not necessarily on production hardware, but on how companies structure production processes and related activities.

Similarly to how ABC and EVA have revolutionized the way companies approach costs, new business and manufacturing management paradigms are being applied that stress QSIFF enhancement as well as cost reduction.

Optimizing Automation for New Operating Strategies

Manufacturing companies in many industries have discovered that one key to satisfying customers is to produce to demand, not to stock. In particular, they are using "flow manufacturing," the general adaptation of the Toyota Production System, which in turn was developed from the original concept of the assembly line pioneered by Henry Ford. Flow manufacturing allows production to order by compressing lead times. It also helps to slash the costs of inventory, over-production, and stock-outs. It improves quality because each step in the production process immediately validates the previous step (similar to total quality management). And finally, producing to order increases the potential for product customization.[4]

Traditional manufacturing focuses on making and then selling products. It optimizes resources (equipment and people) by trying to make sure they are always working to capacity. This focus on "utilization" encourages batch and queuing operations with significant movement of material among WIP locations, where material can be lost, get damaged, or become obsolete. Traditional manufacturing often included a step at the end of the process where inspectors would evaluate the quality of the final product. Rejected material would either be sent back for rework or scrapped.

In contrast with batch and queue, flow manufacturing focuses on process, product, and materials, and searches for waste by identifying idle or underutilized inventory. The basic idea is that product continuously flows down an assembly line, and each step of the manufacturing process is performed at roughly the same rate. Flow manufacturing is the central tenet of lean manufacturing, which emphasizes the following principles: eliminating nonvalue-added activity (*muda*), establishing a process pulse rate (*takt* time), pull scheduling (*kanban*), just-in-time inventory control (JIT), built-in error detection (*jidoka*), quick machine setups, cellular manufacturing, flexible manufacturing systems, and balanced operations.

To be sure, most manufacturers in most industries still do not have lead times short enough to build every component to a specific, final order. In many cases pure build-to-order may never be feasible, and buffer inventory is commonly held for the final product. Moreover, the application of lean manufacturing as described here will have limited impact on production that must occur in batches (like beer), or on processes that continuously flow out of necessity and are already highly automated (petrochemicals).

Nevertheless, great changes are coming along the supply chains in every industry, including among suppliers and intracompany operations. Manufacturers as diverse as Boeing, Parker Hannifin, and Batesville Casket Company are moving toward worldwide implementation of demand-pull flow systems that are eliminating WIP and meeting rigorous targets for cost, quality, speed, and flexibility. Though this movement is spreading rapidly, for most discrete product manufacturing the flow transformation has just begun, and it will have a great influence on the design and application of automation technologies.

As companies progress through lean implementations, automation projects will be a part of the solutions if they are part of a systemwide strategy that has real bottom-line impact. Manufacturing engineers will be looking for automation to provide simple and affordable solutions to the following:

1. Help individual procedures become better synchronized with the overall process pace (*takt* time)
2. Enable faster setup and tool changes
3. Enhance the effectiveness, flow, and ergonomics of human effort
4. Verify the consistency of processes and the quality of the results
5. Transfer product between steps
6. Enhance the information flow along the value chain.

Envision, for the moment, a hypothetical machining cell. Perhaps its role is the creation of a component of a larger product made within the factory. The cell performs six separate processes on raw material to fabricate the part. Such a cell might be set up so that human operators perform the operations requiring greater dexterity, such as machine loading and operation, via a human-machine interface. Since they are less complex tasks, machine unloading and part transfer might be done by simple and affordable machines. Tests of very tight tolerances might require automated equipment. Human visual inspection might be sufficient for other validations. The point of this example is that within the flow manufacturing environment, manufacturing managers and, often more important, the lean-enabled production workers that work with them will be searching for the optimal balance between human activity and automation that supports the overall objectives of the process. And, of course, these goals will most likely be defined in terms of CQSIFF.

To assist their clients on these journeys, automation providers will need expertise and interest in these new methods of organizing production. For example, equipment salesmen will need to understand the manufacturing vision contemplated by a lean implementation by asking to see "current state maps" and "future state maps." Only then can they identify valuable roles for new equipment. Once again, the key is not to regard automation as an end in itself, but as part of a tool kit designed to help manufacturers meet CQSIFF goals within the context of the overall value stream.

The importance of optimizing the value stream is moving beyond the flow of product. Advanced information and communications technology is creating new ways to leverage the complementary flow of data and information across the value stream in order to increase customer value and profitability. This new technology is increasingly embedded in manufacturing and automation equipment in order to assist in the flow and management of data concerning the production process. In fact, this may be the most important trend shaping the automation industry today.

AUTOMATING THE INFORMATION FLOW

Information on the Factory Floor

One of the more important insights of the Toyota Production System that spawned the lean manufacturing revolution was that manufacturing processes consisted of two separate, but equally important, flows: the material/work flow and the information flow. The material flow is familiar. The value creation stream consists of the series of operations, such as part fabrication and product assembly. As shown in figure 6-1, product flows downstream (to the right) along this chain, as represented by the darker arrows. Toyota's insight was that the efficiency of this entire process depended on how the information flowing back upstream (the lighter arrows) was used to shape the behavior of the component processes. More specifically, feedback flowing back through the chain was designed to (1) "pull" production along the chain, and (2) provide validation for the previous step.

In contrast to automated production, the automation of information flows started from a less developed base and evolved in interesting and unexpected ways. From the early 1970s to the mid-1990s, the application of electronic information technology to control operations within facilities grew rapidly, especially with the advent of low cost, off-the-shelf components such as video displays, PC technology, local area networks, and open systems. These technologies made possible computer-integrated manufacturing, which contributed greatly to productivity over the late 1980s and into the 1990s. But just as some mistakes were made in production automation, so some information automation has turned out to be ineffective. Often, managers and workers are overwhelmed with data that cannot be interpreted in a useful fashion. Worse, many existing systems are designed around the detailed planning and execution models of traditional build-to-stock systems.

Indeed, flow manufacturing is stimulating a complete reevaluation and reengineering of how information flows within a factory. The new thinking insists that a well-designed and well-implemented information system gets ***the right information to the right person (or machine) at the right time.*** While such a system is the key component for meeting new standards of cost, quality, speed, and customization, it does not necessarily have to be electronic. Visitors to many lean facilities see that designers of pull and JIT systems are relegating the computers to a minor role and turning off the

Figure 6-1
Manufacturing Value Stream

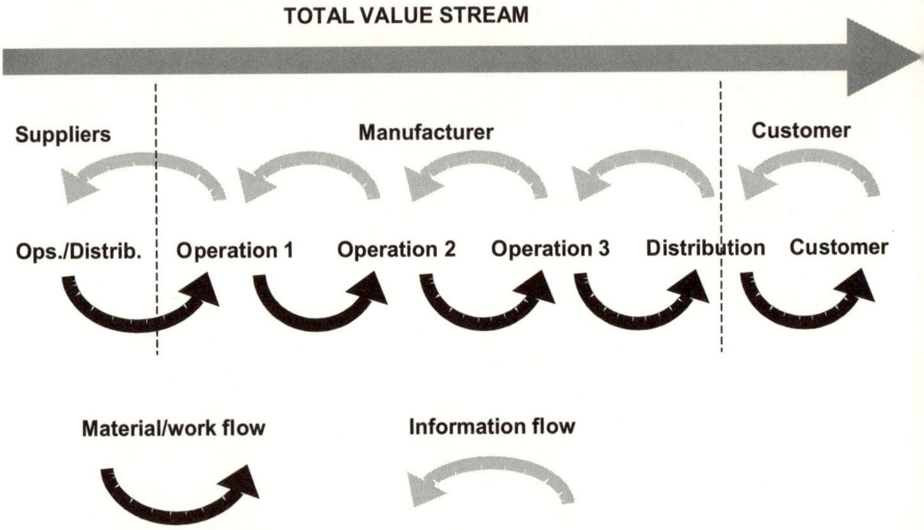

Source: Manufacturers Alliance/MAPI Inc.

manufacturing module of enterprise resource planning (ERP) systems. Traditional resource planning systems are being replaced with simpler but more effective automatic environmental information systems such as *kanbans* or component containers with refill lines drawn on them.

Nonetheless, electronically automated information continues to play new and important roles on the factory floor. Machine-embedded error detection processes often use lights and switches to alert workers and, in some cases, the rest of the automated line to problems. Associated software designed for individual machines and specific processes is needed to analyze the information. Manufacturing researchers are working to build "intelligent systems" that will use machine models, real-time measurements, and predictions of future behavior to automatically control and correct machinery production processes.[5] From now on, most automation solutions will have to incorporate some of the data-handling and information analysis capabilities that these more intelligent systems require.

Local networks also will have increasingly important uses in this context. Among myriad possibilities, performance metrics, schedule changes, customized assembly information, supplier status, and new work ideas can be easily distributed. Presumably during their breaks, employees can even check their retirement accounts, the local sports scores, and the global news via an Internet portal! In fact, once one considers that the typical value stream actually encompasses activities well outside the factory floor, the potential of automated information flows rises dramatically.

Automating Information Flow Across the Value Chain

If it is not happening already, someday soon someone will place a requisition on the Internet, and somewhere a machine will start processing material to fill the request. Perhaps, in fact, the starting noise of the machine will be the first signal to a human that an order has just been entered thousands of miles away. At the same time, marketing, manufacturing, logistic, and financial records in far-flung computers will be automatically updated. In turn, other manufacturing lines might be activated, each a component process of a supply chain stretching across many factories, across several companies, and across a few continents. How could such a vision be realized without automation?

Firms increasingly regard the business process as a long chain of component value-added activities, each of which needs to be balanced and synchronized with the entire chain. Examine, again, figure 6–1. The boundaries between processes and between suppliers are dotted, in order to denote the fact that they are arbitrary and, under fairly common circumstances, easily shifted. Companies will want to move into the areas of the chain where they have particular competence, and to outsource the activities in that chain where they do not. To make this work, collaboration along the supply chain will require seamless information connectivity. In fact, while the manufacturing procedures might be very simple, the information coordination activities are exceedingly complex, and are becoming more so.

With the dawn of the Internet, its common standards, and the new supply chain methodologies that these enable, the automation of and reliance on global communication will continue to expand dramatically. But organizing and controlling data flows involves great complexity, and turning enormous quantities of data into useful information will require great insight. Perhaps the biggest constraint in managing the vast complexity of supply chain information is software. For many managers, current ERP systems have fallen short of their promise to bring the entire company under one information umbrella. Possibly because they do not recognize how product flows in the value stream environment, or because they were designed for batch and queue, or maybe because no one asked the operating engineers, many ERP systems have proven to be too inflexible for planning and executing manufacturing operations, especially in the flow environment. Managers' biggest complaint is that while most software can spout out a lot of data, many systems cannot translate the data into the information they need to run their business. Instead, companies have had to devote massive resources to construct "middleware" that links more suitable "manufacturing execution systems" with the enterprise software.

Where there is chaos, there is opportunity. Software development provides some of the most important challenges for improving the smooth coordination and functioning of the supply chain. Automation software, since it can connect the factory floor with the customer, the raw material supplier, and the boss in the corner office, can play an ever-increasing role in this revolution. Integrated and open software systems are needed to connect design, strategy, planning, control, maintenance, and collaboration from the customer to the factory floor and to the corner office. Moreover, these systems will need to combine inclusive services with modularity so that new capabilities or changes in one function can be implemented without changing other functions. Some visionaries speak of new systems that contain artificial intelligence capabilities that will automate many more activities. Most manufacturing managers would settle for dumb software that could be used intelligently.

Software that helps integrate operations and supply chains will also have to function within networks that incorporate increasing degrees of security. The computer network of any modern organization is under constant danger of a variety of threats, both internal and external. Companies are learning that the security schemes needed to protect most network operability and critical information require highly integrated, comprehensive, and top-down approaches. For instance, it is not sufficient to have firewalls, identification tools, and password policies. Such arrangements need to be backed up with constant monitoring processes and strict accountability policies if they are to be effective. Therefore, new software tools will not only need to operate with various security hardware and software environments, they will also have to support and conform to the various "social engineering" schemes that companies will use to prevent human error from causing security breaches. This aspect may be especially true for any software embedded in human-machine interface equipment.

Precisely because of the need to secure, standardize, and integrate manufacturers' most critical information systems and networks, the software field is going to become increasingly competitive. Current application suites will attempt to migrate into other functions along the value chain, and much of this migration will occur via consolidation. For example, e-business programs will move upstream from the customer and downstream from the purchasing department in order to capture greater functionability. Enterprise systems will try to better implement effective manufacturing environments. Automation software providers will be playing in this competitive arena. It may not be enough to defend current market positions through constant upgrades of existing products. Rather, these systems will have to be retooled to fight for automated control of the customer value chain.

The Definition and Scope of Automation Is Broadening

It may be argued by some that many of the new information and communication technologies do not come under the purview of "automation," at least as it may be traditionally and narrowly defined. Yet, one of the most important themes of this chapter is that as existing business paradigms are redefined, the tools of doing business are also being redefined. In particular, one cannot limit the scope of automation technology to its traditional realm, the factory floor, because fewer and fewer pieces of manufacturing equipment will be installed without an explicit electronic information link to the universe outside that realm. Factory equipment is not only being linked to the greater supply chain, it is increasingly monitored by outside providers of preventive maintenance, diagnostic, and repair services.

Beyond the rough road maps described above, it is difficult to visualize how the next generation of automation tools will develop, especially beyond a ten-year time horizon. But one fact seems certain: the best of the new automation solutions will work to meet profitability objectives through integrating and coordinating different functions along a value chain that might stretch across the street or across the globe. In this world, the borders among functional departments are becoming more and more blurred. A historical example may best illustrate this fact.

Since the 1980s, the most significant advances in manufacturing have come about through computer-aided design (CAD), computer-aided engineering (CAE), and computer-aided manufacturing (CAM). These technological marvels allow developers to drastically cut the design, prototyping, and tooling stages, and are the primary enablers of the ever-compressing product cycle. When quality problems are detected, the manufacturing process or the product itself can be redesigned on the fly to correct the trouble. In many cases, customization would be impossible without rapid ways to redesign products and reprogram tools to handle variations. Indeed, thousands of the new products released since the 1980s would have been too complex to conceptualize, design, and manufacture without the aid of computers. Automated engineering tools make feasible many of the goods taken for granted today. Moreover, engineers never cease to be amazed at the continual advancements in this technology. Not a year goes by without significant advancements, each in some way designed to help firms cope with CQSIFF.

Was CAD simply software advancement out of thin air? Was its extension to CAE and CAM an idea that came out of the blue? Certainly not. When CAD first came on the scene, its true potential was appreciated not by the design department, and not by the manufacturing department, and certainly not by those in finance. It was the marketing folks who realized that CAD could make oodles of money by giving customers new and improved models at a much faster rate. A more urgent dialogue was struck up between marketing and design. Engineers could react to last week's car lot conversations, not last decade's. Product cycle compression was born.

But the manufacturing department then had a problem. Design kept throwing new products "over the wall." New models were delayed because it took too long to figure out how to make them. A plethora of new styles, new technologies, and new materials, together with the requisite new production techniques, demanded a new way to automate the development engineering and retooling process. To meet this need, CAD was extended to create CAE and CAM tools, essentially punching holes through departmental walls. In fact, a new term, concurrent engineering, was coined in order to reflect the fact that engineering and manufacturing changes are now made simultaneously with design changes. These days, operations engineers can be found in the design department collaboratively ironing out the manufacturing bugs of complex products designed not last month or last week, but earlier that day. This event may be the greatest triumph of automation to date.

The functional borders of the manufacturing value chain will continue to blur not only within companies, but also among them. With this development, the scope of manufacturing automation is broadening quite rapidly. Starting from the customer, back upstream through to the raw material provider, and back up the other value stream to the original designer, seamless information and product flow are binding operations together. In order to maximize the benefits of its application, automation technology must also be ready and able to reach beyond its traditional borders to meet new and interesting challenges, many of which are still unknown.

If automation technology is blasting through the artificial borders of corporate departments, can it also push through the artificial borders dividing people?

GLOBALIZATION AND AUTOMATION

The concept of a seamless, worldwide supply chain is not really very old and, in many ways, it remains unachievable. Local characteristics, customs, and regulations still play a substantial role in determining a manufacturing facility's structure and competencies. In Europe, less flexibility among the workforce obstructs reengineering and restructuring efforts. In Japan, a floundering financial system impedes growth, and rigid product markets prevent competition. In developing nations, immature institutions and market systems, unskilled workforces, and government meddling increase the difficulties and costs of doing business.

While such differences will remain important, their significance is declining. Decreases in transportation costs, reductions in trade barriers, and the open standards of the Internet are accelerating the development of global markets for many goods and services, and enhancing the exchange of ideas and technology. International competition and the demands for global standards of CQSIFF are gradually forcing firms to install the most advanced technology and the best practice no matter where they are located.

A recent study by Robert Filippini, Andrea Vinelli, and Chris Voss analyzed how eight manufacturing process initiatives, collectively referred to as high performance manufacturing improvements, were adopted by surveyed plants across five developed nations over the course of 25 years.[6] A summary of the survey results is shown in table 6-1. For example, quality management initiatives were widespread only in Japan by the end of the 1960s. Starting in the 1980s, however, Japanese manufacturing success stimulated a rapid migration of quality management through Italy, the United Kingdom, the United States, and Germany. Widespread adoption of each of the other technologies, flexible automation, supplier relations, CAD, JIT, MRP, human resources, and simultaneous engineering occurred as well, though sometimes unevenly. It is interesting to note that while Japan pioneered many of these high-performance technologies, the country's manufacturers appear to have fallen behind, on average. They particularly lag in adopting simultaneous engineering, an especially crucial technology for sustaining innovation and technological change. By the late 1990s, each technology had similar and high rates of adoption across each of the five nations. The authors go on to claim that the recent acceleration of globalization and its associated competition have worked to quicken the pace of technological diffusion.[7]

Indeed, a similar migration of production technology is also occurring from developed nations to less developed nations, albeit to a somewhat lesser extent. The lower relative cost of labor still influences the choice of production technology, especially for activities that are not core to global characteristics. Where low labor costs are important, labor-saving automation might be less intensive. On the other hand, while low direct labor cost might remain an important reason for establishing a manufacturing "footprint," it is not necessarily a good reason to adopt less automated processes. First of all, most of the manufacturing located in the less developed world is dedicated to making products for those markets. In most circumstances, these facilities will be competing against producers situated in regions with similar costs. Therefore, any competitive edge that affordable and effective automation can make possible will be pursued. More important, downstream customers increasingly demand the same global product standards regardless, of where a product is delivered. And, as stressed throughout this chapter, the objectives of quality, speed, and flexibility are often just as important as cost. In many cases, firms located in less developed nations will not be able to compete on those characteristics without state-of-the-art automation technology.

In particular, as manufacturing multinationals expand their market presence and manufacturing footprints across the globe, they are finding it more and more useful to develop and install in each location global solutions not only for production techniques but for electronic data exchange as well. In many instances, the economies of scope and scale gained by adopting consistent technology and methods across global locations trump cost and other considerations. For instance, a geographically diversified portfolio of similar

Table 6-1
Manufacturing Improvement Initiatives Adopted, by Year and Country
(percent)

	Quality Management	Flexible Automation	Supplier Relations	CAD	JIT	MRP	Human Resources	Simultaneous Engineering	Average of all Technologies
Italy									
1973	6	9	3	3	0	0	0	0	3
1983	31	22	6	12	0	34	12	9	16
1988	69	44	25	72	22	59	37	18	43
1993	100	75	62	97	62	78	81	41	75
1998	100	86	85	99	80	84	92	68	87
United Kingdom									
1973	0	8	8	8	0	8	0	0	4
1983	8	33	8	33	0	33	0	0	14
1988	42	50	25	67	8	50	25	8	34
1993	83	67	75	92	67	75	83	67	76
1998	96	75	91	98	88	86	98	86	90

United States									
1973	5	4	0	0	4	8	8	0	4
1983	12	28	4	32	16	24	12	0	16
1988	44	68	12	64	40	60	28	8	41
1993	72	88	56	92	72	80	76	44	73
1998	85	95	79	98	90	87	90	70	87
Japan									
1973	62	5	40	2	0	12	52	5	22
1983	85	50	62	42	50	32	75	17	52
1988	87	70	65	77	65	50	80	27	65
1993	88	87	70	90	75	60	82	42	74
1998	89	94	73	95	83	68	84	55	80
Germany									
1973	13	10	0	17	0	10	20	0	9
1983	30	33	0	43	7	40	33	0	23
1988	40	70	13	73	20	47	43	7	39
1993	70	90	47	93	43	63	77	40	65
1998	85	95	75	98	78	75	85	70	83

Source: Roberto Filippini, Andrea Vinelli, and Chris Voss, "Paths of Improvement in Plant Operations," in *High Performance Manufacturing*, Roger G. Schroeder and Barbara B. Flynn, eds. (New York: John Wiley and Sons, 2001).

manufacturing equipment and facilities allows companies to easily vary the location of production according to variations in market conditions, input prices, and currency values. Indeed, conversations with operating executives reveal that, at the very least, most intend to work toward uniform technologies and strategies for core processes, regardless of location.

Yet despite this desire for common processes and product, most companies still have much change and work ahead in their quest to become truly global. In some cases, regional differences and biases still matter. But more often, it is usually legacy structures and old capital equipment that stand in the way of establishing a global culture and homogeneous manufacturing processes. ***Automation providers and capital equipment manufacturers have a lucrative opportunity to help their customers execute the globalization process. To do this, they must be ready to supply world-class, standardized equipment and services anywhere across the globe. They must understand global problems and local nuances, and be able to design flexible manufacturing solutions that can adapt best global technology to local practices. Moreover, these facilities must integrate smoothly into a global supply chain. In other words, to excel in the global environment, automation providers must be global corporations themselves.***

The "global corporation" goes beyond establishing a presence across world regions. A truly globalized corporation regards the entire world as its potential operating locale. It markets, manufactures, conducts research, raises capital, and purchases supplies wherever it can get the job done best. Yet, global corporations must also be able to recognize when national boundaries, regulations, and/or customs are important. They often have to serve customers set in local ways, to adhere to local product standards, and to face competitors on their home ground. When necessary, they must be prepared to deal with such local and regional differences and, when advantageous, exploit them. In short, the modern company must be able to "think globally and act locally." In order to accomplish this task competitively, global companies must develop human resources and analytical systems that can identify and evaluate durable trends, changing opportunities, and dangerous risks. Finally, since the globalization culture must become ingrained, global corporations must be ready to establish diverse and talented workforces from all around the world.

The need for global reach means that some corporations may have to become larger, expanding across regions organically or by mergers and acquisition. This approach might be especially appropriate where the products and services provided by the capital equipment supplier are particularly complex or proprietary. In other cases, however, large corporate size may not be required. Just as commercial boundaries among nations are becoming blurry, so globalization is redefining the concept of enterprise. Providers of industrial equipment and services can engage in joint ventures, alliances, and licensing schemes in order to furnish the goods and services to key clients throughout the globe. Often, national partners in new markets can leverage local knowledge to provide important commercial advantages for multinational manufacturers. In fact, many companies are rediscovering the value of traditional distributor networks for serving important customers in other regions, albeit, perhaps, with new solutions-orientated business models. Indeed, while globalization might encourage homogenization of processes, it does not mean the standardization of organizational models. Indeed, global corporations are finding that a key challenge is to optimize the mix between cultural and organizational consistency and diversity.

Chapter 7

The Rapid Globalization of Markets for U.S. Manufacturing

by Ernest H. Preeg and Jeffrey F. Werling

Since the mid-1980s, international trade and investment have grown far more rapidly than global gross domestic product (GDP), with the manufacturing sector as the dominant center of this "globalization" process, especially for trade. The U.S. manufacturing sector has more than doubled its trade engagement since 1982 (see table 2-4 in chapter 2), and the challenge for U.S. corporate leadership is how to maximize the gains from this ever-deeper engagement in international markets. There are two basic and interacting dimensions to this challenge: maximizing the sales opportunities and other dynamic gains from expanding markets, and meeting new globalization-induced competitors around the world.

The first section of this chapter introduces the broad quantitative dimensions and the principal dynamic forces in play, first for trade and then for the more complicated investment relationships which can involve both trade and cross-border technology transfer.

The second section of the chapter distinguishes three geographically oriented paradigms within these evolving trade and investment relationships. The first paradigm, "The Even Playing Field: Europe and Japan," is distinguished by roughly comparable labor costs; technical, environmental, and other standards; and other common characteristics of the advanced industrialized economies. The transatlantic relationship is more heavily oriented toward investment than trade, with investment principally "horizontal," that is, mergers and acquisitions to gain a presence in these large, affluent markets.

The second paradigm, "Converging Playing Fields: The Emerging Market Economies of East/South Asia, South America, and East/Central Europe," involves high growth in U.S. economic relationships, where labor and other systemic cost differentials are still substantial and international investment tends more to be "vertical," through supplier plants to reduce aggregate global production costs. The key adjective "converging" refers to the dynamic growth process under way in these economies whereby, through economic reforms and international engagement, they are converging toward industrialized country status.

The third paradigm, "The Integrated North American Market," is a hybrid of paradigm 1 (for Canada) and paradigm 2 (for Mexico), with the important distinction that economic convergence between the United States and Mexico, in particular, is moving forward at an especially rapid pace.

A fourth paradigm, relating to the poorest countries in Africa and parts of South Asia and the Caribbean Basin, is not addressed in this chapter. Clearly, for some of these countries, the bleak economic outlook suggests more divergence than convergence. This fourth paradigm is not addressed, however, because the absolute amounts of trade and private investment involved are relatively small, while economic relationships are driven largely by official financial support rather than private-sector investment.

The third section of the chapter has a somewhat provocative title, "The U.S. Trade Deficit as the Achilles' Heel for U.S. Manufacturing," and explains why this is so. The final section of the chapter, "The Management Response to Deepening Globalization," pulls together the various interrelated components presented to derive conclusions as to how corporate management can best respond to the fast-moving challenges and opportunities of economic globalization.

THE OUTLOOK FOR MANUFACTURING TRADE AND INVESTMENT

Patterns of U.S. Trade in Manufactures

The central and rapidly growing role of manufactures in world trade was presented in broadest terms in chapter 2: from less than half of total trade in 1960 to 63 percent in 2000; with growth more than three times that of global GDP during the 1990s; and thus almost a doubling of the level of world exports of manufactures from $2.4 trillion in 1990 to $4.6 trillion in 2000.

This section looks more closely at evolving trade patterns in manufactures, with a particular focus on U.S. trade. Table 7-1 breaks down world exports of manufactures by major country and region during the 1990s. U.S. exports more than doubled from $290 billion in 1990 to $650 billion in 2000, while global market share rose from 12.1 percent to 14.0 percent. Noteworthy shifts in regional trade growth during the decade were the following:

1. The West European share (over half of which is internal European Union [EU] trade) declined sharply from 55 percent in 1990 to 45 percent in 2000, with

Table 7-1
Exports of Manufactures by Major Country and Region, 1990 and 2000

	1990		2000	
	$ billions	Percent of World Exports	$ billions	Percent of World Exports
World Exports	2,390	100.0	4,630	100.0
United States	290	12.1	650	14.0
Canada	73	3.1	176	3.8
Mexico	25	1.0	139	3.0
NAFTA Subtotal	**388**	**16.2**	**965**	**20.8**
EU (15)	1,203	50.3	1,831	39.5
Switzerland/Norway	71	3.0	154	3.3
Czech Republic, Poland, Hungary	29	1.2	75	1.6
Turkey	9	0.4	22	0.5
Western Europe Subtotal	**1,312**	**54.9**	**2,082**	**45.0**
Japan	275	11.5	450	9.7
South Korea	61	2.6	155	3.3
China	44	1.8	220	4.8
Hong Kong (domestic exports)	27	1.1	22	0.5
Taiwan	62	2.6	141	3.0
ASEAN 5*	84	3.5	324	7.0
East Asia Subtotal	**553**	**23.1**	**1,312**	**28.3**
Brazil	16	0.7	32	0.7
India	13	0.5	29**	0.6
Israel	10	0.4	30	0.6
Russia	22***	0.9	25	0.5
All Listed Countries Subtotal	**2,314**	**96.8**	**4,475**	**96.7**

* Indonesia, Malaysia, Singapore, Philippines, and Thailand.
** 1999.
*** 1995.

Source: World Trade Organization, International Trade Statistics 2001, Table IV31.

corresponding increased shares of 5 percent each for North America (from 16 percent to 21 percent) and East Asia (23 percent to 28 percent).

2. The North American increase is largely a result of trade growth stimulated by the North American Free Trade Agreement (NAFTA), with Mexico showing the most dramatic increase of manufactured exports, from $25 billion in 1990 to $139 billion in 2000, and a corresponding increase in its share of world exports, from 1 percent to 3 percent.
3. Within East Asia, the Japanese share of world exports declined from 11.5 percent

to 9.7 percent, which was more than offset by large increases by China (1.8 percent to 4.8 percent) and the Association of Southeast Asian Nations (ASEAN) (3.5 percent to 7.0 percent). It is noteworthy that manufactured exports of "Greater China"—China/Hong Kong/Taiwan—increased from less than half the Japanese level in 1990 to 86 percent of Japanese exports in 2000, and should pass Japan by 2003, if not sooner.

4. These three regions—North America, Western Europe, and East Asia—together accounted for 94 percent of world exports of manufactures in 2000, and global competition is thus almost exclusively among them. Brazil, India, and Russia, in contrast, while major countries in other respects, together account for less than 2 percent of world exports of manufactures.

Table 7-2 takes a closer look at U.S. trade in manufactures, both exports and imports. Noteworthy in this case are the following:

1. North American trade has grown fastest and is by far the largest export market, up from 34 percent of total U.S. exports of manufactures in 1995 to 38 percent in 2000 (24 percent to Canada and 14 percent to Mexico); imports from Canada and Mexico, however, constitute a relatively smaller share of total imports, rising from 25 percent in 1995 to 28 percent in 2000.
2. Trade with Organization for Economic Cooperation and Development (OECD) Europe has been more level in terms of market shares, 24 percent to 25 percent of exports and 21 percent of imports, while the share of manufactures trade with Japan has dropped sharply, with exports down from 10 percent to 7 percent and imports from 20 percent to 15 percent.
3. Other East/South Asia shows an uneven trend, with the U.S. export share down from 17 percent to 14 percent (well below half of that of North America), while the import share holds steady at 25 percent. The reason for this uneven trend, of course, is the growing trade deficit with East Asia, discussed in the third section of this chapter.
4. South America accounts for a relatively small share of overall manufactures trade, but is decidedly larger for U.S. exports, 5 percent of total exports in 2000, than for imports, at 2 percent. One implication of this is the potential for substantial gains for U.S. manufactures trade if a Free Trade Area of the Americas is brought to fruition.

The overall trend of U.S. trade in manufactures, also shown in table 7-2, highlights the very rapid growth during the late 1990s, with exports and imports together surging 60 percent, from $1.0 trillion in 1995 to $1.6 trillion in 2000. Then came 2001, when the serious recession for U.S. manufacturing included an absolute decline in both manufactured exports (down by 8 percent from 2000) and imports (down by 6 percent), and the downward trend continued during the first half of 2002. This is another manifestation of the more volatile cyclical swings in the manufacturing sector within the high-tech, more globalized new economy. For the same reasons,

Table 7-2
U.S. Trade in Manufactures by Destination
($ billions)

	1995		2000	
	$ billions	Percent of World	$ billions	Percent of World
A. U.S. Exports				
World	394.4	100	661.2	100
Canada	99.1	25	157.9	24
Mexico	37.0	9	94.0	14
Japan	39.1	10	47.4	7
OECD Europe*	99.9	25	157.5	24
South America	27.5	7	32.8	5
Other East/South Asia	65.8	17	92.5	14
Other	26.0	7	79.2	12
B. U.S. Imports				
World	623.4	100	961.1	100
Canada	106.9	17	158.3	16
Mexico	48.4	8	110.6	12
Japan	124.4	20	141.4	15
OECD Europe	129.4	21	206.5	21
South America	11.0	2	16.1	2
Other East/South Asia	153.0	25	241.4	25
Other	50.3	8	86.8	9

* European Union, Norway, Switzerland, Turkey, Poland, Hungary, Czech Republic, and Slovak Republic.

Source: OECD, *International Trade by Commodity Statistics*, Volume 2001/2. Manufactures are defined as SITC 5–8. These statistics differ slightly from those gathered by the WTO, contained in Table 7-1.

however, trade in manufactures should resume high growth as the U.S. and other economies get back on a healthy growth track.

A more qualitative question is how the regional trends in U.S. manufactures trade will shape up as economic recovery gathers momentum, and the trends presented in table 7-2 for 1995–2000, by and large, will likely continue. North America will continue to grow in relative importance, headed toward 40 percent of manufactured exports and 30 percent of imports; OECD Europe will hold more steady shares of about 25 percent of exports and 20 percent of imports, overshadowed in broader economic terms by the much larger transatlantic investment relationship; and Japan, which remains in the economic doldrums in the absence of effective economic reforms, will continue to decline in relative trade importance, toward 5 percent of U.S. exports in particular.

This leaves the rest of East Asia as the least predictable trade relationship. Economic strategies throughout East Asia are highly trade-oriented, but how this trade will evolve, including export versus import growth, is less clear. The related key figure in table 7-2 is the huge U.S. trade deficit in manufactures, up from $229 billion in 1995 to $300 billion in 2000. Of this total in 2000, Other East/South Asia accounted for $149 billion and Japan for another $94 billion, or together 80 percent of the entire deficit.[1] Moreover, these deficits increased further in 2001 and 2002. There has been near consensus that such unprecedented trade imbalances are "unsustainable," and the operative questions have related to when and how the point of unsustainability is reached, which is left for the penultimate section below.

Patterns of U.S. Investment in Manufactures

Another important mechanism of globalization is foreign direct investment (FDI). Most foreign direct investment occurs when multinational companies establish an equity-based marketing or operating "footprint" in another economy. This participation can consist of buying existing companies or facilities, constructing completely new or "greenfield" outlets or operations, or reinvesting in existing operations.

While international trade has expanded steadily and rapidly since World War II, FDI is a relatively late arrival to the globalization process. However, starting in the mid-1980s, at least two developments increased the feasibility of direct investment as a corporate strategy. First, with the demise of communist and socialist models, many developed and developing countries started to open or liberalize their domestic markets to foreign competition. While progress in this area is uneven, a broad embrace of market capitalism encouraged governments to provide a warmer welcome to foreign capital in general, and direct investment in particular. These governments know that the advanced technology and management expertise often embodied in direct investment is an important asset to growth and development. Second, new developments in communications and transportation technology have helped to slash drastically the costs and complexities of managing far-flung corporate operations. Figure 7-1 shows that since 1985, global FDI flows increased exponentially from a little over $50 billion per year to over $1,200 billion by 2000, or from less than 0.5 percent of global GDP to 4.0 percent.

Companies expand their operations across the globe the way an investor might structure a portfolio, balancing the parameters of cost, opportunity, and risk to determine the optimal "footprint." Economists identify two broad types of investment that might make up their direct investment portfolio.[2] Horizontal FDI occurs when a multinational firm moves into a rel-

Figure 7-1
Global Foreign Direct Investment Flows, 1970–2000

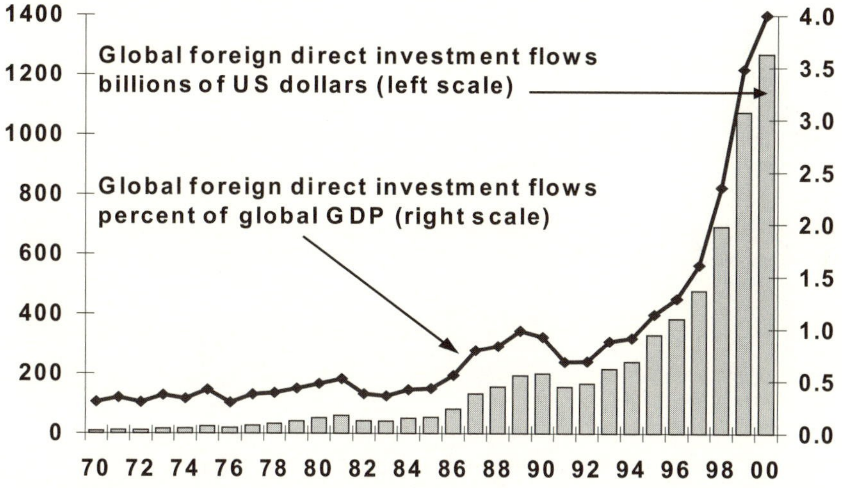

Source: World Bank Development Indicators.

atively developed, high-income economy to take advantage of favorable market opportunities by setting up manufacturing and/or marketing operations. Vertical FDI occurs when multinationals move to less developed regions to take advantage of production cost differentials, especially the lower price of labor vis-à-vis the home country. In practice, of course, the determination of any given firm's footprint is multifaceted, and many foreign operations contain elements of both investment types. In particular, manufacturing multinationals must weigh key factors such as the availability of transport facilities and skilled personnel, the level and complexity of taxation, trade barriers on imported materials and equipment, and the ease of coping with administrative burdens. The rules and implications of regional economic unions, such as the European Union, and free-trade arrangements, such as NAFTA, also figure heavily in the computations.

Table 7-3 shows the historical-cost, accumulated value of U.S. outbound foreign direct investments for selected regions and countries, both in total and for investment in manufacturing establishments.[3] In 1990, U.S. companies owned foreign direct investments costing $424 billion. By 2000 that stake had grown to $1,245 billion, an average growth rate of 19 percent per year. Of this total involvement in 2000, U.S. manufacturing companies (manufacturing parents) held $665 billion, or 53 percent, of these assets. About half of this $665 billion stake, or $344 billion, consists of the ownership of manufacturing infrastructure, up from $164 billion in 1990. The other half of U.S. manufacturing's stake abroad, around $320 billion, is

Table 7-3
U.S. Direct Investment Position Abroad on a Historical-Cost Basis

	Total					Manufacturing Entities				
	1990		2000		avg annual growth (%)	1990		2000		avg annual growth (%)
	$ billions	% share	$ billions	% share		$ billions	% share	$ billions	% share	
All countries	**424.1**	**100.0**	**1244.7**	**100.0**	**19.3**	**164.5**	**100.0**	**344.0**	**100.0**	**10.9**
Manufacturing Parents			665.2	53.4						
Canada	67.0	15.8	126.4	10.2	8.9	31.8	19.3	50.4	14.7	5.9
Mexico	9.4	2.2	35.4	2.8	27.7	7.2	4.4	20.4	5.9	18.3
Western Europe	**211.2**	**49.8**	**648.7**	**52.1**	**20.7**	**83.3**	**50.7**	**177.4**	**51.6**	**11.3**
United Kingdom	68.2	16.1	233.4	18.8	24.2	21.9	13.3	51.0	14.8	13.3
Netherlands	22.7	5.3	115.5	9.3	41.0	6.8	4.1	24.2	7.0	25.6
Germany	27.3	6.4	53.6	4.3	9.7	16.3	9.9	26.8	7.8	6.5
Eastern Europe*	**0.3**	**0.1**	**11.0**	**0.9**	**388.6**	**0.2**	**0.1**	**2.5**	**0.7**	**149.7**
South & Central America	**32.1**	**7.6**	**118.7**	**9.5**	**27.0**	**15.7**	9.6	**28.7**	**8.4**	**8.3**
Brazil	14.9	3.5	35.6	2.9	13.8	11.0	6.7	18.9	5.5	7.2
Argentina	3.0	0.7	14.5	1.2	39.0	1.7	1.0	3.6	1.1	11.6
Chile	1.4	0.3	10.8	0.9	69.3	0.3	0.2	1.4	0.4	39.6
Asia and Pacific	**61.9**	**14.6**	**199.6**	**16.0**	**22.3**	**23.9**	**14.5**	**60.7**	**17.6**	**15.4**
Japan	21.0	5.0	55.6	4.5	16.5	9.9	6.0	15.2	4.4	5.3
ASEAN 5**	11.2	2.6	50.9	4.1	35.4	4.1	2.5	19.5	5.7	37.2
Australia	14.8	3.5	35.3	2.8	13.8	5.8	3.5	8.0	2.3	3.8
Hong Kong	6.2	1.5	23.3	1.9	27.7	1.0	0.6	3.3	1.0	24.5
China*	0.4	0.1	9.6	0.8	235.8	0.1	0.1	5.7	1.6	484.3

* Figures in 1990 columns refer to 1991.
** ASEAN 5 is Indonesia, Malaysia, Singapore, Philippines, and Thailand.

Source: U.S. Department of Commerce, Bureau of Economic Analysis.

devoted to other activities, especially the wholesale marketing, distribution, financing, and after-sales servicing of its exports.

U.S. FDI is spread widely but unevenly throughout the world. By far the largest stake is committed in high-income countries, where equity is relatively easily obtained through mergers, acquisitions, and partnerships. A little over 50 percent of FDI in total and for manufacturing entities is concentrated in Europe. This share has held firm since the 1990s. Considering that Europe's share of global GDP not including the United States is only about 25 percent, these figures show that U.S. companies continue to be deeply involved in European markets. Interestingly, FDI growth, while still buoyant, was slower than average for the United States' two other high-income economic partners, Canada and Japan. Presumably, an already mature relationship and the establishment of free trade between Canada and the United States has made new equity involvement in that market relatively less attractive. In contrast, the declining share of investment moving toward Japan since the 1990s is due to that economy's difficulties and to lingering hostility to foreign investment among the Japanese.

While American companies continue to pursue "horizontal" FDI with Europe, the investment flow aimed toward less developed regions grew even more rapidly in the 1990s. The formation of NAFTA helped the investment stake in Mexico grow from a little more than $9 billion in 1990 to over $35 billion in 2000, an annual growth rate of 28 percent. The fall of the "Iron Curtain" in Eastern Europe stimulated investment from a negligible base in 1991 to $11 billion in 2000. The rush to invest in developing Asia was particularly marked. The total and manufacturing equity stake in Southeast Asia increased by over 35 percent per year. Finally, by 2000, China had become established as one of the most favored destinations of U.S. capital, especially for manufacturing facilities. While the base is still small, at less than $10 billion, flows continue to rise at dramatic rates.

Foreign direct investment ***into*** the United States also has increased rapidly since 1990. Table 7-4 shows that the investment position accumulated by over 30 percent per year both in total and for manufacturing facilities. Most of these investments were made to acquire existing businesses rather than to start new ones. Multinational companies from seven high-income countries—Canada, France, Germany, Japan, the Netherlands, Switzerland, and the United Kingdom—accounted for 75 percent of the foreign equity in manufacturing affiliates. But investment from other countries, especially from the rest of Europe, is growing rapidly.

Indeed, foreign multinationals have powerful incentives to come to the United States. Fast-growing, easily entered, competitive, and dynamic markets characterize the economy. Companies are coming to America not only for market opportunities but also to leverage research and development expertise, high-technology infrastructure, and a liquid and efficient financial system. Finally, the United States has skilled workers and managerial talent

Table 7-4
Foreign Direct Investment Position in the United States on a Historical-Cost Basis

	Total					Manufacturing Entities				
	1990		2000		avg annual growth (%)	1990		2000		avg annual growth (%)
	$ billions	% share	$ billions	% share		$ billions	% share	$ billions	% share	
All countries	396.7	100.0	1238.6	100.0	31.2	157.4	100.0	496.6	100.0	31.5
United Kingdom	102.8	25.9	229.8	18.5	22.4	47.3	30.0	67.9	13.7	14.3
Japan	81.8	20.6	163.2	13.2	20.0	17.2	10.9	43.7	8.8	25.5
Netherlands	69.9	17.6	152.4	12.3	21.8	24.7	15.7	50.8	10.2	20.6
Germany	28.3	7.1	122.8	9.9	43.4	15.7	10.0	59.8	12.0	38.1
France	18.7	4.7	119.1	9.6	63.8	13.7	8.7	66.1	13.3	48.3
Canada	30.0	7.6	100.8	8.1	33.6	9.7	6.1	50.1	10.1	51.9
Switzerland	17.7	4.5	81.7	6.6	46.0	10.4	6.6	36.6	7.4	35.2
Other Europe	13.3	3.4	184.8	14.9	138.5	9.5	6.0	103.2	20.8	108.4
Others	34.1	8.6	84.0	6.8	24.6	9.3	5.9	18.4	3.7	19.7

Source: U.S. Department of Commerce, Bureau of Economic Analysis.

that in many cases can help invigorate an entire global corporation. American industry is one investment that most multinationals want in their portfolio.

THREE GEOGRAPHICALLY ORIENTED PARADIGMS

Economic convergence is the idea that countries with a lower income per capita will tend to have higher rates of growth than their richer counterparts. This tendency means that eventually per capita incomes across countries will become equalized or "converge" to the average income of the highest country. The theory of convergence has its roots in conventional "general equilibrium" trade theory. In this story, convergence works through world trade, capital flows, and technology transfer, as follows. Less developed economies imply lower costs of production, especially for labor-intensive goods. Therefore, all other things being equal, the rate of return on capital investment in those countries will be greater than in rich countries, and capital will flow to those countries. As capital accumulates, the productivity growth of labor accelerates and, therefore, real incomes increase. Foreign direct investments can be especially helpful when they include the transfer of technology and the managerial skills needed to utilize that technology. Moreover, since the capital flowing out of richer countries will tend to have a dampening effect on labor productivity growth there, income growth decelerates, at least relative to the countries catching up.

This mechanism does not imply that incomes need to fall in the richer countries. According to economic theory, the process will also have important positive income effects in developed economies since trade expansion with the developing economies will allow them to exploit comparative advantage. Convergence theory only says that given the relative price of labor to start with, a greater share of the benefits of enhanced trade flows, foreign investment, and technology transfer goes to citizens of the less developed countries.

In fact, however, it is difficult to conclude that income convergence occurs all the time, or even most of the time. There are at least two general reasons why income convergence might not occur in the real world. First, convergence may not occur because shortcomings in legal frameworks, macroeconomic policies, financial infrastructures, trade regimes, business regulations, or education systems impede the pro-growth forces of competitive markets and productivity-enhancing investment.[4] Second, if technology advances in rich nations faster than it can be diffused to developing regions, incomes grow relatively faster in the former. If front-running societies have institutional and cultural advantages that contribute greatly to the development of innovation, even well-managed economies will have trouble catching up. It should be noted that even if technology cannot be perfectly transferred, less developed economies can benefit greatly from technological improvements through trade and investment, even when they are developed and applied primarily within richer countries.

Today's global business environment can be divided into two principal groups of nations. The first group is the high-income, or developed, economies of North America, Western Europe, Japan, Australia, and New Zealand. Together, these economies represent a little over 50 percent of total world GDP, but a little less than 15 percent of world population. The second group, sometimes called the emerging markets, is made up of the "globalizing" economies of East/South Asia, Latin America, and East/Central Europe. It represents about 40 percent of world GDP, and almost 70 percent of the world's population. Each group represents a different paradigm for modern manufacturers. For most U.S. companies, the first group represents the core, less risky business. All other things being equal, the convergence theory would lead us to believe that the faster market growth will be in the less developed regions. But while many U.S. manufacturers indeed see much of their future growth coming in these markets, they know that the operating risks there are much higher. We examine each group in turn.

Paradigm 1—The Even Playing Field: Europe and Japan

The advanced economies of North America, Europe, and Asia are characterized by similar long-established democratic and capitalist institutions, high labor costs, and relatively high social and environmental standards. Important differences among these economies influence the growth and business potential of each region. Figure 7-2 shows the per capita income, in purchasing power parity, relative to that of the United States, for selected advanced nations in 1999. Given our hypothesis of convergence, the disparity in income among these economies is surprisingly large. In fact, each of the United States' G-7 partners—Canada, Japan, France, Germany, Italy, and the United Kingdom—have, by this measure, per capita incomes of only 65 to 80 percent of that in the United States.

While these countries did grow faster than the United States during most of the post-World War II period, the growth rates of several major advanced nations have slipped recently, at least relative to the United States. Figure 7-3 shows the average annual growth per capita of real GDP for selected developed nations from 1981 to 1990, 1991 to 2000, and 1996 through 2000. Comparing the first two periods, growth quickened significantly in the Netherlands and Spain, and was about the same in the United States and Canada. Per capita income growth fell a little in Sweden, France, and the United Kingdom, and rather substantially in Germany, Italy, Switzerland, and Japan. This sluggishness was mainly due to very low growth, and in some cases contraction, of employment as a proportion of the population.[5]

In the second half of the 1990s, the period of the so-called "new economy," growth per capita accelerated sharply for the Netherlands, Spain, the

Figure 7-2
Relative GDP Per Capita, Purchasing Power Basis, 1999
U.S. = 100

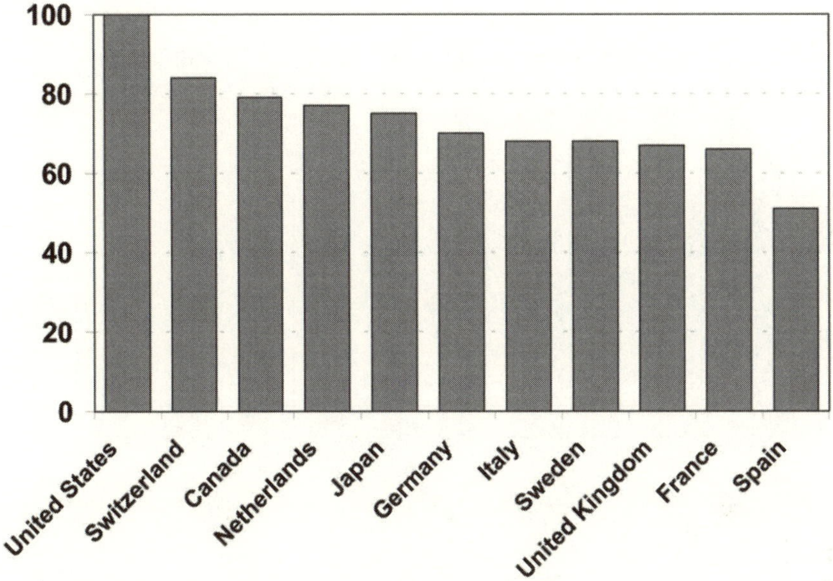

Source: OECD, *The New Economy: Beyond the Hype* (Paris: OECD, 2001).

United States, Canada, Sweden, France, and the United Kingdom compared to the early 1990s. But income expansion remained in the doldrums for Germany, Italy, Japan, and Switzerland. It remains to be seen whether the accelerated expansion of GDP per capita can be sustained once the major economies come out of the current slowdown. But many observers are encouraged by the fact that large stocks of productivity-enhancing innovations have yet to be applied in the developed world. Questions, however, are being raised about how ready and willing some advanced economies are to accept such innovations. Concerns are particularly focused on Europe and Japan.

European Union.—As 2002 dawned, many (but not all) of the countries of the European Union (EU) were putting the finishing touches on the European Monetary Union (EMU), replacing their national currencies with the euro at the retail level. But the EMU always meant much more than the adoption of a single currency. To many, it is the key component of a single European market that has been put into place since 1993. But for every two steps forward that the EU takes in liberalizing its "single economy," it seems to take a step back. Business is still waiting on many important integration and liberalization measures. National governments have often failed to live up to existing promises or have undermined new efforts.

Figure 7-3
Real GDP Per Capita Growth

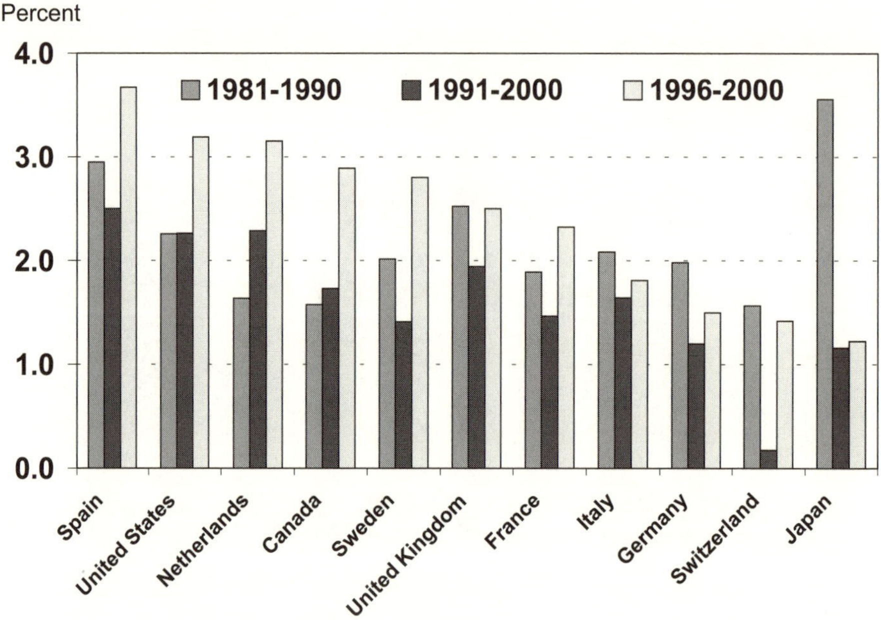

Source: International Monetary Fund, World Economic Outlook Database.

At the March 2000 Lisbon summit, EU leaders promised to recharge the effort by committing to the adoption of several policies aimed at making the Union the "most competitive and dynamic economy" in the world by 2010. The important measures that would push the EU in this direction include tighter integration of financial markets, harmonization and simplification of business regulations, deregulation of labor markets, and liberalization of energy, communication, and transport industries. Unfortunately, since the summit these new ideas have met stubborn obstacles at even advanced stages of approval.

Much of the opposition to moving forward on these initiatives comes from Germany and France, the two nations that are the traditional drivers of most EU efforts. Meanwhile, other countries in the Union such as Spain, the Netherlands, and the United Kingdom, have combined intra-EU integration and liberalization with extra-EU opportunities for trade, investment, and technology to reach higher levels of performance. They have shown that, to be successful, the EU must be leveraged as a catalyst to promote Europe's competitiveness in world markets, not as a device for turning inward. U.S. manufacturing business has a large stake in the outcome of this process.

Japan.—At the turn of the 21st century, the Japanese economy is trapped in a decade-long recession and a deflationary spiral. This state of affairs is particularly troubling because Japan has many things going for it, including an educated and talented population, many world-class corporations, a high savings rate, and well-developed financial and product markets. Yet despite the dramatic growth and development that the country displayed in the post-World War II era through 1989, or perhaps because of it, Japan developed some very serious political and economic rigidities. The maze of stifling economic regulation, government intervention, and institutionalized protectionism has prevented the Japanese economy from adjusting to economic shocks, technology changes, globalization, or even gradual economic evolution.

Japan's economy is split into two segments. The first part consists of a liberalized, world-class export sector dominated by transnational corporations, such as Toyota, Honda, and Sony. By developing modern technology and management techniques and, more recently, by moving offshore, these companies are competitive, profitable, and inextricably linked with the global economy. Within Japan, however, these companies coexist with uncompetitive small enterprises, an inefficient service sector, a construction industry that doubles as a public welfare agency, and staunchly protected farmers. This larger part of the economy has developed around and in collaboration with the network of government guidance and regulation, with its bias toward producers at the expense of consumers. Moreover, cozy relations between the liberalized and administered parts of the economy, Japan's commercial banks, and the government planning ministries have complicated any attempts at deeper economic liberalization.

Much has been made of the Japanese government's ineffective attempts to alleviate the banking crisis, reform and restructure the economy, and rein in government deficits. But forcing bankruptcies and debt write-offs and cutting inefficient government spending, while no doubt desirable in their own right, will exacerbate the recession and complicate the overall reform effort. Without new liberalization and restructuring efforts, it is impossible to build a foundation for better long-term growth. While some experts believe that Japan can muddle along this road indefinitely, this outcome seems increasingly improbable. It is more likely that a sudden and significant crisis, probably involving the financial system, will finally make change essential. If and when it comes, however, a major financial and economic crisis in the second largest economy on the globe will present a great challenge to the rest of the world as well.

Low-growth economies.—Figure 7-4 displays historical growth averages since 1990 and GDP growth forecasts from 2000 to 2010 for major economies of the developed world. Outside of North America, the 1990s were the slowest decade of growth in the postwar period. Not only was the proportion of the population at work falling, but population growth is stagnating in most of Europe and in Japan. Therefore, for most of these nations, eco-

Figure 7-4
Advanced Nation Real GDP Growth History and Forecast

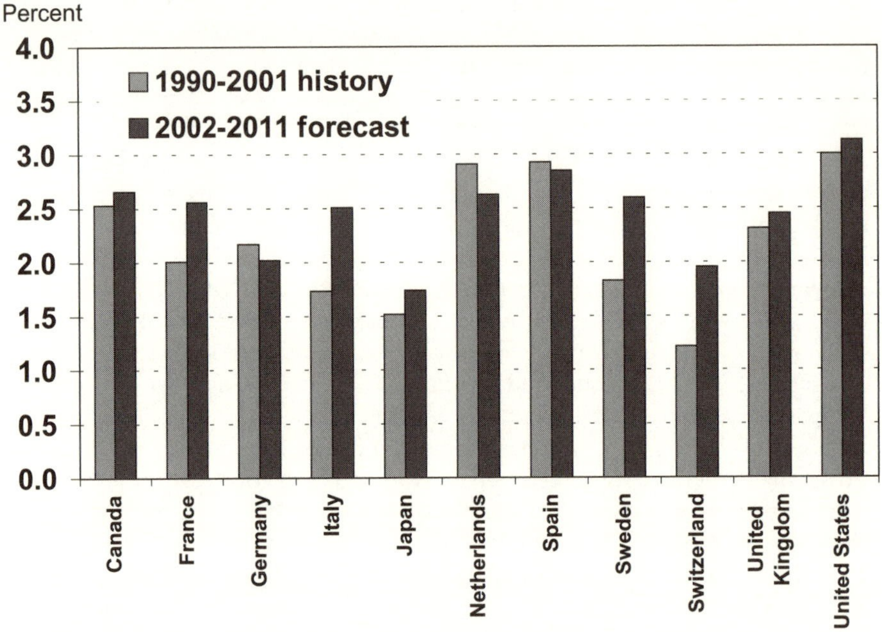

Source: International Monetary Fund, Consensus Economics, 2002.

nomic growth in the next decade is forecast to be about the same as in the last. Only France, Italy, Sweden, and Switzerland are expected to post noticeable accelerations in growth. Moreover, only the United States, with its relatively rapid labor force growth, is expected to post growth at 3.0 percent.

These long-term forecasts come from a survey of economists provided by Consensus Economics. It is worth noting that the projections, for whatever reasons, assume little in the way of a lasting pickup in productivity growth in Europe and Japan. Even in the United States, productivity growth per employee is expected to grow by around 2.0 percent per year over the decade ending in 2010, down from recent performances exceeding 2.5 percent. Such assumptions run counter to the more optimistic economic literature which claims that productivity growth can continue at its accelerated path, at least in open liberalized economies like the United States. Certainly, adding only 0.5 percent in annual productivity growth rates to the assumptions presented here would make a substantial difference in the market outlook in these societies. Indeed, whether or not Europe and Japan can obtain and sustain higher levels of productivity growth is one of the key questions for the business environment through 2010.

Figure 7-5
Emerging Market Real GDP Growth History and Forecast

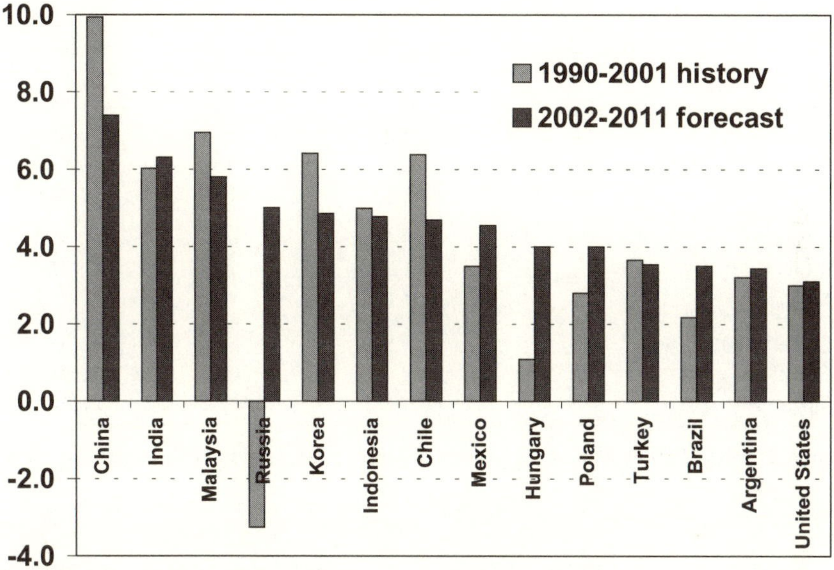

Source: International Monetary Fund, Consensus Economics, 2002.

Paradigm 2—Converging Playing Fields: Emerging Markets

Because of their large size and high per capita income levels, the developed economies of North America, Europe, and Japan will continue to constitute the largest markets for global manufacturers for the foreseeable future. However, it is the emerging economies of Asia, Latin America, and Central Europe that offer the best market ***growth*** potential for manufacturing industry. Assuming that income convergence works at least most of the time and in most places, developing nations will continue to display higher rates of economic growth. Figure 7-5 shows historical and forecast GDP growth for several major emerging market countries. Clearly China claims the best recent growth track record and holds the most promise. It is expected to continue expanding at an average rate of 7.0 percent over the next decade. India is next on the list, followed by Malaysia, Korea, and Indonesia. Russia, recuperating from the disastrous decade just past, should also grow quickly over the next ten years. The next tier includes Latin American and Central European countries, each expected to grow in the 3 percent to 6 percent range. Each of these major emerging markets is expected to grow faster than the United States.

Besides aggregate income growth, several other important economic and demographic trends in emerging countries will have a tendency to drive both

Table 7-5
Population Growth in Selected Countries, 1990–2030
(Annual average percentage growth)

	1990–2000	2000–2010	2010–2020	2020–2030
Brazil	1.5	1.2	1.0	0.8
Mexico	1.9	1.4	1.1	0.8
Poland	0.1	−0.1	−0.1	−0.3
Turkey	1.9	1.3	1.0	0.8
China	1.0	0.7	0.6	0.3
India	1.9	1.5	1.1	0.9
Malaysia	2.5	1.8	1.3	1.1
United States	1.1	0.9	0.8	0.7
Germany	0.3	−0.1	−0.2	−0.3
Japan	0.3	0.1	−0.2	−0.4

Source: United Nations Population Division, World Population Prospects, Population Database.

consumer and government budgets toward higher consumption and investment patterns. In turn, this implies steady gains in the purchase of manufactured products. Such trends include the following.

Population growth.—Though decelerating, population growth rates in most emerging market countries will remain well ahead of those in the developed world. Table 7-5 shows United Nations population growth projections for selected countries until 2030. While populations in Japan and Europe (Central and Eastern Europe included) will be stagnant or could actually decline over the period, growth will be at least 1 percent per year in major nations of Latin America and Asia through 2020. One exception is China, which is forecast to see growth of between 0.5 percent and 1.0 percent. Population growth is the most fundamental driver of economic growth and of the consumption of manufactured goods. Each additional person requires the basics of food, clothing, and housing, each of which is either manufactured directly or needs manufactured goods or equipment to be produced.

Age demographics.—The current populations of most emerging market countries in Latin America and Asia are very young. Over the period to 2020 large cohorts of young people will be moving into their prime income-earning years. Table 7-6 shows that in developing nations the proportion of the population between the ages of twenty and sixty will rise from below 50 percent in 1990 to levels of around 55 percent to 60 percent by 2020, about the current level in developed nations now. These demographic transitions are similar in scale to the coming of age of the "baby boomers" that occurred in the developed world over the period since 1970. Meanwhile, the aging

Table 7-6
Prime Working Age Population in Selected Countries, 1990–2030
(Percentage of population between the ages of 20 and 60)

	1990	2000	2010	2020	2030
Brazil	48.5	53.2	56.7	56.0	54.3
Mexico	43.4	49.7	53.5	55.5	54.8
Poland	52.5	55.6	60.0	55.6	53.5
Turkey	46.8	51.4	54.6	56.7	55.3
China	53.1	57.1	60.1	58.1	53.1
India	46.6	48.9	52.5	55.5	56.2
Malaysia	47.7	49.2	52.1	54.9	55.0
United States	54.6	55.1	55.2	52.5	49.7
Germany	57.9	55.6	56.0	53.6	47.2
Japan	56.1	56.2	51.4	48.9	46.7

Source: United Nations Population Division, World Population Prospects, Population Database.

of the "boomers" means that the proportion of the population between the ages of twenty and sixty in developed countries is decreasing. While these relatively older populations in developed nations will be devoting large budget shares to medical, entertainment, and travel services, the emerging middle-aged populations of Brazil, Mexico, Poland, Turkey, China, Malaysia, and India will be more interested in new and better housing, motor vehicles, furnishings, food, and clothing.

Urbanization.—One of the most important trends worldwide is the influx of migrants from the countryside to cities. According to a recent United Nations report on urbanization, of the 2.0 billion increase in world population expected to occur between the years 2000 and 2030, virtually all of it, or 1.9 billion, will be absorbed by the urban areas of less developed regions.[6] Indeed, table 7-7 shows that while the proportion of people living in urban areas is expected to increase everywhere, urbanization has much further to go in developing nations, particularly in China and India, where the process will become greatly accelerated. Urbanization's impact on the economies of these developing countries might be even more important than it was in the history of the currently developed regions. At the least, great challenges lie ahead for emerging market governments trying to keep up with the infrastructure needed to support cities. This opens opportunities for manufacturers involved with providing material and equipment for road and building construction, water systems, and telecommunications.

Education, health, and environmental attainment.—As income grows, consumers will demand higher education levels, health quality, and environ-

Table 7-7
Urbanization in Selected Countries, 1990–2030
(Percentage of populations living in urban areas)

	1990	2000	2010	2020	2030
Brazil	74.8	81.3	86.0	88.9	90.5
Mexico	72.5	74.4	76.6	79.2	81.9
Poland	60.7	65.6	64.8	68.5	72.5
Turkey	61.2	75.3	69.9	73.7	77.0
China	27.4	32.1	45.2	53.4	59.5
India	25.5	28.4	30.3	34.7	40.9
Malaysia	49.8	57.4	63.8	68.6	72.7
United States	75.2	77.2	79.7	82.2	84.5
Germany	85.3	87.5	89.2	90.5	91.7
Japan	77.4	78.8	80.5	82.6	84.8

Source: United Nations Population Division, World Population Prospects, Population Database.

mental standards. Though progress is unevenly distributed across time and place, these patterns are becoming realized in emerging economies. Young people are staying in school longer and learning more, they are looking forward to enjoying better medical services and living long lives, and they are becoming increasingly interested in environmental issues. In turn, the provision of educational, medical, and environmental services requires the technology and equipment that have been pioneered and already widely applied in developed economies.

Decreasing household size.—As populations become more affluent, educated, and urbanized, young people marry later, the number of children per woman decreases, and older people remain independent longer. These tendencies mean that the average household size in most emerging markets is decreasing. Therefore, while population growth may be decelerating in Latin America, Asia, and Central Europe, the growth in the number of households remains high. So while population growth in nations may decelerate a half or a full percentage point per year through 2010, the growth in the number of households—the relevant buying unit for many manufactured goods—will remain rapid for a longer period. Therefore, demand for products specific to households such as housing units, appliances, and automobiles will be robust.

Taken in total, income growth, demographic patterns, social progress, and consumer preference changes in the emerging countries will combine to produce fertile markets for global manufactured products. History shows that as households move from the poorest income levels to the lower and middle rungs of the middle class, they will devote larger and larger proportions of their expenditures to mass-produced manufactured goods of all types (automobiles, refrigerators, computers, packaged food, etc.). And there are a large number of households just now reaching middle-income levels in Asia, Central Europe, and Latin America. Brazil, for instance, had approximately 50 million households in 2000. Out of this total, an estimated 15 million, or 30 percent, earned more than $20,000 per year on a purchasing power equivalent basis. On current growth trends, this total could increase by at least another 10 million households by 2010, qualifying 25 million households, or over 40 percent of the total in Brazil, as middle class.

While China is a much poorer country, it is much larger. If China were to sustain its current growth rate for another ten years, the number of households over the $20,000 income threshold would grow from only a few million currently to around 250 million by 2010, a number twice the size of all the households in the United States. A surge in the number of households earning over a moderate $20,000 will not push per capita ownership of televisions, automobiles, and computers in emerging markets to developed-country levels within the next 10 or 20 years. Nevertheless, as hundreds of millions of households move from very basic living standards to new levels of affluence, their demand for many basic manufactured goods will grow dramatically.

It stands to reason, then, that global manufacturing activity will continue to expand briskly. Of course, the location of the new production to meet this demand will be determined by myriad factors. In some industries, customer intimacy and speed of delivery will mandate that final assembly and service operations take place close to the final markets. Supply chain activities requiring high levels of skill and technology, such as research, development, and the manufacture of advanced components, will continue to take place in developed economies. But many other activities will continue to migrate to the emerging economies, not least of all because markets will be growing particularly fast in these regions. Labor-intensive manufacturing, back-office and administrative service operations, customer call centers, global logistics, research, and design activities are all candidates for outsourcing to developing nations. In any case, companies that want to take advantage of the coming boom in manufacturing production need to be ready to operate globally.

Interplays between changes in historical circumstances, institutional infrastructure, government policy, and capital and trade flows create a dynamic and unpredictable business and investment environment in emerging markets. The determination of a company's footprint in emerging markets must consider more than growth. Risk looms large in the equation. At a minimum, companies must consider the following:

1. Sovereign risk: The government defaults on its debts, decreasing domestic liquidity and impacting the level and quality of government services.
2. Transfer risk: Liquidity or exchange regulations prevent the repatriation of profits or capital.
3. Currency risk: Fluctuations in currencies materially impact the value of profits and investment.
4. Economic risks: A decline in growth or profit opportunities occurs, due to general economic difficulties.
5. Political/institutional risks: Changes in government regulations, taxes, or legal framework, or changes in the government itself, as a result of war or revolution.
6. Intellectual property risk: Indigenous enterprises steal proprietary ideas and designs.

Certainly, these risks loom large for the countries identified above as high-growth prospects. China, for instance, faces many substantial challenges, political and social, as well as economic. Membership in the World Trade Organization (WTO) presents a whole set of new and difficult problems not only for China but for its trading partners as well. A flood of imports into the economy could rapidly dislocate workers by the tens of millions. Optimists correctly perceive this economic integration as an essential vehicle for bringing China into the community of democratic nations. At the same time, however, the global economy's burgeoning stake in the Chinese economy poses an increasing risk if the transition were somehow to go wrong. It is an understatement to describe the expanding mountain of investment in China as risky.

At the other end of the spectrum is Argentina. In the early 1990s the country was the darling of investors. However, its inability to adapt its fiscal arrangements, its labor market regulations, and, most crucially, its exchange rate regime, to the realities of the competitive global environment proved catastrophic. According to the forecast presented here, the nation will be hobbled for several years to come.

Nonetheless, taking on risks in emerging markets can often produce rewards. Figure 7-6 shows the average annual return on foreign direct investment by U.S. firms from 1996 to 2000 for selected countries. This ratio is the net income, minus taxes, divided by the historical cost position of the investment. The largest returns were produced by investments in Hungary, Malaysia, Indonesia, Turkey, Mexico, China, and Korea. Below-average returns are characteristic of advanced economies like the United Kingdom and France, where the bulk of U.S. foreign direct investment resides. But low returns are also characteristic of some developing countries in some periods, in this case India and Russia.

The portfolio model of foreign direct investment is illustrated clearly. In

Figure 7-6
Average Annual Returns* to U.S. Investors from Foreign Direct Investment, 1996–2000

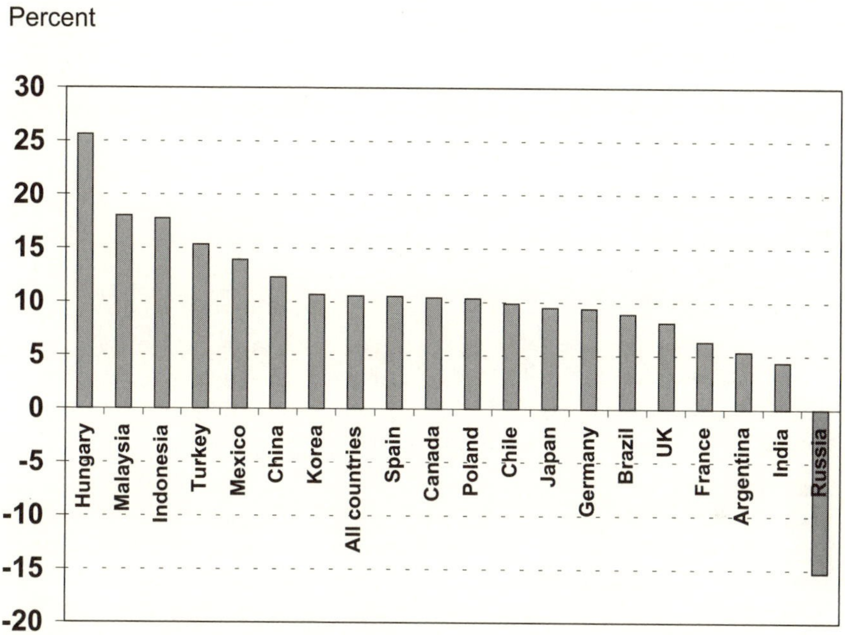

* Return is defined as net income, less taxes, divided by the historical cost basis of the investment.

Source: U.S. Department of Commerce, Bureau of Economic Analysis.

trading off risk and reward, firms are diversifying across the risk/return spectrum. Investments in less risky but low return economies still predominate. Today's multinationals are increasingly willing to seek higher returns in riskier locations. As globalization and convergence proceed, opportunities in all parts of the spectrum will multiply. Competitive manufacturers will pursue these prospects vigorously.

Paradigm 3—The Integrated North American Market

Almost total free trade and investment within North America, as a result of NAFTA, has resulted in the most dramatic surge in regional trade and investment ever recorded, and this trend will continue. Free trade between Canada and the United States has been progressing for decades, dating from the bilateral automotive sector free trade agreement in 1964 through the U.S.-Canada Free Trade Agreement of 1988. Canadian trade and investment is 80 percent to 90 percent with the United States, and the degree of eco-

Table 7-8
U.S.-Mexico Merchandise Trade
($ billions)

	1996	2001	Percent Change 1996–2001
U.S. Exports			
Total	56.8	101.6	+79
Manufactures*	46.5	85.2	+83
Machinery and transportation	(26.6)	(51.4)	+93
Mineral fuels	1.5	3.3	+120
U.S. Imports			
Total	73.0	131.4	+80
Manufactures*	58.0	108.7	+87
Machinery and transportation	(40.7)	(78.3)	+92
Mineral fuels	6.8	10.2	+50
Trade Balance			
Total	−16.2	−29.8	+40
Manufactures*	−11.5	−23.5	+104
Machinery and transportation	−14.1	−26.9	+91
Mineral fuels	−5.3	−7.0	+32

* SITC 5–8.

Source: U.S. Bureau of the Census.

nomic dependence continues to deepen, driven principally by private-sector initiatives to lower costs. The analytic framework for this economic integration is similar to the level playing field paradigm for Western Europe and Japan, described above, although in the case of the United States and Canada it is far more advanced. For U.S. manufacturing companies, the United States and Canada are essentially one integrated market.

The U.S.-Mexican economic relationship within NAFTA, in contrast, is a far more dynamic paradigm 2 relationship of converging economic systems with wide-ranging opportunities to reap both static and dynamic gains from trade,[7] focused heavily within the manufacturing sector, as shown in table 7-8. U.S. manufactured exports to Mexico increased from $46.5 billion in 1996 to $85.2 billion in 2001, with the machinery and transportation sector alone rising from $26.6 billion to $51.4 billion. Manufactured imports from Mexico likewise increased sharply, from $58.0 billion in 1996 to $108.7 billion in 2001. Much of this almost doubling of two-way trade is integrated in terms of supplier relationships involving both exports and imports to gain comparative cost advantages. Another key aspect of U.S.-Mexican trade is the growing dominance of manufactures, up to 83 percent of total merchandise trade in 2001. In parallel, the petroleum share of U.S. imports from Mexico declined from almost half of total imports during the early 1980s to only 10 percent in 2001. Finally, the United States had a $29.8 billion trade deficit with Mexico in 2001, including $23.5 billion in manufactures.

Foreign direct investment in Mexico has grown rapidly since the inception of NAFTA. Annual FDI in Mexico increased from $3.7 billion in 1989–1993 to $10.7 billion in 1994–2000, then rose to $25 billion in 2001. Almost 70 percent of this investment is by U.S. companies. The sectorial composition of the investment varies greatly from year to year because a few large investments tend to dominate the figures, such as the Citibank purchase of Banamex in 2001. Overall, for the period 1994–2001, about half of foreign investment in Mexico was in manufacturing, which is relatively high, especially compared with Brazil, the other principal FDI recipient within the Western Hemisphere.

The dynamic forces of "economic convergence," as defined here, are driving this burgeoning and highly interactive trade/investment/technology transfer relationship with Mexico. U.S. manufacturing investment in Mexico, in particular, tends to incorporate close to, if not the same, technology and environmental, labor, and other standards as in American facilities.[8] Lean manufacturing strategies are also being adopted south of the border, including reported Six Sigma certification for national employees. These advances reinforce the competitive cost advantage of U.S. companies vis-à-vis traditional national and third-country competitors.

The net result is that average costs are going down in Mexico, while wage rates are rising relative to U.S. levels due to large increases in peso earnings and a strengthened peso resulting from the Mexican trade surplus and FDI inflow. From 1995 to 2000, the hourly compensation for production workers in manufacturing in Mexico increased from $1.51 to $2.46 (63 percent), compared with a 16 percent increase in the United States. Looking ahead, the convergence of wages should continue at a relatively rapid rate compared with other emerging market economies, but at an uneven pace as the free-floating peso vis-à-vis the dollar moves up and down somewhat, although nothing close to the 50 percent plunge that took place in Brazil and the 70 percent plunge in Argentina.

The overall rapid economic integration of the U.S. and Mexican economies will likewise continue, including the convergence of wage rates and other cost differentials through across-the-board productivity gains in Mexican industry. It will nevertheless be a bumpy path because considerable regulatory and cultural barriers to complete free trade remain in Mexico. Prominent among these barriers are inflexible labor laws; restrictions on investment in electric power, gas exploration, and telecommunications; and shortcomings of the judicial system related to mercantile law. The inability of President Vicente Fox to enact economic reforms, in the absence of a majority in the legislative branch, and growing urban crime rates are other impediments to convergence. American companies need to take all these factors into account when assessing the profitability of particular investments in Mexico. Nevertheless, over the medium to longer term, the die is cast for close-to-full North American economic integration, driven by the extraordinarily powerful momentum of free trade and investment unleashed by NAFTA.

THE U.S. TRADE DEFICIT AS THE ACHILLES' HEEL FOR U.S. MANUFACTURING

The total U.S. trade deficit, including both merchandise and services, set a record of $376 billion in 2000, declined slightly to $345 billion in 2001, and then rose to $418 billion in 2002 as a result of the relatively rapid economic recovery in the United States and the delayed trade impact of a strong dollar, which during 2001 rose about 10 percent on a trade-weighted basis and 15 percent against the yen. Moreover, the large trade deficit is not a short-term, cyclical phenomenon, but has now been going on since the 1980s.

The dimension of the trade deficit highlighted here is its predominant impact on the U.S. manufacturing sector. Between 80 percent and 90 percent of the deficit is borne by manufacturing, and since manufacturing is ten times more engaged in trade than is the services sector, the adverse impact on output and jobs—that is, fewer export-related jobs and a larger market share held by imports—falls almost entirely on manufacturing. The National Association of Manufacturers estimated that 500,000 manufacturing jobs were lost from the sharp decline in U.S. manufactured exports during 2001 and the first half of 2002. These adverse effects were generally ignored during the high-growth 1990s, but in light of the severe recession in U.S. manufacturing during 2001–2002, the impact has become more acute and a broader assessment is clearly in order. Most directly, the positive results from a downward adjustment of the dollar and the trade deficit would be more stimulating for sustained economic recovery: for U.S. automotive companies to regain market share vis-à-vis Japanese competitors; for Boeing vis-à-vis Airbus; and for U.S. technology-intensive machinery and allied products companies across the board.

Even more important, in view of the central theme of this study that a more deeply trade-engaged U.S. manufacturing sector remains the dominant engine of growth for the entire U.S. economy, a broader national interest is in play than simply the number of trade-related jobs won or lost in manufacturing industry. Unfortunately, however, public policy discussion of the trade deficit and the related question of a strong dollar have often been misguided, including some obfuscation over the years by the U.S. Treasury. The official one-line policy mantra that "a strong dollar is in the U.S. interest" was not really a policy but a value judgment, and a highly debatable value judgment at that. A strong dollar is clearly very good for the banking sector and for U.S. consumers, who benefit through lower cost imports, but an overly strong dollar also can have substantial adverse consequences for U.S. manufacturing industry.

The brief presentation here can only highlight the principal reasons why the record and chronic trade deficit is a problem both for U.S. manufacturing and for the broader U.S. national interest and, from that, specify what the real policy issues are that could influence the course for the trade deficit ahead.[9]

There are two principal reasons why a chronic external deficit on the projected order of 5 percent or more of GDP should be a national concern. The first is its direct impact on manufacturing industry. A return to trade balance in the manufacturing sector could lead to an increase in output of about 10 percent, offset by a small decline in the services sector share of GDP. In the context of the secular decline of the manufacturing sector, the trade deficit since the early 1980s has accelerated the decline significantly, and it is highly doubtful that this acceleration has been in the U.S. interest in view of the central role of manufacturing industry in generating technology-driven growth.

The second reason for concern about the deficit is its cumulative impact in turning the United States from the largest net creditor nation in the mid-1980s to an unprecedented net debtor nation approaching $3 trillion, headed toward $5 trillion by about 2010. The fact is that a current account deficit (a somewhat broader measure than the trade deficit) must, by definition, be offset by net borrowing abroad, which in turn tends to increase the U.S. net debtor position (i.e., the balance between U.S. financial assets held abroad and foreign assets held in the United States). What this foreign debt buildup means is that we are currently living beyond our means by $400 billion to $500 billion per year, while paying for it through foreign borrowing. Most of this surfeit of spending is devoted to immediate consumption, not to the capital investment that leads to innovation and productivity growth.[10] The resulting $3 trillion to $5 trillion buildup in foreign debt is then left to our children and grandchildren to service indefinitely or pay off. With a younger generation of Americans already concerned about paying the rising Social Security and Medicare commitments to the current older, high-consumption generation, the foreign debt buildup is one more intergenerational income transfer being undertaken essentially by stealth.

With these adverse consequences stemming from the chronic trade deficit, what can or should we do about it? There are two principal remedies. The first is to increase domestic savings, thereby reducing the need to borrow abroad. This should involve basic changes in tax and other laws to stimulate domestic savings. Principal trading partners would likewise have to move in the opposite direction, stimulating domestic consumption so as to reduce savings. For trade, the net result would be that the United States would export a larger share of GDP and others would import more, while the principal price incentive for bringing about this restructuring of trade accounts would be downward movement in the dollar exchange rate. None of this would be easy, quick, or painless, but it was done in the mid-1980s without lasting adverse consequences.

The second way to reduce the trade deficit is to restrain others from "manipulating" their exchange rates to commercial advantage, as explicitly proscribed under International Monetary Fund (IMF) rules and explained more fully in chapter 9. In our now mostly floating-rate financial system, some foreign governments do this by buying large amounts of dollars so as to keep their exchange rates lower than they would be if based on market forces alone. In any event, a country with a persistently large trade surplus and an inflow of foreign direct investment should not be buying dollars, since this only results in an even larger trade surplus (and a larger U.S. deficit). Unfortunately, such currency manipulation (the IMF term of art) has been rampant in recent years among a number of Asian exporters to the United States, even while in 2000, $264 billion of the $319 billion U.S. deficit in manufactures was with Asia.

Japan, with the largest trade surplus in the world, is the outstanding example of such manipulation, with more than $321 billion of official foreign exchange purchases (almost all dollars) from 1998 through May 2003, including $43 billion in May 2003 alone, when market forces were putting strong upward pressure on the yen. South Korea is a more recent example: the Korean central bank bought $18 billion of foreign exchange during 2002, while recording a $9 billion trade surplus and $12 billion of new FDI commitments. Meanwhile, the Korean won depreciated 5 percent against the dollar.

Chinese exchange rate policy is an important special case which spells currency manipulation in a different but even bigger way.[11] The Chinese currency has a fixed rate to the dollar but is nonconvertible on capital account. During 2001, China had a $20 billion trade surplus and a $45 billion inflow of FDI, and the central bank purchased $40 billion of foreign exchange. Without the central bank purchases, that $40 billion within the Chinese economy would have put strong upward pressure on the yuan in formal and informal markets.[12] Central bank purchases continued at over $6 billion per month during 2002. What all this means is that the Chinese yuan is substantially undervalued and certainly should not be depreciated, as the Chinese government has occasionally threatened to do.

This brings the discussion to what the policy issues really are with respect to the trade deficit and the strong dollar. The domestic policy question is whether we continue to accept a low savings rate with the consequent need to borrow abroad. In fact, in recent years, actual policy has been, on balance, more in the opposite direction, with tax reforms often designed to stimulate more rather than less consumption.

The international policy issue concerns exchange rate policy. U.S. policy for the dollar is close to a free-floating exchange rate, presumably permitting the dollar to strengthen or weaken as market forces determine. But the critical issue is whether the United States continues to condone—contrary to IMF strictures—exchange rate manipulation to commercial advantage by others, particularly in East Asia and most prominently by Japan and China. This results in a much larger trade deficit than would prevail through market forces alone, with a consequent adverse impact on U.S. manufacturing industry in particular.

The outlook for the decade ending in 2010 is thus either to continue U.S. benign neglect of the trade deficit, while we continue to consume beyond our means at home, and East Asians, in particular, continue to pursue essentially mercantilist policies (that is, the pursuit of a large trade surplus as a national policy objective), or to adopt a concerted strategy to reduce the deficit through adjustments in national savings levels and related exchange rate policies. The impact of either of these alternatives for the United States would fall predominantly on the manufacturing sector. The latter strategy of gradually bringing down the trade deficit from $400 billion to $300 billion to $200 billion over several years would, of course, have a highly concentrated stimulative effect throughout the U.S. manufacturing sector.

The alternative course of benign neglect is more difficult to predict, especially with respect to timing. Almost all political and economic analysts agree that the current U.S. deficits are "unsustainable" indefinitely. If the U.S. foreign debt is permitted to rise from $3 trillion to $5 trillion and higher during the decade ahead, the point will come when others will hesitate to lend the projected $500 billion to $600 billion to the United States each year, at least at current interest rates, and growing anticipation of a depreciation of the dollar, in turn, will increase the hesitation and hasten the depreciation. This already began to happen for the dollar rates vis-á-vis the euro, the Canadian dollar, and some other currencies in 2002 and 2003.

Specific recommendations for a concerted strategy to reduce the deficit through adjustments in national savings levels and related exchange rate policies are made in chapter 9. But in any event, the record U.S. trade deficit, especially if allowed to grow larger as economic recovery in the United States outpaces growth elsewhere, is the Achilles' heel to the central theme of this work: that the U.S. manufacturing sector will continue to be the principal engine of economic growth within the overall U.S. economy. Sooner or later, something has to give—and already is giving—which will almost certainly include a substantial decline in the dollar exchange rate, with some adverse impact on U.S. inflation, interest rates, and perhaps growth, at least in the short term. The silver lining behind this ominous storm cloud, however, is that, once and however it plays itself out, the U.S. manufacturing sector would benefit greatly.

THE MANAGEMENT RESPONSE TO DEEPENING GLOBALIZATION

Bringing together all of the foregoing observations, five conclusions about the strategic response by corporate management are appropriate:

1. All corporate strategy is becoming global, and the dichotomy between domestic and international operations is history. Global products and global standards are the wave of the future. Within companies, the integration of domestic and international divisions is happening at all levels of organization up through top management. This also happened in 2001 for the Manufacturers Alliance/MAPI council structure, when the long-standing Council on International Business was shut down for lack of member commitment. Separation of international from domestic strategy is simply no longer practical.
2. Foreign markets, nevertheless, are highly diverse and constantly changing, especially in the rapidly growing emerging markets of Latin America, Asia, and Eastern Europe. Country-by-country market assessment is essential, but this assessment process requires some form of regional or country grouping approach as well in order to maximize gains from scale in a systematic way where similar market characteristics exist. The three paradigm groupings introduced here are an example of such grouping related to similar market characteristics. Within shared characteristics of these broad paradigms, however, distinct subgroupings also need to be related to management decisions, as is evident from distinctions drawn here between Europe and Japan within paradigm 1, Canada and Mexico within paradigm 3, and among the various emerging market economies within paradigm 2.
3. The central ***analytic*** conclusion from the current course of globalization is that traditional comparative cost gains from trade based on lower wage rates abroad and more capital- and skill-intensive U.S. production are of declining relative importance. Rather, the driving force for profit maximization in global markets is shifting to "dynamic change" stemming from new investment with embedded new technology, together with the organizational skills summarized as "lean manufacturing." Success in international markets remains, in part, based on the classic comparative cost model, but increasingly, and in many industries now to a dominant degree, profits derive principally from having a technology and lean manufacturing edge over competitors from all directions. Moreover, the realization of such profits can require an integrated strategy including exports, foreign suppliers, and direct investment abroad.
4. The central ***operational*** conclusion from the current course of globalization is the need to respond to the trade-offs between rapidly expanding market opportunities around the world and corresponding growth in risk and global competition. This balance can vary considerably from industry to industry and from one country or regional market to another. As explained in chapters 5 and 6, the highest payoff

will come in markets where the U.S. company is ahead of the curve with a distinct or customized product based on leading-edge technology and leaner production costs. Dependence on "commodity" products, in contrast, can result in low or nil profit margins in the face of ever-widening global competition.

5. The central ***organizational*** challenge from the current course of globalization is how to develop a decision-related information system to assess the diverse and constantly changing market opportunities and competitive pressures throughout the world. In effect, this constitutes a globalization of "lean enterprise" and opportunistic marketing strategies. The challenge has many organizational facets, including a more powerful and flexible automated information system for global market decision-making.

Chapter 8

The Changing Nature of the Firm

by Donald A. Norman

Manufacturing firms are undergoing profound changes as they relocate production and assembly outside the United States and outsource activities that traditionally were part of most firms. At the same time, many firms have acquisition programs resulting in ever-larger organizations. Finally, flatter, leaner organizations incorporating management teams are replacing hierarchical managerial structures.

These changes are a consequence of increased competitive pressures faced by manufacturers. In response, firms are shedding low-margin activities and focusing on developing and exploiting core competencies that enable them to compete in global markets. The outlook for manufacturing is positive, given the projections of rising incomes in highly populated developing countries. Firms adopting a global strategy will have a competitive advantage in world markets, especially since their major competitors have become or are becoming global. This chapter elaborates on these themes, drawing on the analyses in the previous chapters.

THE TRADITIONAL FIRM AND ITS BOUNDARIES

Modern discussions on the nature of the firm start with Nobel laureate Ronald Coase's famous 1937 article that asked what the firm is and what determines the scope of activities brought under its umbrella.[1] Anyone organizing the creation, production, and distribution of a product can rely on market transactions, facilitated by contractual arrangements, rather than making these activities a part of the firm. Indeed, a firm like Topsy Tail, with just three employees, has annual sales in the neighborhood of $100 million.[2]

These employees conceive new personal appearance products and then, using contractual relationships, arrange for their production and distribution.

What determines which activities are brought inside the firm? Coase observed that there are "transaction costs" associated with market-based contractual relationships, just as there are managerial coordination costs when activities are brought inside the firm. For one thing, it is costly to specify and enforce every contingency in a contract. Also, rigidities in long-term contracts make reliance on contractual integration less attractive. When the costs of using the market are greater than the costs of coordinating production within a firm, an activity will be brought into the firm. As obvious as this might seem, it was not until Coase's article that much attention was focused on why firms are organized as they are.

While there has always been a rich variation in the structures of firms, a list of the activities that were cumulated within manufacturing firms through the first three-quarters of the 20th century provides a benchmark from which to discuss the changes that have occurred in recent years. During this period, manufacturing firms were (and still are) composed of a wide range of activities, including product research, product design and development, production and assembly facilities, distribution, and marketing. Firms also had employees engaged in support activities such as human resources, accounting, legal services, and planning.

In some manufacturing industries, firms are vertically integrated throughout all stages of production, including the supply of raw materials or critical components. The petroleum industry is a good example. Major oil companies are engaged in exploration, production, transportation, refining, and marketing of crude oil. However, the extent to which oil companies are vertically integrated has declined in recent years as they have sold off assets. Some have sold refineries, while others have divested themselves of onshore producing properties in the lower 48 states.[3]

Vertical integration is one solution to a problem created when a firm makes a fixed investment in something whose value is contingent on its use by another firm. For example, independent suppliers may be reluctant to make investments in a production line dedicated to a specific product for another firm, for fear that they will be subjected to "opportunistic" behavior by the firm purchasing the product.[4] Likewise, a firm purchasing a product may fear that reliance on a particular supplier could make it hostage to similar behavior. The motivation behind General Motors' acquisition of Fisher Body in 1926 is said to have been General Motors' dissatisfaction with Fisher's unwillingness to make investments that would lower costs.[5]

Another characteristic that has distinguished firms is the extent of their diversification into other product lines. In some instances, this diversification was "horizontal," in the sense that firms expanded into products that bore some relationship to their traditional product line. At other times, diversification activities were wide-ranging and without a particular pattern. For

Table 8-1
Trends in the Number of Manufacturing Establishments, 1958–1999

	Number of Manufacturing Establishments	Number of Manufacturing Establishments With 20+ Employees	Value of Manufacturing Shipments (billions $1996)	Value of Shipments per Establishment (billions $1996)
1958	303,303	095,310	1,555.7	5,129,194
1963	311,931	102,296	1,828.3	5,861,232
1967	311,410	110,256	2,211.0	7,099,965
1972	320,710	114,195	2,377.4	7,412,928
1977	359,928	118,699	3,017.6	8,383,899
1982	358,061	123,163	2,958.5	8,262,559
1987	368,904	126,302	3,131.4	8,488,387
1992	381,696	124,822	3,271.7	8,571,481
1999	360,244	119,410	3,403.9	9,448,999

Source: Bureau of the Census, *Annual Survey of Manufactures, Statistics for Industry Groups and Industries, E-Stats*, June 8, 2001; NIPA Tables, *Economic Report of the President*, 2001.

example, General Electric and Tyco are two firms that have diversified into a broad array of product lines, many of which are unrelated.

THE NUMBER OF MANUFACTURING ESTABLISHMENTS AND MANUFACTURING PROFITABILITY

Chapter 3 provided detailed background on changes in the manufacturing sector as well as some projections of future growth by 2010. Additional information is provided by the historical series on the number of manufacturing establishments in the United States and the trend in the profitability of the manufacturing sector in recent years.

The number of manufacturing establishments peaked at 381,696 in 1992 (table 8-1). The number of establishments with 20 or more employees peaked in 1987, and by 1999 was down to an estimated 119,410, a decrease of 5.5 percent since 1987. Despite the decline in the number of establishments, the total inflation-adjusted value of shipments from the manufacturing sector has increased. The value of shipments per plant also has increased over time, indicating that plants are becoming more productive and probably larger. As chapter 4 pointed out, plants are more productive because manufacturers have invested in capital equipment, technology, and improved production processes. Thus, the trends in table 8-1 are consistent with the fact that U.S. manufacturing operations are becoming increasingly capital-intensive and technologically sophisticated.

Figure 8-1
After-Tax Rate of Return on Stockholders' Equity, 1988–2001

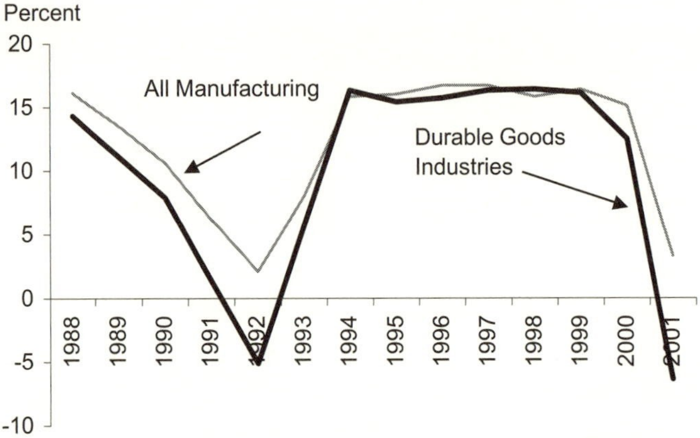

Source: Council of Economic Advisers, *Economic Report of the President,* 2002, Table B-94.

Following the 1991 recession, the profitability of the manufacturing sector, as measured by the rate of return on stockholders' equity, rose quickly and remained stable, averaging 16 percent between 1994 and 1999 (figure 8-1). During the most recent recession in the manufacturing sector, which began in the middle of 2000, profitability again dropped quickly. For the first three-quarters of 2001, the rate of return on equity for all manufacturing was 3.3 percent. For durable goods industries, the rate of return averaged −6.4 percent. This drop in profitability is consistent with the typical cyclical pattern observed during recessions. Although profitability will recover as the manufacturing sector rebounds, the low rate of profitability in 2001 added to the pressure firms are under to improve performance. Performance can be improved by lowering production costs, but firms have always been under pressure to do this. The increasingly competitive environment in which firms operate, means that they must seek other ways to improve performance. That they are doing so helps to explain why the structure of manufacturing firms is changing.

INCREASING COMPETITION

A central theme of this chapter is that manufacturers are operating in an increasingly competitive environment. This is not to say that the environment was in some sense less than competitive in the past. One test of competitiveness is whether an industry is able to earn above-normal rates of return on investment or equity for an extended period of time. If an industry is truly competitive, then above-normal rates of return will be competed for as new competitors enter the market. Although a few early studies found that highly concentrated industries tended to be more profitable than average, evidence from some later studies showed that there was little persistence of above-normal profitability.[6]

The conjecture here is that manufacturers face greater pressures than ever to reduce costs and to develop new products. Profits attributable to efficiency gains and the introduction of new products are being competed away more quickly than in the past.[7] Many executives certainly believe that there has been an increase in the pressure felt by firms to continually reduce costs, to improve products, and to react ever more swiftly to changing market conditions. As the chief financial officer of one large company put it recently, "business just isn't as much fun as it used to be." A number of factors coalesced in the 1990s to make increased competitive pressures perceptible.

The Revolution in Information Technology

Developments in information technology enable individuals to obtain and disseminate information at an incredible speed. As a result, buyers can quickly canvass and compare prices of many sellers. Also, information has become more visible within firms because managers can easily obtain data on current operations. Increased and faster access to information contributes to collapsing managerial hierarchies and speeds reactions by managers.

The growth of e-business and experiments with how best to use the Internet are changing the way firms conduct business. Firms can use the Internet to search for and coordinate with their suppliers, and arrange for production and delivery. At Brady Corporation, a customer can go into the firm's Web site, design a sign, and then order it. The order is then sent directly to a machine that makes signs. Some firms conduct on-line auctions that allow potential suppliers worldwide to compete for business. These firms can specify standards and even provide blueprints for parts they want produced. In terms of Coase's analysis, information technologies have lowered transaction costs so that firms are motivated to increase their reliance on markets for coordinating activity.

Increased Openness of Global Markets

As discussed in chapter 7, the lowering of barriers to trade and reduced transportation costs have increased international trade flows. This globalization of markets means that manufacturers are better able to take advantage of labor cost differences across countries. It also facilitates foreign direct investment as the mobility of capital is increased.

At the same time, increased openness makes it easier for foreign companies to compete against domestic manufacturers. One aspect of the increased openness of world markets is the rise of truly global firms that produce and sell throughout the world. These firms make strategic decisions regarding where production and assembly are carried out. Further, their products are marketed across a broad range of countries with vastly different languages and cultures. They also have created managerial organizations and cultures that enable employees from different countries to work together.

The service sector in the United States, while also facing increased competition, has a degree of protection owing to differences in languages and cultures that makes competing against American firms more difficult. Even here, however, barriers are falling as foreigners providing services become more adept at reading and speaking English and as information technologies enable those providing services to do so from abroad. For example, some credit card firms and telemarketers have established phone and computer centers in countries such as India, where labor costs are very low and education levels are high.

The Strength of the Dollar

The rise of the dollar from 1995 through February 2002 made U.S. exports less competitive while making imports more competitive. The dollar remained surprisingly strong throughout this period despite low interest rates, a large and growing trade deficit, and the recession that for the manufacturing sector began in mid-2002. By itself, a growing trade deficit should induce an adjustment in exchange rates. Such an adjustment was slow in coming, but beginning in March 2002 the dollar finally began to fall in value. As of May 2003, the Federal Reserve Board's dollar index showed that the dollar had fallen by 17.6 percent against a basket of currencies of our major trading partners. Against the euro, the dollar declined by 24.6 percent between February 2002 and May 2003.

While the strength of the dollar has declined in the past year and a half, the fact remains that its strength in the late 1990s posed a problem for U.S. manufacturers. The strength of the dollar induced various responses by manufacturers. Some firms moved production abroad so that they were not penalized by the high value of the dollar. Angell Manufacturing Company, a maker of auto parts, opened a joint venture factory in Germany.[8] According to Angell's chief executive, this move was prompted by expectations that the value of the dollar would stay high, thereby making it too expensive to produce the parts in Kentucky and ship them to Germany. Firms like Automatic Feed, a manufacturer of heavy machinery used by automobile manufacturers, began redesigning products to reduce their production costs, and other firms have beefed up their sales forces and marketing efforts.[9]

Deregulation

Countries as diverse as Norway, Chile, New Zealand, the United Kingdom, Germany, and Korea, as well as the United States, have deregulated or at least reduced the regulation of industries such as transportation, energy, electricity, and telecommunications. Firms that once operated in a protected environment and were guaranteed a "reasonable" rate of return on their "prudent" investments find themselves forced (or enabled) to compete. J. R. Hicks, another Nobel laureate in economics, observed long ago that managers of monopolistic firms are unlikely to be concerned with minimizing costs and maximizing profits. As he put it, the best of all monopoly profits is a quiet life.[10] It would be fair to include in his definition of "monopoly" firms sheltered from competition by regulation. Deregulation has increased competition in formerly regulated industries, thereby forcing managers who once led a relatively quiet life to become more cost-conscious because they no longer have the regulatory backing to pass along costs to captive customers. As a result, deregulated firms have become more aggressive in seeking lower prices when purchasing manufactured goods and equipment used in their businesses. This is one reason that final prices for goods and services in deregulated industries generally have fallen.[11]

Innovative Activity

Between 1959 and 2000, industry spending on research and development (R&D) in the United States, measured in constant dollars, grew by an average annual rate of 5.5 percent; real gross domestic product (GDP) grew by an average annual rate of 3.4 percent over the same period.[12] As a result, industry R&D as a percent of GDP more than doubled, from 0.8 percent to 1.8 percent. R&D spending by industry accounted for 67 percent of total U.S. R&D spending in 2000, including R&D spending by the federal government.[13] Since as much as 70 percent of total business R&D spending is accounted for by the manufacturing sector, manufacturing's role in promoting economic growth is substantially more important than is suggested by its share of total employment or value added. And, although the percentage of GDP accounted for R&D expenditures is relatively small, William J. Baumol[14] argues that a much larger share of the labor force is at least peripherally involved in activities related to or affected by innovative activity.

Competition: Structure Versus Rivalry

Traditional analyses of competitiveness focused on the structural characteristics of an industry. Perfectly competitive industries were those in which there were a large number of small firms, each of which took the market price as given. The surprising paradox is that firms in perfectly competitive industries do not in fact compete in the sense of engaging in rivalrous behavior. They are merely passive entities producing at that scale in which marginal production costs are equated with the product price. In contrast, industries dominated by a few large firms were deemed oligopolistic. Their very structure was supposedly a sign that the firms did not actively compete against each other and instead tacitly coordinated prices, to the detriment of consumers.

The modern view is that structure is not a key determinant of an industry's competitiveness. As long as a market is contestable, that is, as long as a market is open and subject to being contested by a potential entrant, existing firms are effectively constrained from exercising market power, say in the form of pricing decisions.[15] Baumol's recent analysis adds to this insight by emphasizing the role of innovation in forcing even large oligopolistic firms to compete in order to survive. According to Baumol, technology consortiums among large firms, including firms that compete with each other, are justified by the fact that they enable more rapid diffusion of new innovations and, because firms gain by sharing knowledge or their innovations, help overcome the disincentive to invest in R&D created by their inability to capture all the direct benefits from such investment.

The implications of Baumol's analysis go beyond technology consortiums. The traditional view of price discrimination, that is, selling the same product at different prices to different customers, was that its very existence was a sign that the seller possessed market power. In contrast, Baumol views price discrimination as being "thrust" on firms and necessary for recovery of the fixed costs of innovating. Without it, there would be less innovation, and hence slower economic growth.

For Baumol, the rise in spending on R&D over time is an indication that competitive pressures have increased.

THE RESTRUCTURING OF MANUFACTURING FIRMS

One way in which firms have responded to increased competitive pressures has been to move some production offshore. Firms also are outsourcing an increasing number of activities and functions. That is, they are divesting themselves of activities that traditionally were carried out within the firm. There is a distinction between moving production offshore and outsourcing. When moving production offshore, a firm sets up a manufacturing establishment that it owns and operates in another country. Outsourcing refers to "hiring" another firm via a contractual relationship to undertake some activity—manufacturing or support service—previously carried on within the firm by its own employees. An outsourcing activity may be performed domestically or abroad.

At the same time, many firms have active acquisition programs that bring additional activities, including new product lines, into the firm. These two trends—outsourcing and acquisitions—may seem contradictory, except that the nature of what is being divested and what is being acquired is usually quite distinct. Finally, firms are changing the way in which activities are managed as they move from traditional hierarchical structures to flatter team environments.

Offshore Production

Competitive pressures motivated many manufacturers to expand and/or relocate production after World War II from the North and the Midwest to the Sunbelt. This was simply a case of taking advantage of the lower labor costs there. Moving production to Mexico and offshore to Asia and Eastern Europe is merely an extension of the movement to the Sunbelt. It also is consistent with the flow of activity predicted by the economic principle of factor cost equalization. By this principle, the movement of economic activity in response to differences in factor costs (such as labor) tends to reduce these differences. However, as long as there are barriers to trade, restrictions on labor mobility, cultural and language differences, and differences in the productivity of labor forces, a complete convergence of factor costs will not occur. Nonetheless, as discussed in chapter 7, trade barriers have declined over time, with the result that firms are motivated to take advantage of international differences in labor costs.[16] As trade barriers are reduced, price levels and labor costs converge, and the labor cost component of production diminishes. Then such relocation will become less important.

International differences in labor costs are in fact changing, in some cases rapidly. Table 8-2 presents average hourly compensation costs for production workers, measured in dollars, and production worker cost indexes for selected countries. The indexes are based on the U.S. index set equal to 100. For example, in 1990, the index for labor production costs in Japan was 86, indicating production worker costs were 14 percent lower than in the United States. By 1999, Japan's index had risen to 109, indicating that production worker compensation costs were 9 percent higher than in the United States. In Korea, the index rose from 25 to 35, indicating that the production worker costs there are significantly lower than in the United States, but that the labor cost advantage there has declined. Mexico's labor compensation costs, relative to the United States, appear to have remained stable between 1990 and 1999. This is misleading, however, because the peso was pegged at an unsustainable and overvalued rate relative to the dollar in 1990. Since 1995, the peso has floated, with the result that the labor cost advantage in Mexico has declined.

Labor cost differences reflect differences in the productivity and skills of the labor forces as well as local supply and demand conditions in labor markets. With falling trade barriers, firms are better able to take advantage of lower labor costs, but in doing so they tend to bid up wages. However, lower wages do not measure the gains from moving production offshore because they also reflect the lower productivity of the labor force. In fact, since productivity growth in the United States has generally been higher

Table 8-2
Compensation Costs for Production Workers in U.S. Dollars, 1990 and 1999

	1990		1999	
	Hourly Labor Costs (*U.S. dollars per hour*)	Index (*U.S.=100*)	Hourly Labor Costs (*U.S. dollars per hour*)	Index (*U.S.=100*)
United States	14.91	100	19.21	100
Canada	15.95	107	15.60	81
Mexico	1.58	11	2.12	11
Japan	12.80	86	20.89	109
Korea	3.71	25	5.44	35
Taiwan	3.93	26	5.68	29
Germany (West)	21.88	147	26.93	140
Italy	17.45	117	16.60	86
France	15.39	104	17.98	94
United Kingdom	12.20	85	16.56	86

Source: U.S. Department of Labor, Bureau of Labor Statistics.

than that of its main competitors, it has gained a considerable advantage since the 1980s in terms of unit labor costs in manufacturing. When compared to its main competitors, between 1979 and 2000, unit labor costs in the United States grew 15.5 percent less than those in the 12 competitor countries. For example, while these costs grew by 29 percent in the United States in that time period, they grew by 40 percent in Japan, 69 percent in the United Kingdom, and 108 percent in Taiwan.[17] As developing countries invest in the education and training of their labor force, workers will become more productive and wages will rise.

At the same time that U.S. manufacturers have moved production offshore, foreign firms have set up significant manufacturing operations here. South Carolina, a state with relatively low wages and a good port, has been very successful in attracting foreign-owned manufacturing operations, including BMW, Honda, Michelin, and Fuji Film since the mid-1970s. In 2000, Haier, a Chinese producer of refrigerators, opened a $35 million factory there. The motivation for setting up operations in the United States is largely to gain access to markets here, as well as to benefit from reduced transportation costs.

Outsourcing

Widespread outsourcing by U.S. firms began in the 1980s, although it started earlier. In 1972, for example, Pyrotronics, a California manufacturer and distributor of fireworks, began purchasing fireworks from China and reducing its own production. The fireworks were shipped to California, where they were packaged along with domestically produced fireworks on an assembly line. By the mid-1980s, the Chinese firms were producing and packaging all of Pyrotronics' retail fireworks. Very quickly, Pyrotronics moved from being a producer, assembler, and distributor of fireworks to being primarily a distributor.

Today, manufacturers of automobiles and equipment are among the leaders in outsourcing. As Hanson et al. observe, these kinds of manufacturing processes are made up of distinct stages, such as component production and assembly, that are physically separable and amenable to being carried out in different locations.[18] Japanese automobile manufacturers were outsourcing production to other firms before outsourcing caught on in the United States. One reported difference between the Japanese and American automobile firms is that the goal of Japanese firms was to improve the efficiency and quality of their manufacturing processes, whereas American firms primarily were interested in using other firms to produce items at lower unit cost and to reduce their own fixed costs.[19]

Outsourcing is not without problems. When production is outsourced to a number of firms, each of which supplies a component, the firm must coordinate activities so that production runs and deliveries coincide with the assembly process. Further, a firm engaged in outsourcing must ensure that quality standards are maintained. Some firms find that they end up working very closely with outside suppliers to facilitate coordination and to ensure that new technologies are applied to components. Hence, despite outsourcing, a degree of integration remains intact.

Successful outsourcing is facilitated by the reputation of suppliers and their relationships with firms that seek to outsource. In Japan, the automobile producers outsource on the basis of long-term business arrangements. Concern that nonintegrated suppliers will not make specific investments for fear of being held "hostage" is alleviated by continuous renegotiations that effectively substitute for integration.[20] Japanese suppliers work to build their "reputational" capital so they can establish a long-term relationship.[21] Finally, Japanese firms tend to rely on a relatively small number of suppliers compared to their American counterparts, although American automobile firms are reducing the number of suppliers.

As discussed earlier, the information technology revolution has lowered the cost of finding customers and suppliers. This facilitates outsourcing, but it also can destroy the reputational capital that is built up by repeated business transactions. Successful outsourcing ultimately depends on more than having something produced at the lowest cost. Another potential problem is that firms may lose their technological edge after a few years if they "lose control" over their process technology.[22]

Outsourcing is a component of a global strategy. At the same time, it is facilitated by the increased openness of world markets. According to John McLaren, international openness "thickens" markets, making it easier for firms to find suppliers.[23] By this, McLaren means that the likelihood a downstream manufacturer will be "held up" by a supplier is reduced because the downstream manufacturer knows that, with open markets, there is a larger number of potential suppliers. Hence, increased international trade can lead to a decrease in the extent to which manufacturing activities are vertically integrated.

Automobile producers are not the only manufacturers that are outsourcing. Nucor has made a single firm its sole supplier of scrap metal, relying on a contractual relationship. At one time, producers of finished steel products were vertically integrated as far back as the mining and processing of ores, such as taconite, used to make raw steel. Nike and Benetton outsource their production abroad and focus on developing their brand names and marketing their products.

Outsourcing involves activities other than manufacturing and assembly. An increasing number of firms are outsourcing their legal, accounting, and human resources departments, activities that once were an integral part of any large manufacturing company. In the 1980s most large companies had strategic planning departments. At the time Jack Welch became the CEO of General Electric, the firm had a corporate planning staff of 200. Welch eliminated this group, as did many other firms. While firms cut back drastically on formal and permanent corporate planning activities, strategic planning did not disappear; firms employed consultants to undertake these activities when needed. Other firms have reinstituted internal strategic planning activities in recent years as they seek to restructure their operations and redefine their corporate strategy.

An important motive for outsourcing nonmanufacturing activities seems to be the desire to reduce fixed costs. Firms are more vulnerable to swings in final demand the greater their fixed costs are as a proportion of total costs. By definition, variable costs fluctuate with the level of a firm's activity, whereas fixed costs are more difficult to cut because they cannot easily be "laid off." Outsourcing makes the cost of some activities variable and, hence, easier to adjust as a firm's business fluctuates.

The fact that some manufacturers reduce their fixed costs does not mean that these costs magically disappear. The firms that become the suppliers must invest in production facilities, and thus bear fixed costs that presumably make them vulnerable to the same swings in product demand. The crucial difference is that in an open global market, specialist supplier firms can produce and assemble for more than just one manufacturer. If a supplier finds that an outsourcing arrangement is terminated due to slow demand for one firm's final product, it can compete to be another manufacturer's supplier. The potential to diversify reduces the vulnerability of a supplier firm's fixed investments to fluctuations in the demand for a specific product.

Acquisitions

While firms are outsourcing a wide range of activities that tend to reduce the size of the firm, many active acquisition programs enlarge the firm. A number of factors were behind the wave of mergers and acquisitions during the 1990s, including the desire to maintain growth, globalization, operational efficiencies, technology, size advantages, and deregulation.[24] Another factor is "strategic," meaning that firms want to take advantage of what economists call ***economies of scope***. With strategic acquisitions, a firm can leverage its core competencies over a broader array of products.[25]

The essence of a core competency is based on a firm's knowledge and skills. It is something specific to the firm, and hence something that cannot be easily imitated or commoditized. It also is the source of a firm's comparative advantage in competing against other firms. Core competencies can pertain to a number of activities, including engineering, process control, production planning, finance, distribution, and marketing.

Some acquisitions are made with the intent of extending a firm's core competencies over a broader range of activities and products. Instead of ***shedding fixed costs*** (as with outsourcing), firms can ***spread the fixed costs*** associated with the development of their core competencies by leveraging them to additional activities. By so doing, they achieve economies of scope.

As firms focus on their core competencies, the overall mix of employees found in manufacturing firms should change. Core competencies like the development of production systems, the design of new products that provide enhanced services, finance, and the coordination of disparate activities rely on what Peter Drucker has called "knowledge workers."

Employees classified as "production" workers, that is, those who actually make and assemble products, will likely decrease in relative importance in the United States as firms adopt a global strategy. Data on manufacturing employment and production workers show that between 1949 and 1984, the number of production workers as a percent of total manufacturing employment fell from 79.4 percent to 65.7 percent. This understates the relative decline in the importance of production workers because there have been parallel declines, especially since the 1980s, in middle management in addition to the outsourcing of services previously carried on within the firm. As shown in figure 8-2, the production worker share of value added in the manufacturing sector fell from 39 percent in 1950 to just 18 percent in 2000. This corroborates observations that the focus of manufacturing activity is shifting away from production and assembly, and toward activities encompassing higher value-adding core competencies.

Many large manufacturing firms have active acquisition programs and a formal process for screening potential acquisitions to ensure they will "fit in" with the firm's core competencies. The process of integrating acquisitions

Figure 8-2
Production Worker Share of Manufacturing Value Added, 1950–2000

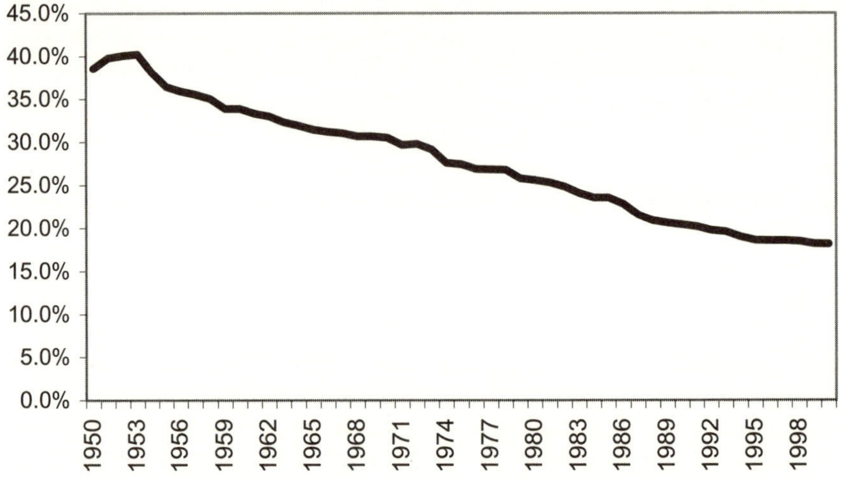

Source: U.S. Department of Commerce, Annual Survey of Manufactures, 1993, 2000.

also is systematized so that accounting systems, salary scales, and such are quickly aligned with those of the parent company.

There is an ongoing debate regarding whether companies are able to capture economies of scope. While General Electric and Parker Hannifin have been successful with their acquisitions, the academic literature on diversification calls into question whether such benefits actually exist. Until recently, most researchers believed that there was a 10 percent to 15 percent "diversification discount," meaning that companies with a multidivisional structure were valued 10 percent to 15 percent less in the stock market.

Several reasons for this diversification discount have been suggested, including the loss of financial transparency and the rising difficulty of managing growing multidivisional firms.[26] In addition, diversified firms may not allocate capital investment efficiently. In a diversified firm with many divisions, bureaucratic processes in which capital investment among divisions is evened out rather than allocated to the best prospects replace purely profit-based decision-making.[27] As a result of this cross-subsidization, weak divisions end up investing more than their nondiversified industry peers.

Recent empirical studies have challenged whether there is in fact a diversification discount. Hadlock et al. suggest that any investment inefficiencies as described above are offset by the increased information regarding markets and opportunities generated by diversification.[28] Their empirical evidence fails to find a diversification discount. Similarly, Graham, Lemman, and Wolf find that the companies that are acquired tend to be underperformers.[29]

Figure 8-3
Capacity Utilization Index for All Manufacturing, January 1999–April 2003

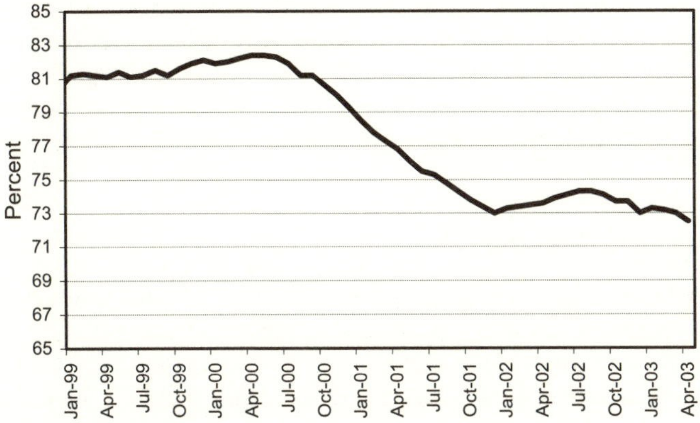

Source: Federal Reserve Board, "Industrial Production and Capacity Utilization," Federal Reserve Statistical Release, G. 17 (419), May 15, 2003.

When this is accounted for in empirical work, the evidence for a diversification discount disappears.

Acquisitions and Capacity

As discussed earlier, a number of factors explain the merger and acquisition activity of the 1990s. One other factor is industry consolidation. Consolidation is a response to the low capacity utilization rates that manufacturing industries have experienced in recent years, especially since the downturn in manufacturing activity that started in September 2000. Globalization and the movement of production offshore also have contributed to lower utilization rates in the United States.

The rapid increase in industrial capacity since 1995 also has contributed to the low level of capacity utilization. From 1967 to 1988, the capacity of durable goods manufacturers grew by an annual average rate of 3.4 percent. Since 1995, the industrial capacity of durable goods manufacturers has increased by an average annual rate of 7.3 percent.[30] In 2000 alone, this capacity increased by an astonishingly large rate of 8.3 percent. Since then, the rate of capacity growth has slowed markedly. In 2001, durable goods capacity grew by 4.6 percent and in 2002 the growth of capacity slowed to just 2.3 percent.

The net result of increased capacity, increased competition from abroad, and the slowdown in manufacturing has been a decline in capacity utilization. As shown in figure 8-3, the capacity utilization rate in the manufacturing sector fell steadily from June 2000 through December 2001. It edged up from January 2002 through August 2002, but has declined slowly since then. As of April 2003, the rate of capacity utilization stood at just 72.5 percent. This is almost as low as it was in the depth of the 1982 recession, when it fell to 71.8 percent. Acquisitions enable firms to retire capacity that is relatively inefficient. Given the excess capacity that currently exists, aggregate capacity expansion by the manufacturing sector over the next five years likely will be slower than it was in the 1990s.

Management Organization

The changing nature of firms necessitates concomitant changes in managerial organization if a firm is to realize all the potential gains from its new structure. Many firms, inside and outside of manufacturing, have moved or are trying to move from a hierarchy to a leaner, flatter, team-oriented organization. Manufacturers also are setting up shared service centers to handle activities, such as accounting, for all their divisions. For example, Deere has set up a shared service center for its accounts receivable. The goal is to learn from this experience so that the shared services can be expanded to other accounting activities. Shared service centers hold out the promise of reducing the cost of these activities by spreading the service provided by a center across all of a firm's divisions. That is, they are another way of spreading fixed costs.

Restructuring management can improve a firm's efficiency just as changing its structure confers benefits. It is important to note that there are variations on what is meant by team organizations. Some companies have established a relatively large number of teams and have given them wide discretion to pursue their goals. Others have created a limited number of teams and continue to rely on strong leadership at the top for overall direction of the firm's activities. A potential problem faced by any organization implementing any new management structure is the resistance to change by those who are impacted. Some resistance originates from a dislike for something new, but it also exists because some employees find their role diminished or even eliminated when a company switches to a leaner team-oriented management organization.

THE GLOBALIZATION OF THE AUTOMOTIVE INDUSTRY

The changing structure of the automotive industry and its companies typifies what it means to become truly global. In the 1970s, automobile manufacturers around the world were based in their home country, meaning that virtually their entire operations were located domestically. They began their transformation by establishing production facilities in other countries where they could take advantage of lower labor costs and use their local presence as a way of entering foreign markets.

In recent years, the major automobile producers have become truly global by purchasing foreign producers and by strategically locating engineering, design, and production facilities throughout the world.[31] In addition to adding significant production and assembly facilities in the United States, foreign manufacturers are establishing design and engineering centers there. U.S. automobile producers are becoming global entities as they acquire or invest in foreign producers. Thus, Ford owns Mazda (Japan), Volvo (Sweden), and Jaguar and Land Rover (United Kingdom). Chrysler is part of Daimler (Germany), and DaimlerChrysler owns a controlling share of Mitsubishi Motors (Japan) and a small share of Hyundai Motors (Korea).

Honda has a significant production base in the United States and is planning to produce cars in China for export to Asia and Europe.[32] Twelve automobile producers already have plants in China where cars are turned out for its domestic market.

In addition to acquiring foreign producers and locating facilities strategically throughout the world, the automobile producers have a rich variety of relationships with their suppliers. That is, they carefully outsource the production of specific components to specialist suppliers. These suppliers work closely with the producers and often locate their own facilities near assembly plants.

All this raises the question of just what defines the nature of a global automobile producer. Essentially, the global producer's core competencies include the planning, coordination, and financing of a vast and complex set of tasks that go into the design, engineering, production, assembly, and marketing of an automobile. Many of these tasks—like design, engineering, and research—are done within the firm, while some tasks are left to specialist suppliers. The global firm, thinking strategically, decides where, from a global point of view, these tasks are best carried out.

Globalization is a response to, as well as a force for, increased competition. The result of globalization in the automobile industry has been a significant improvement in automobiles, an incredible variety of products to choose from, and lower prices.[33]

THE OUTLOOK FOR MANUFACTURED PRODUCTS

According to the analysis in chapter 5, rising incomes in the United States help to explain the faster growth of the service sector relative to manufacturing. Penetration rates for appliances like refrigerators and washing machines, as well as for automobiles, already are high so that the growth in unit sales is largely governed by the population growth rate. Consumers are interested in the features and services attached to goods rather than in more goods.[34] For example, one can purchase refrigerators that make ice, provide cold filtered water, and monitor the humidity of the interior, as well as keep food cold. Whirlpool has teamed with Cisco Systems and Sun Microsystems to develop networked home appliances that can be controlled using the Internet.[35] Similarly, automobiles with sophisticated sound systems are mini symphony halls (or rock palaces). They include a host of new safety features, engines designed to burn gasoline so that harmful emissions are minimized, and even sophisticated navigation systems. Thus, the real growth potential for manufactured goods in the United States is not so much in terms of numbers as it is in terms of the additional features and services embedded in these goods.

Given projections of economic growth in developing countries, the worldwide outlook for manufactured products in terms of the numerical growth of unit sales is positive. The low penetration rates for automobiles and appliances in countries like China and India, and in Eastern Europe and South America, where billions of people aspire to a higher standard of living, are measures of the potential of markets for manufactured goods. For example, the penetration rate of refrigerators in India was estimated to be just 11 percent in 1999, up from 4.6 percent in 1990.[36] In rural India, which has 71 percent of the nation's population, the penetration rate of washing machines is 0.5 percent.[37] As incomes rise in these countries, unit sales of basic appliances, as well as manufactured products used in producing goods, will increase significantly in absolute terms.

COMPETING IN GLOBAL MARKETS

U.S. manufacturers face the challenge of operating in an increasingly competitive environment. While contributing to these competitive pressures, the opening of world markets and the expansion of trade also create opportunities, in that markets for manufactured goods will expand as incomes in highly populated developing countries increase. To take advantage of these opportunities, U.S. manufacturers must adopt global strategies, especially since other manufacturers throughout the world have done or are doing so themselves.

A global strategy goes far beyond the traditional firm's concentration on achieving production cost efficiency through economies of scale. Firms must develop and market core competencies that are unique to their firm. By leveraging core competencies across other products and activities in world markets, firms can capture the value inherent in their skills. Also, the products they offer must provide enhanced services. Although production efficiency remains a necessary condition for profitability, it is not, by itself, sufficient to ensure survival in a global economy. The critically important tasks are developing and leveraging skills and knowledge, and providing products with services that other firms cannot easily or quickly imitate.

In the late 1970s and early 1980s, there was widespread concern that U.S.

manufacturers would be overwhelmed by their Japanese competitors, which seemed to have an insurmountable edge with respect to production costs and quality. American manufacturers successfully responded to this challenge. Productivity grew at a very healthy pace in the 1990s and especially in the late 1990s. Quality also improved. By the mid-1990s, domestic manufacturing had returned to sounder footing. The recession in manufacturing that began in June 2000, coupled with an increasingly competitive environment, has challenged American manufacturers once again. Their responses are changing our conception of what activities define a manufacturing firm, and in the end will contribute significantly to a growing economy and a higher standard of living.

Chapter 9

The Engine for Growth in a Global Economy: An Integrated Policy Response

by Thomas J. Duesterberg and Ernest H. Preeg

INTRODUCTION

The manufacturing sector does not exist in a vacuum: it operates in and is affected by the political, cultural, and social environment of which it is an integral part. Economists from Hayek and Schumpeter to North and Friedman have elucidated some of the fundamental nonmarket factors that affect the performance of the industrial sector. Among the most important of these are the policy and related institutional frameworks within which manufacturing must operate. A stable and effective rule of law, efficient tax and high-performance educational systems, and a benign regulatory climate are crucial for the success of the type of manufacturing model we have described. Alternatively, the policy and institutional environment can hinder the most productive development of this sector in many ways. While it is our contention that the overall environment in the United States is among the best in the world for nurturing modern, innovative manufacturing, there are certain problems and impediments which can and should be addressed.

The policy response to nurture and support the U.S. manufacturing sector as the engine for growth in a global economy needs to be both comprehensive and integrated so as to produce mutually supportive results. Specific policy issues are often addressed in isolation, within a zero-sum game political context—winners versus losers—and with insufficient consideration of broader national objectives. In fact, the overall engine for growth strategy is a highly positive-sum game, and the policy response in support of it should be developed on this basis. In the global market which has evolved since the 1950s, the owners of capital will not be the only, or perhaps even the primary, beneficiaries of reforms to improve economic performance. A large portion of the benefits will go to workers through higher pay and the creation of new jobs. Huge benefits also accrue to consumers in the form of better products and higher living standards.

Such a strategy is presented here in summary form, beginning with a statement of broad objectives. Specific policy proposals to strengthen support for the objectives are then elaborated. The ten areas of policy addressed are selective, representing the highest priorities that collectively would have the most important positive impact on the objectives. The final section of the chapter explains the need to communicate the engine for growth strategy, and its policy implications, more effectively at home and abroad, with examples of how this might be done.

The Broad Policy Objectives

There are six broad policy objectives which together can greatly strengthen the performance of the U.S. manufacturing sector as the engine for growth within the U.S. economy and, to a large extent, for the global economy as well. There are many interrelationships between these objectives and the specific policy proposals contained in the following section of this chapter, and for each of the objectives key interrelationships are highlighted.

1. Wider freedom for creativity and innovation.—This is the vital core of the engine for growth, from the sprouting of new ideas to their developmental research and commercial application. Indeed, as William Baumol has argued, innovation has become systematic and "routinized" in modern corporate practice, and is crucial to the dynamic growth characteristic of modern capitalism, especially in the United States.[1] As we have shown throughout this book, manufacturing is the cradle of a large majority of research, development, and innovative activity. As described in preceding chapters, a uniquely positive symbiosis has evolved in the U.S. manufacturing sector between an innovation-oriented private sector and a generally supportive policy framework. There is also a wide range of mutually supportive innovations among the private sector, public-sector research programs, and academic work. The United States is the global leader by far in such creativity and innovation. Other nations, however, seek to broaden and deepen their capability, which offers both cross-border opportunities for global economic growth and increased competition for American companies. The European Union (EU), for example, has set as an explicit goal increasing research and development (R&D) spending to become the most competitive knowledge-based economy in the world by 2010. But a gap of nearly 1 percent of the gross domestic product (GDP) in research spending still separates the EU from the United States.[2]

In any event, the United States needs not only to maintain its current primary role but also to strengthen further the stimuli for creativity and innovation in an ever more technology-intensive economic setting. Particular policy areas for improvement include education, deregulation, and tort reform.

2. A sustained high level of productive investment.—A strong and vigorous investment sector is crucial for sustained economic growth and continued productivity gains. These relationships have been corroborated and amplified by research on the high rates of growth in the late 1990s and are reviewed in chapter 4 of this book. This involves, in quantitative terms, increasing the aggregate level of investment from the doldrums of the 2001-2002 recession in manufacturing and, in qualitative terms, ensuring that investment is utilized in the most productive way for increasing output. We should add that investment can be in the form of both physical capital and human capital, including that related to research.

The priority on stimulating productive investment is broadly recognized, but there is no integrated policy response for doing so. The "economic stimulus" packages signed into law by President George W. Bush in early 2002, providing an additional 30 percent depreciation for most capital equipment investment for a three-year period and in early 2003 reducing the tax rates on capital gains and corporate dividends, were steps in the right direction. But they hardly constitute a comprehensive policy. Almost all of the specific policy areas discussed here have some impact on investment decisions.

3. An increased rate of domestic savings.—We are currently living beyond our means, borrowing almost 5 percent of GDP abroad per year to pay for current levels of consumption and, to a lesser extent, investment, with a consequent buildup of foreign debt approaching $3 trillion. Personal savings rates have fallen to the low single digits consistently since the mid-1980s. A higher rate of personal and corporate savings should be a priority national objective. A return to a balanced federal budget would also increase the national savings rate. Higher domestic savings would facilitate, among other results, a consistently higher and more stable rate of investment.

Fiscal policy reform is the major area for stimulating increased savings, although in recent years tax relief or reform has tended to stimulate greater consumption rather than savings.

4. A more highly educated and flexible labor force.—There is consensus that primary and secondary school education standards need to be raised, particularly for math, science, and reading. Raising the quality of teacher training is an important component of this challenge. Another issue is negative attitudes about the future of manufacturing on the part of K-12 teachers and administrators. Such attitudes contribute to the problem of motivating students in higher education to follow careers in science and engineering. Less well understood but of comparable importance are joint initiatives from the private sector and university-level training facilities to strengthen and upgrade job-related skills in an increasingly technology-oriented labor market. Another dimension of labor productivity is the need to facilitate flexibility in the workforce, among firms and industry sectors, as the structure of the overall economy evolves at a brisk pace.

Educational reform at the federal, state, and private-sector levels is central to this objective. Other areas of policy, however, including fiscal incentives and more mobile retirement and health care programs, can also contribute significantly.

5. *More open international trade and investment.*—The U.S. manufacturing sector is heavily engaged in international trade and investment, which reduces input costs and increases growth opportunities in many ways. R&D and initial investment costs are spread more broadly, on a global basis, and export markets are growing rapidly, especially in the newly industrialized regions. Moreover, exposure to international markets is a primary stimulus to continuously improving productivity and innovation.

U.S. liberal trade policy has been stalled in recent years, but circumstances are now more favorable to pursue free trade and investment in the manufactures sector, in conjunction with an orderly decline in the large U.S. trade deficit in manufactures. The passage of the Trade Promotion Authority in 2002 gives the president the capability to pursue trade agreements, as well as the political momentum needed to complete them.

6. *A reduced and more market-oriented government regulatory role.*—The uneven course of government deregulation since the late 1970s has responded to the ever more dynamic course of technology-driven growth, centered on the manufacturing sector. While some regulatory oversight is needed to ensure the smooth functioning of markets, too often overeager regulators can have a negative impact on initiative and investment. Government regulators tend to be behind the innovation curve, and misguided regulations can inhibit necessary economic restructuring for growth. One lesson repeatedly learned is that when government regulatory objectives are deemed appropriate, market-oriented price incentives are vastly preferable to highly legalistic performance standards as a means to accomplish the objective.

Deregulation is usually industry-specific and direct, but other policy areas, especially tort reform, can also play an important role.

Specific Policy Proposals

A policy agenda for advancing these broad objectives is presented here in terms of ten priority target areas for action which, if pursued in parallel, would have a substantial, mutually supportive, positive impact on the manufacturing sector as the engine for growth in a global economy. No attempt has been made to establish a comprehensive agenda. Rather, the most critical, near-term changes needed to support an economy based on high growth, productivity, and innovation is outlined. The sequence of the ten policy targets moves from more broadly based policies, such as fiscal and financial market reforms, to more functional targets, and to the concluding three issues of international economic policy.

1. Fiscal reform.—The federal tax structure has an overriding and pervasive impact on the degree to which the manufacturing sector is the engine for economic growth. The existing structure, especially the federal tax system, tends to favor incentives for consumption at the expense of productive investment, while the myriad narrowly defined tax exemptions create widespread distortions in the efficient allocation of resources. Moreover, the current tax regime puts a higher burden on the capital-intensive manufacturing sector than on other sectors of the economy. Although the gap has narrowed in recent years, manufacturers still pay 36.8 percent of all private business income in taxes, compared to 31.8 percent for the services sector. The marginal rate for manufacturing is 51.9 percent, compared to 43.3 percent for services. The higher capital intensiveness of manufacturing is one reason for this gap; another is the double taxation of corporate income when part is paid out in dividends to shareholders. The services sector is not as heavily incorporated as manufacturing, and thus has a lesser incidence of double taxation.[3] Higher incidence of corporate taxation than in many other countries has in recent years driven manufacturing firms both to incorporate outside the United States and to move some research activities offshore.[4] Finally, the federal tax code as applied to depreciation of assets is woefully outdated in today's rapidly moving economy. This is especially true in the high-technology sector, where advances in computing power, for example, make equipment such as telecommunications switches or machine tools obsolete more rapidly than they can be depreciated. The tax relief package signed into law on May 28, 2003 goes part way to relieving, on a temporary basis, the problems of double taxation of dividends and outdated depreciation schedules. Fundamental tax reform should thus be a top priority for sustained productivity-driven economic growth.

Tax reform should be pursued within a framework of restoring fiscal balance and of moving toward radical tax simplification. The balanced budget objective not only is the starting point for restraint in government spending, but also is particularly important at this time for raising the national savings rate and thus reducing the need to borrow abroad. Tax simplification through consolidation and convergence of rates and phaseout of exemptions would reduce distortions in resource allocation and garner widespread public support from all except tax lawyers. Within this framework, specific targets for tax reform should include the following:

a. *Shift toward a consumption-based tax structure*. The purpose is to encourage a higher level of national savings to finance investment. The modality for such reform could be made comprehensive through a shift in tax structure from income-based to consumption-based taxes or more selectivity in applying higher taxes on consumption while easing income tax rates. A particularly effective incentive to raise savings is through more generous tax preferences for 401(k) and other retirement-oriented savings vehicles.

b. *Reduce the excessive tax burden on business.* The United States applies an unusual double taxation on corporate business, first on profits and then on after-tax profits distributed as dividends to shareholders. One result is reduced incentives to invest. Another is a competitive disadvantage in trade with nations that tax business only once. The best remedy would be to abolish the corporate profit tax, which in the process would greatly reduce the cost and serious legal problems of tax compliance through the elimination of complicated rules for depreciation and other profit-related deductions. A second-best solution would be to eliminate the double taxation of corporate dividends. The tax burden on business could also be alleviated through a reduction in the capital gains tax in conjunction with greater emphasis on consumption-based taxes. This latter course was partially, though temporarily, accomplished by the 2003 Tax Relief Bill.

c. *Encourage research and development.* This is currently done through a combination of private-sector tax credits, government-subsidized research programs, and the protection of intellectual property rights (IPRs). A cost/benefit review of how to improve the existing incentive system would be useful. One objective would be to move toward greater reliance on competitive incentives within the private sector. In view of the rapid globalization of markets, the uneven international application of IPRs and copyright piracy are of growing importance for the international competitiveness of American companies. Such piracy is estimated to cost American companies between \$20 billion and \$22 billion per year.[5]

d. *Move toward complete expensing of capital investments.* A particularly useful change in corporate taxation for manufacturing (in the event that elimination of the corporate profit tax is not feasible) would be to move toward complete expensing of capital expenditures. While some might object to complete current year expensing, especially if it encouraged overbuilding of structures, its application to business equipment and software, the keys to innovation, would be especially helpful to manufacturing.

e. *Move toward a territorial system of taxation.* Because U.S. firms are taxed on a global basis, they are at a disadvantage with EU and other foreign-based firms that are taxed only on income generated within national borders. A move toward a territorial system would reduce this disadvantage, help stop the exodus of corporate headquarters from the country, and solve a long-festering trade dispute with the EU.

f. *Restructure the Social Security system toward contribution-based and market-oriented retirement accounts.* In addition to offering employees the opportunity for a higher rate of return on their contributions, there would be a more efficient allocation of capital compared with the current Social Security system and a higher rate of savings.

2. Financial market standards and transparency.—Corporate finance has recently benefited from a monetary policy of low interest rates in line with low inflation and continued strong growth in productivity. However, financial markets have suffered a serious loss of confidence as a result of the Enron/Andersen, WorldCom, and other scandals, and the related broader issues of adequate disclosure and potential conflicts of interest. Actions to improve investor confidence are clearly in order and under way. Not the least of the reasons for restoring confidence is to maintain the participation of the millions of individual investors who entered the equity markets in the 1980s and 1990s.

In some instances, needed actions can take the form of strengthened and improved regulatory practices, as provided in some ways by the 2002 corporate accountability legislation (Sarbanes-Oxley Act, Public Law 107–204). In most cases, however, private-sector initiative would be preferable. Indeed, the highly competitive U.S. market economy has reacted quickly to adjust and to impose new disciplines on financial markets which will strengthen it in the long run. Among the priority changes to be adopted are the following:

a. *Improve corporate governance*. Through private-sector initiatives, corporate boards should become more professional and more independent of management. Former Intel leader Andrew Grove recommended separating the function of chairman from that of CEO in order to improve the "checks and balances" inherent in corporate governance.[6] Audit committees especially should be more professional and independent. Shareowners should become more active in oversight and election of board members, and board members should engage in the sort of continuing education now practiced by management.

b. *Reduce conflicts of interest*. This is an area where a counterproductive overreaction by official regulators (or legislators) needs to be resisted through credible private-sector initiatives. In the area of audits, the Securities and Exchange Commission needs to implement improved regulations with credible competence, which requires a stronger staff capability. The newly created SEC Public Accountability Board should help achieve this. For the important potential conflict of interest when the auditing firm also provides lucrative consulting services, the corporate clients, in compliance with the 2002 legislation, need to sharply limit such consulting services to those directly related to improved accounting procedures. Periodic rotation of auditing firms might also increase public confidence in audit reports. Corporate boards, through more independent audit committees, should take the initiative for giving explicit direction to management. In parallel, private-sector organizations can adopt voluntary codes of good practices that include such changes, with recognition given to those members who comply. Similarly, investment banking and securities companies should adopt good and effective practices to ensure objectivity by securities analysts in providing advice to investor customers. The securities industry and its regulators need to do a better job of overseeing the behavior of investment houses and their analysts.[7]

c. *Report profits on a more uniform and clearly understood basis*. A one-size-fits-all formula for reporting profits is not feasible, but a simpler approach, with two or three clearly defined models to choose from, would boost investor understanding of and confidence in profit reports.

d. *Move toward international accounting standards*. This would serve both to improve on existing standards and to reduce costs through a uniform set of global standards in parallel with the deepening globalization of markets. U.S. participation in the International Accounting Standards Board would entail negotiation, principally with European regulators, of some compromise provisions, and a broadly shared mutual interest could lead to early agreement.[8]

3. Tort reform.—Long-term, growth-generating investment can thrive only within a reasonably receptive and predictable legal framework. Indeed, the strength, comprehensiveness, and stability of the U.S. legal system is a competitive advantage vis-à-vis much of the world. However, the major debilitating weakness in the U.S. legal framework is tort litigation with unlimited punitive damages. Such litigation is currently spiraling out of control and undermining both economic vitality and the U.S. system of justice.[9] A report of the President's Council of Economic Advisers estimates annual direct costs to business of $180 billion, or nearly 2 percent of GDP, and tort costs are growing rapidly. Asbestos-related litigation continues to bankrupt companies only remotely related to long-past production or use of asbestos. The proliferation of class action lawsuits, which now includes plaintiffs with exposure to asbestos but no symptoms of disease, clearly exacerbates the problem. Recent multibillion dollar settlements with tobacco and tire companies have motivated (and provided the financing for) tort lawyers to target class action suits against a series of other industries. Plaintiffs, directed by a tort bar with vast resources at its disposal and incentives to bring even frivolous suits, increasingly congregate in local jurisdictions known for their tendency to favor tort claimants. Some products, especially in the medical technology arena, are simply not developed or brought to market due to fear of tort or related product liability litigation.

The threat of tort litigation is thus the single largest direct impediment to innovation and new product development in the U.S. economy. Moreover, the U.S. tort system is by far the most expensive in the world, more than double the average cost in other industrialized nations, and is thus a significant competitive cost disadvantage for U.S. companies in international markets. Recommended steps to rectify current investment-debilitating practices include the following:

- In the class action context, adoption of specific standards for closer judicial scrutiny of class certifications, settlement agreements, and attorneys' fee awards.
- Expansion of the jurisdiction of federal courts over multistate class actions.
- Abolishment of joint and several liability in most cases.
- Adoption of objective medical criteria for asbestos-related impairment, and a tolling of the statute of limitations for those who may later develop such illnesses or diseases.

- Restrictions on forum shopping by requiring that civil suits be filed in venues where plaintiffs reside or where there is a substantial connection to the injury.
- Limitation of punitive damages to cases where defendants acted with actual malice and require that they be proven by clear and convincing evidence.
- Limiting the ability of the government to sue private companies to achieve policy objectives that normally require regulation or new laws.
- Reining in the use of junk science in the courtroom.
- Organized public pressures against the most out-of-control state legal practices adverse to business.
- More detailed and current information on the costs of tort litigation for corporate profits, jobs, and consumers.

4. Higher educational achievement.—The professional and technical skill requirements of the U.S. labor force are moving steadily upward as the economy becomes more technology-intensive, and a growing gap exists between supply and demand for such skills. As the Hudson Institute concluded: "Unless the education and skill levels of the American workforce are upgraded, America's productivity and prosperity will grow less quickly than is desirable."[10]

Three central challenges for improvement need to be addressed. First, the failures of U.S. primary and secondary education have been repeatedly documented since the 1980s, but with limited remedial improvement achieved. Second, job-related education is now a continuing process throughout most career paths, and needs to be addressed more rigorously through mutually supportive private- and public-sector initiatives. And, third, the structure of the labor force is subject to more rapid change as a result of applied new technologies and shifting markets on a global basis, which requires greater labor market flexibility.

A more effective response on all three counts should be based on two underlying principles. The first is increased freedom for parents, students, and workers to choose the best available education and advanced training and the most productive career paths. The second principle is decentralization of responsibility for education to the state and municipal levels, which is more important than ever as the educational needs of the country become more diverse and technically complex. And with local control should come rigorous accountability of the leadership of schools and school systems. Regrettably, federally mandated educational provisions over the past several decades have often done more harm than good, including wide-ranging incentives for tort litigation to the detriment of local school budgets and teacher morale.

Specific ways to meet these educational requirements include the following:

a. Primary and secondary school vouchers for parents who prefer to send their children to private schools. Such parental choice is largely limited to affluent families. Since the Supreme Court has now approved such programs, broader experimentation and adoption are warranted.

b. Greater encouragement for the gifted and talented. These are the students most likely to provide the necessary innovation and related skills to the economic engine for growth, but their programs have been curtailed as a result of cost-cutting. Part of the problem is competition for funds from ill-conceived federally mandated requirements, with high administrative costs for compliance, that respond more to the imperatives of current intellectual fads than to the needs of basic literacy and numeracy or the needs of the job markets.

c. Increased support for skill-related programs between the private sector and junior colleges. Outstanding achievement in this area is usually the result of community-oriented (i.e., decentralized) collaboration between local firms and schools.

d. Incentives for corporate "universities" and other in-house training. These are proliferating throughout the private sector, and could be encouraged through targeted public support. For example, training in skills assessed to be a high priority could receive some form of government support at the federal or state level, depending on whether the priority needs are national or regional.

e. Special efforts at both the local and the national levels to strengthen and broaden science, engineering, and mathematics education up through the graduate level.

f. Greater flexibility for worker health and retirement programs, especially encouraging either portability or individual ownership of plans. This would facilitate labor force flexibility and improve the incentives for retraining. Targeted tax incentives might also improve motivation for the retraining needed by a fast-moving and fast-changing workforce in the innovative economy of the 21st century.

g. Encouragement of student interest in careers in the manufacturing sector. Misconceptions about manufacturing that persist among teachers and administrators, particularly in kindergarten through grade 12, but also at the community college level, have led to their common reluctance to train students for jobs in industry or encourage them to pursue careers in manufacturing. The changing nature of manufacturing and the aging manufacturing workforce make it incumbent upon individual companies to take the initiative with K–12 school systems, community colleges, and universities in order to ensure that they can attract, train, and retain the workers they need for the future.

5. *More cost-effective health care services.*—Health care is by far the fastest-growing cost component for business, just as it is for the entire economy. Annual national health expenditures were $1.5 trillion in 2001 and will top $2 trillion by 2006. They have grown from 5.3 percent of GDP in 1960 to 13 percent in 2000 and, on a per capita basis, are now more than double that of other Organization for Economic Cooperation and Development (OECD) countries. The quality of care is generally among the best in the world, but the insurance and payment system gives clear incentives to overuse and excessive cost. Companies are struggling to contain double-digit

annual percentage increases in costs, and a reduction in employee benefits is often the primary issue in labor negotiations.

A basic problem is that the U.S. health care sector is neither market-oriented, with customers paying for services received from competing suppliers, nor socialized through government-salaried health providers. In some ways, the result is the worst of both worlds. Maximum services at maximum prices are provided at little or no cost to recipients, with third parties paying the bills. Skyrocketing legal costs from tort litigation also add substantially to overall health care costs, including overuse of tests and care to avoid lawsuits. One major adverse impact on U.S. business is the progressive decline in international competitiveness because trading partners have much lower health care costs which are often paid for by the government, through socialized programs, rather than by the firms. The reason for the employer-based U.S. system was largely an accident of history, whereby the government granted tax exclusion for employer-paid health benefits that allowed business to increase compensation without violating World War II wage controls.

Employer-provided health care has involved employers in a complex market that they have little knowledge of. Separating the payer from the recipient eliminates an effective force for ensuring the proper trade-off between quality and cost, contributing to the inflation in health care costs. Throughout much of the 1990s this inflation was contained, mainly by involving employers more directly in the health care options available to their employees. But in recent years spiraling costs have returned, partly as a result of standards for care imposed on employers and health maintenance organizations by federal administrative action or legislation.

There is no simple solution to this growing problem. The general direction, however, should be to have greater participation by health care recipients in funding their normal expenditures, with full coverage insurance limited to unusually high-cost services, such as major surgery. Increasing use of medical savings accounts or other defined contribution plans would enhance consumer responsibility and gradually help shift the cost from employers to beneficiaries. Policies that encourage recent trends in this direction and extend equal tax treatment to individual health plans should be encouraged. In parallel, corporate strategies for selecting health care providers should be restructured to encourage more competitive and cost-effective programs for employees to choose from. Tort reform also has a role to play, as, for example, when California recently limited legal settlements for "pain and suffering," which can be in the tens of millions of dollars in other states, to $250,000.

6. Improved environmental policies.—Environmental objectives and policies are often formulated without taking full account of all national interests involved, including economic growth, jobs, and national security. The 2002 congressional debate over protection of caribou versus increased oil production in Alaska was poorly informed on both counts. Problems regularly arise from the Endangered Species Act when the protection of a particular species automatically takes precedence over other legal rights, without full consideration of the ensuing economic impact. Environmental laws can also be counterproductive when clean new investment at abandoned industrial sites is discouraged because of uncertainty about unknown cleanup costs from past polluters. Instead, industry locates on valuable (often undeveloped greenfields) real estate while the old sites remain unutilized eyesores. And yet again, environmental laws have been drafted in ways that encourage a proliferation of tort litigation. Moreover, by extension of the concept of joint and several liability beyond all reasonable limits, more and more companies are being severely penalized for actions they had little or nothing to do with. Thus liability has been extended to acquiring companies, or to predecessor companies, and maximized beyond any relation to actual responsibility for a given wrong.

A restructured approach to pursuing environmental objectives should be based on more thorough and objective cost/benefit analysis of all affected interests, including the economic impact on business and jobs. There should also be greater flexibility in how environmental laws are implemented, so as to be able to adjust objectives as new information on costs and benefits emerges. New investment, in particular, should be protected against cleanup penalties for past pollution by others, unknown at the time of investment. Specific measures includes the following:

a. Establish a more objective cost/benefit review process for environmental laws and regulations, updated on a periodic basis, that takes full account of adverse impacts on business and jobs.
b. Revise existing laws and regulations so as to provide greater flexibility, in the context of such improved cost/benefit analysis, to the executive branch of government for implementation of environmental objectives.
c. Appropriate adequate funding for environmental cleanup in cases where the perpetrators of past pollution either were operating legally at the time or are no longer available to pay.

7. Continued deregulation.—The progressive deregulation of the U.S. economy since the late 1970s is a continuing struggle that should move forward and, in some areas, be accelerated. The process of further deregulation should, to the maximum extent feasible, shift to price rather than quantitative targets whose impact cannot be predicted and are, therefore, to a large extent arbitrary. Pollution reduction and energy conservation are important examples where price incentives are far preferable to command-and-control solutions. Price incentives also are far less prone to tort litigation than are quantitative targets.

There are two basic components involved in the deregulation process. The first is the very large number of new or revised regulations being processed by executive agencies that are based on existing legislation. Close to 5,000 such "rules" are in the pipeline at any one time, and more than 100 of them are likely to cost business $100 million or more per year if implemented.[11] The total cost of accumulated government regulations, including the voluminous paperwork involved, has been estimated at more than $800 billion per year. The objective should be to reduce and streamline the huge accumulation of government regulation, but it is a daunting challenge. It should involve better scientific analysis, more public involvement in rulemaking, and a more aggressive review and central decision-making process within the executive branch.

The second component of deregulation involves more systematic initiatives to deregulate particular industries. Rapid technological change and related information flows make government regulation of industries more and more difficult, if not impossible. New technology can engender private- sector competition where a public-sector monopoly was earlier believed to be preferable or necessary. In this respect, one remaining monopoly clearly past its prime is the U.S. Postal Service. It makes little sense to retain this monopoly when the overwhelming and growing mass of communication and document transmissions is being sent electronically by the private sector. Monopolistic profits from first class mail should not be used to subsidize competition with private package delivery and electronic bill payment systems. Many industries should thus be continually reassessed with a view to deregulation.

A related point is that in a rapidly innovating market structure, antitrust authorities should exercise extreme caution and forbearance in pursuing actions against perceived monopolies or collusive behavior. In the first place, monopoly is often temporary or transitory, as rival firms rapidly adapt new products or production processes, or find newer products which rapidly displace the old. Second, as Baumol has shown, in today's competitive environment, it is highly beneficial to both firms and the general welfare for firms to enter into various forms of cooperation, be it research consortia, technology licensing, or teaming on individual projects. Most of the advantage gained from new inventions is quickly undermined by other products or better production and dissemination. In this environment, Baumol concludes, ". . . it follows that the antitrust authorities' willingness to show forbearance in their toleration of research joint ventures and technology licensing is fully justified."[12]

Our presentation here is limited to the two sectors whose size and importance to the modern economy make them crucial to growth and innovation: energy and telecommunications. Other areas where attention is needed include the medical technology industry, where slow regulatory approval and product liability issues retard introduction of innovative new products, and export control requirements which are often out of date and disadvantage U.S. suppliers of technology, such as computers, in international markets:

a. *Energy*. Energy supply and demand are heavily regulated, including through publicly regulated private monopolies. Such regulation is principally at the state and local levels, which can create serious price distortions on a regional basis. The economics of such heavy regulation are no longer valid in a sector with rapidly evolving new technologies and the potential for far lower cost energy supplies through effective competition. To take but one example, the technology for small-scale electrical generation at competitive prices already exists, and small-scale gas electricity generators are being used at plants and in some homes. This means that competition to the electric power generation and distributor monopolies can be developed from the natural gas distribution system. A reduction in energy consumption, for national security and environmental reasons, also can be more effectively achieved through market-based price incentives than through quantitative technical standards and government-established prices, whose impact is unpredictable and whose actual results can be counterproductive.

   Implementation of a broadly based deregulation strategy for the energy sector, as pursued at the federal, state, and local levels, would be highly complex. Only three general guidelines are offered here:

   (i) A clear and analytic statement by the president that broadly based deregulation of the energy sector to achieve comprehensive and effective private-sector competition is in the national interest, and that the executive branch will be fully supportive of state and municipal deregulation programs.

   (ii) More objective and fuller analysis at all levels of proposed deregulation, to ensure that "partial" deregulation is not merely counterproductive reregulation, as happened in California when the misleading term "deregulation" was applied to a complex form of managed competition in the electricity sector.

   (iii) A systematic reassessment of all quantitative standards and public pricing policies, with a view to shifting to market-oriented incentives of comparable effect. The latter, for example, could include tradable vouchers for reduced industrial pollution and tax incentives for renewable energy sources and higher gas mileage automobiles.

b. *Telecommunications*. The telecommunications sector (due to its size, its crucial role, and the rapid technological change which characterizes it) is central to the most advanced economies. Unfortunately, it remains one of the most highly regulated sectors of the U.S. economy, and indeed around the world. As a direct result of regulation, this sector has become the poster child of the boom and bust cycle of 1995–2002. If the United States is to return to the type of growth path experienced in the late 1990s, this sector will have to be repaired.

The telecommunications sector, in all its major components, has been tightly regulated since the first period of its rapid expansion in the early part of the 20th century. Deregulation began with the breakup of the AT&T monopoly through an antitrust settlement in 1984, which itself was driven by competition resulting from technological progress. In 1996, a major revision of the Telecommunications Act had the goal of moving to a deregulated, highly competitive marketplace. This law was, however, compromised by an insatiable urge on the part of both legislators and regulators to maintain their grip on the enormous and growing industry. Thus an attempt was made to manage competition through a new system of highly specific mandates, especially in the wire line, cellular phone, and cable television segments of the industry.[13]

The advent of new opportunities for entry into the communications business coincided with the flowering of the Internet, the rapid growth of wireless communications, general prosperity, and giddy optimism in financial markets. All told, some $880 billion was invested in telecommunications ventures in the late 1990s, including some $500 billion in new local phone companies. The latter was aided by the regulatory requirement for facilities sharing on the part of Bell operating companies. Spectrum auctions were held to encourage competition in cellular telephony. By the height of the boom in 1999 and 2000, total information technology (IT) spending represented 20.3 percent and 46.8 percent of all capital investment in the United States and increased GDP by almost 1 percent.[14] But the subsequent economic slowdown and stock market free fall exposed the poor business plans of most of the newer telecom firms, which could not survive in the face of intense competition and the increasing technological efficiency of communications networks and fiber-optic transmission systems which drove prices down relentlessly. The investment boom quickly turned into a bust, with IT investment declining by over 60 percent in 2001 and continuing into 2003.[15]

The Darwinian selection of strong and weak telecommunications providers after 2000 was headlined by the WorldCom and Global Crossing cases. While mismanagement was perhaps more of a symptom of the underlying problem of overcapacity and failure of projected demand to materialize, inappropriate and heavy-handed regulation also contributed to the problems and discouraged a long-term solution. The carnage of the telecommunications meltdown masks at least two important regulatory bottlenecks in the industry that impede growth in usage and the future health of both service and equipment firms.

The first of these is the problem of providing affordable and reliable high-speed broadband connectivity to consumers. Although fiber-optic lines provide ample "backbone" capacity for Internet data and voice communications traffic, high-speed connections to the home have been very slow to materialize. High-speed connections are seen as necessary to promote both new investments in communication equipment and new upgrades to computer systems. There are some technical problems involved, but the main impediment has been regulation.[16] The Federal Communications Commission (FCC) requires telephone companies to resell any broadband connections at uneconomic wholesale prices to competitors, thereby muting their enthusiasm for the large capital expenditures needed to provide such service. Cable companies are not subject to the same regulatory requirement, but are under threat by both federal and state regulators of being forced to share their capacity with competitors. In February 2003, the FCC announced some remedial action to relieve local operating companies of the requirement to resell broadband communications at a cheap discount. It remains to be seen if this action is sufficient, especially in the face of opposition by state regulators, to unleash needed investment in fast connections.

The FCC has long labored under an antiquated view of competition which blinds it to the technological and market forces of the contemporary environment. The FCC (and most state regulators) want to force competition ***among*** both wire line and cable carriers by requiring line sharing. Alfred Kahn exposed the flaw of such thinking in the following way: "If rivals can share use of whatever network facilities they ask for at prices explicitly intended to recover only the minimum cost of employing the most modern technology, it cannot but have a fatally discouraging effect on their own initiative and innovation efforts. When every applicant can be a free rider at such minimum prices, who is going to build the vehicle?"[17]

A better way to proceed would be simply to recognize that competition is arising primarily from other modes of communication and is likely to be sufficiently robust to satisfy regulators and antitrust authorities. That is, the high-speed service of wire line operators will compete with those of cable and, if the second bottleneck is solved, wireless operators. Other types of wireless systems based on point to multipoint technologies are being explored. At some point it is even conceivable that data-driven demand will be so robust that fiber-optic cable will be laid to homes, providing another source of competition. The need for and promise of broadband connectivity is so clear that as early as 1999 the computer and software industry urged Washington to ease the regulation that has discouraged its spread to homes and small businesses.[18] In 2002 a federal court of appeals overturned the FCC requirement for reduced pricing of shared network equipment, but further actions are needed by either the Congress or the FCC to eliminate altogether the requirement to share broadband facilities and to eliminate the anachronistic distinction between local and long-distance data traffic.[19]

The second area where reduction of "managed competition" by regulators would yield positive results for broadband deployment and renewed investment in infrastructure concerns the way in which the radiomagnetic spectrum is allocated. Although new technologies have been perfected which reduce the danger of overuse and infringement of radio frequencies by multiple users, the FCC, largely backed by the Congress, persists in keeping tight control over the allocation and use of the spectrum. Average monthly minutes of use of cellular phones grew from 1.6 billion in 1993 to over 37 billion in 2001, and existing cellular systems are reaching capacity. This was vividly demonstrated on September 11, 2001, when it became nearly impossible to get a cellular connection. As wireless operators begin to offer data services and attempt to introduce high-speed (so-called third generation or 3G) services, the capacity problem becomes acute.

In the United States, much of the spectrum designated by international consensus for 3G systems is currently utilized by military and local education users. Other available spectrum has been tied up in court disputes resulting from auctions the FCC held in 1996, or simply has been held from use by inaction of the FCC. When new spectrum has been made available through auctions, the artificial scarcity imposed by regulatory authorities has driven prices so high that companies have difficulty raising capital to build the needed infrastructure. Other spectrum was granted to television operators by Congress in 1996 for high definition television (HDTV) but remains unused as the broadcast industry delays the introduction of HDTV.

The regulatory authorities need to adopt new spectrum management approaches and move toward eventual market allocation of this resource. A system of full property rights for spectrum holders, preferably sold by auction, and including the right to deploy it for the most efficient purposes, should be the goal of regulatory reform. Given the long entrenched interests, including huge sunk costs in existing cellular and broadcast systems, it almost certainly will take time to manage a transition to property rights for the spectrum. Priority should be given to making the spectrum available in the near term for 3G uses. This would alleviate the voice capacity problems while providing competition to wire line systems for broadband applications.

These are the principal ways that government policy can contribute to a solution to the "last mile" broadband problem. In spurring competition, these policies would help revitalize the technology sector and ensure another period of growth and increasing productivity. There will, of course, be a transition period, especially as the excess capacity problem is addressed, during which time authorities will need to be mindful of the possibility of pockets of market dominance by the survivor. Ultimately, of course, the industry will have to right itself by working off the excess inventory of equipment and spurring broader utilization of infrastructure such as fiber-optic capacity. But action by regulators could help revive the "animal spirits" that Keynes famously identified as essential to putting capital at risk and testing innovative ideas. It would also help launch another virtuous cycle of innovation and growth in related industries such as software and content development, thus multiplying the economic impact in ways impossible to foresee.

8. Free trade in manufactures.—U.S. manufacturers export $600 billion in goods each year, and a further opening of foreign markets would permit solid growth from this baseline. The most dramatic export expansion in recent years involved trade with Mexico, as a result of the 1994 North American Free Trade Agreement, but since then U.S. liberal trade policy has been stalled. With the passage of the Trade Promotion Authority legislation in 2002, however, new opportunities arise to move to free trade in manufactures through bilateral agreements and, multilaterally, through the new Doha round of negotiations within the World Trade Organization (WTO).

The U.S. strategy should be to pursue both the bilateral and the multilateral free trade tracks as mutually reinforcing building blocks of global free trade in manufactures. Bilateral free trade agreements with Singapore and Chile should be followed by others with responsive candidates, such as Australia and the Central American grouping.

Multilateral free trade in manufactures in the Doha round is a far more ambitious objective, but it is feasible and the United States proposed it in November 2002. Such an initiative could be a centerpiece of the Doha round and provide the strong, business-led impetus needed to bring the round to a successful conclusion. The reasons for such an initiative at this time are (1) to reap unprecedented trade gains from the already rapidly growing world exports of manufactures, now approaching $5 trillion per year; (2) to consolidate the growing number of regional and bilateral free trade agreements into a more efficient multilateral framework, and thus avoid the foreign policy pitfalls of adversarial regional trading blocs; and (3) to support the U.S. foreign policy objective of building a coalition against international terrorism through a major cooperative economic undertaking among all market-oriented democracies.

U.S. exports would benefit particularly in the rapid growth emerging-market economies of East Asia and South America, where tariff and other border restrictions on manufactures are much higher than in the United States. At the same time, East Asians, in particular, have large trade surpluses in manufactures with the United States and would be eager to obtain permanent duty-free access to the U.S. market. Free trade participation by the OECD industrialized nations and the emerging market economies of East Asia and South America would result in immediate coverage of over 90 percent of world trade in manufactures, and poorer countries elsewhere could be permitted more gradual movement to free trade. As for the far more protected agricultural sector, which has slowed down the pace of bilateral free trade agreements, the multilateral Doha round has separate negotiating groups for manufactures (i.e., "industrial trade") and agriculture. Hence, this structure would permit the complete free trade objective in the former and more limited trade liberalizing objectives in the latter.

As in past multilateral trade negotiations, political leadership by the largest trading nations, beginning with the United States, is the key, and the United States is doing its part, in the context of the growth-oriented themes presented in this volume, to achieve multilateral free trade in manufactures.[20]

9. A greatly reduced trade deficit.—The chronic and now record U.S. trade deficit of over $418 billion in 2002, 80 percent to 90 percent of which is in manufactures, was assessed in chapter 7 as the Achilles' heel for the continued prosperity of the U.S. manufacturing sector. The causes for the trade deficit were explained to be (1) too little savings in the United States, coupled with too much savings in chronic trade surplus economies, and (2) "currency manipulation" by some trading partners, particularly Japan and China. The principal adverse impacts on the U.S. national interest are a weakening of the growth-generating U.S. manufacturing sector and a buildup of net foreign debt approaching $3 trillion, headed to $5 trillion by 2005.

A forceful strategy is thus overdue for an orderly reduction of the trade deficit, at least by half and perhaps back to trade balance for the first time in over 20 years. The strategy needs to begin with clearly stated recognition by the president and congressional leaders of both parties that the chronic trade deficit is a substantial problem for U.S. interests, and that steps should be taken to reduce it. Regrettably, over the years the trade deficit has been largely ignored or rationalized away on specious grounds, as explained in chapter 7.

Once the problem is recognized, the strategy implementation would be in two parts. First, steps would be taken to increase the national savings rate, principally through fiscal measures as described under "Fiscal reform," above. This would proceed in parallel with international consultations within the International Monetary Fund (IMF), the G-7 finance ministers grouping, and bilaterally, to develop a concerted approach whereby countries with consistently large trade surpluses (or, even more pointedly, trade surpluses together with FDI inflows) should take steps to increase domestic consumption and thus reduce surplus savings. Japan and China would be at the top of the list for such consultations.

The second part of the strategy relates to exchange rate policy.[21] The basic policy of market-based exchange rates—already practiced de facto by the United States, the EU, Canada, Mexico, and others—should be explicitly adopted. At the same time, the United States, together with the EU and other free floaters, should act to curb "currency manipulation" by Japan, China, and some others. IMF Article IV states that members shall "avoid manipulating exchange rates to gain an unfair competitive advantage," and the principal indicator of such manipulation, under IMF surveillance procedures, is "protracted large scale interventions in one direction [official purchases of dollars and other foreign exchange] in the exchange market." Clearly, at least Japan and China are manipulating their currencies as defined by the IMF, and the United States and others should press them, through IMF procedures and bilateral consultations, to cease such action.

10. A reassessment of trade remedy laws.—The most controversial area of trade policy is "trade remedy" policies in three specific areas: (1) countervailing duties to offset export subsidies by foreign governments; (2) antidumping duties to offset predatory export pricing by foreign companies; and (3) temporary import restrictions to avoid injury to domestic industry from import surges. All three are permitted within the WTO trading rules, although with considerable flexibility given to importing countries in their application.

The problem arises from the proliferation of such import-restricting actions in recent years. Worldwide antidumping restrictions alone have more than doubled since the 1980s, from about 150 to more than 300 per year. Moreover, while the United States and EU used to be the principal invokers of trade remedy action, China, India, Mexico, and Brazil have become far more frequent users, often with more closed procedures than practiced in the United States. Earlier actions were concentrated heavily in the steel sector, and U.S. antidumping and countervailing duty actions in this sector are still frequent, but the proliferation of trade remedy actions by others is wide-ranging by industry, with U.S. exporters facing more and more numerous actions against them.

The assessment of foreign practices and injury to domestic industry from all three causes—export subsidies, dumping, and import surges—is technically complex, and should be pursued without bias among the conflicting interests involved. Within the U.S. economy, the conflict is between domestic industry facing import competition and other industries and consumers who buy the imports. For instance, many domestic U.S. industries which use steel as an input to their production have complained about higher prices and short supplies after the imposition of 30 percent duties on certain imported steel in early 2002. Internationally, the conflict is between the domestic industry seeking protection and foreign exporters to the market. A frequent criticism of trade remedy practices is that they favor the protectionist interests of domestic industries, and thus tend to undermine a liberal trade policy. The policy issue has come front and center as the result of recent U.S. actions and the inclusion of trade remedy laws on the agenda for the Doha round of WTO negotiations.

The U.S. debate over how to respond to the proliferation of trade remedy import restrictions is highly politicized, with little constructive discussion as to how current practices might be improved. One way out of this impasse would be through the convocation of a presidentially appointed commission of distinguished members to analyze the subject and make recommendations to the president. The presidential commission mechanism for seeking resolution of deeply troubled areas of policy can be used only sparingly, for truly important policy challenges. The conclusion here is that the current troubled outlook for proliferating trade remedy actions throughout the world, and the wide range of U.S. interests affected by them, warrant a presidential commission initiative.

Communicating the Engine of Growth Strategy

Action on all or almost all of the foregoing ten targeted areas of policy would have a substantial positive impact on the U.S. manufacturing sector as the engine for growth in the U.S. economy and, to a large extent, on the global economy as well. No attempt has been made to quantify the cumulative impact, but it could well add 1 percent or more to annual economic growth through higher productivity-enhancing investment, more efficient use of the labor force, and curtailment of nonproductive or counterproductive activities by government bureaucracies and litigation courts. The U.S. manufacturing sector is already the global lead engine for growth, as explained in earlier chapters, and what we present here in conclusion is a ten-point program enabling manufacturing companies to do significantly better in the years ahead while maintaining their global leadership.

Another way of expressing this is that further steps to stimulate innovation and growth in manufacturing is a very positive-sum game for all segments of the economy, from business to labor to agriculture, and from students to senior citizens. Employment in manufacturing is more highly compensated than in the services sector, and more efficient production leads to better products at lower prices. The only long-term losers would be a relatively small number of tort litigation attorneys, but in view of recent fees of more than $800 million for one attorney from several tobacco company lawsuits, most should have an adequate financial cushion to see them through transition to more productive forms of legal work.

And yet this very positive-sum game is not well understood or appreciated in the United States or internationally. The policy issues addressed here are often debated in a narrow context of immediate winners or losers rather than as integral parts of a longer-term aggregate strategy in which all boats rise with the tide of productivity-induced growth. A highly competitive economy will have its short-term ups and downs, and short-term winners and losers. There is a Schumpeterian element of creative destruction in play as new technologies, new products, new job skills, and new industries replace the old. There are also the relatively rare bad apples in corporate management—as within Enron, WorldCom, and Global Crossing—that emerge and need to be dealt with. But of over 10,000 listed U.S. companies subject to annual audit reports, only a very small number have been found to have significant problems. The vast majority of companies remain in good standing in terms of financial accounting and transparency, but they receive little notice in the media or elsewhere.

Much of this positive story about manufacturing as the engine for growth has been described in earlier chapters. But how can the story be more effectively communicated in support of the proposed policy agenda for further improvement?

One way is to undertake a more detailed and ongoing assessment of the unique role of manufacturing industry for growth in an ever-more-technology-driven and global economy. Within the United States this could be done by one of the independent economic research institutions, such as the National Bureau of Economic Research. At the official level, the congressional Joint Economic Committee could do a regular assessment that would receive wide public attention. It could also be a featured chapter in the annual report of the President's Council of Economic Advisers.

Manufacturing as the engine for growth phenomenon should receive more pointed international appraisal. The OECD is the appropriate body to do this for the industrialized country grouping, now including South Korea, Mexico, and Poland as members, which constitutes the dominant core of the international economy. The interests of the populous developing regions that, though still less fully engaged in international trade and investment in manufacturing, have potentially the most to gain, could best be examined by the World Bank research staff.

First and foremost, however, private-sector leaders should be more assertive in explaining the highly positive contributions to growth by the manufacturing sector. The tendency is often to be defensive in the face of carping criticism from many directions. This is nothing new. The least productive members of society have long tended to be the most outspoken critics of the most productive. Without trying to over-analyze this endemic problem in free societies, it does nevertheless place greater responsibility on the more productive members to speak out forcefully and positively about what is really taking place.

The point of departure for the response to the antibusiness critics is that we are the most affluent economy in history, and the reason for this is that we have the most productive and growth-oriented private sector ever assembled. Moreover, the central engine for this growth—in terms of developing new technologies, investing in plant and equipment to apply these technologies, and producing the new products that will generate economic growth and jobs in all sectors—is the manufacturing sector. It is not an easy business, and indeed it is ever more competitive in an increasingly global marketplace. Firms can make a profit for their shareholders only if they stay at the front of the curve for new product and process development, offering the highest quality products at the lowest prices. Indeed, Baumol puts the matter even more bluntly: ". . . What differentiates the capitalist economy most sharply from all other economic systems is free-market pressures that force firms into a continuing process of innovation, *because it becomes a matter of life and death to them*."[22] If impediments to such leading-edge performance arise, such as from excessive taxes or debilitating lawsuits, some firms can falter or fail. But overall, so far, so very good for all segments of the U.S. economy, and we should all work together to do even better in the years ahead.

This is the message we are developing within the Manufacturers Alliance/MAPI. We have 32 councils of senior corporate representatives engaged in addressing, in a positive and forward-thinking way, a wide range of emerging challenges of a technical, market, or management nature. The deliberations of the councils on strategic planning, manufacturing, marketing, research and innovation, human resources, environmental management, and business ethics have all been especially relevant and helpful to the authors of this volume. The results are striking and important, and we now need to communicate this positive message more widely and effectively.

Endnotes

CHAPTER 1

1. For example, see Michael K. Evans, "U.S. Headed for 'Hollow' Economy: Manufacturing Leads the Way for Plunging Profits," *IndustryWeek*, August 2002, p. 80.

2. The Manufacturers Alliance/MAPI countered this theory in a seminal book by George Terborgh, *The Bogey of Economic Maturity* (Chicago: Machinery and Allied Products Institute, 1945).

3. For example, see Robert Scott, "Fast Track to Lost Jobs: Trade Deficits and Manufacturing Decline Are the Legacies of NAFTA and WTO," Briefing Paper, Economic Policy Institute (2002), www.epinet.org, or Alan Tonelson, *Race to the Bottom* (New York: Westview Press, 2000).

4. A leading proponent of this view is Peter Schwartz, Peter Leyden, and Joel Hyatt, *The Long Boom: A Vision for the Coming Age of Prosperity* (New York: Perseus, 2000).

5. See Fred Zimmerman and Dave Beal, *Manufacturing Works: The Vital Link Between Production and Prosperity* (Dearborn, MI: Dearborn Trade Publishing, 2002), pp. 14-15.

6. Terborgh, *Bogey of Economic Maturity*, p. 4.

7. Figures derived from "GDP by Industry" data collected by the Bureau of Economic Analysis, U.S. Department of Commerce.

8. Zimmerman and Beal, *Manufacturing Works*, chap. 2.

9. See Organization for Economic Cooperation and Development, "Trends and Recent Developments in Foreign Direct Investment," in *International Investment Perspectives* (Paris: OECD, September 2002), pp. 16, 23.

10. See "International Investment Position of the United States at Yearend, 1976-2001" (Washington, DC: Bureau of Economic Analysis, U.S. Department of Commerce, July 2002).

11. See John Thornhill, "Asia Awakes: The Region's Middle Classes Are Spending and Borrowing More," *Financial Times*, April 2, 2002, p. 14.

12. Gregory Tassey, *R&D and Long-Term Competitiveness: Manufacturing's Central Role in a Knowledge-Based Economy* (Washington, DC: National Institute of Science and Technology, 2002), p. 1.

13. I explored this relationship in an earlier work: Thomas J. Duesterberg, *Manufacturing in the Era of the New Economy: Evidence for Sustainable Productivity Gains* (Washington, DC: Manufacturers Alliance/MAPI, 2000).

14. See Dale Jorgenson, "Projecting Productivity Growth," presentation to the Manufacturing Institute, June 17, 2002, www.nam.org.

15. See Bob Davis, "Why Europe Trails U.S. in High-Tech Innovation," *The Wall Street Journal*, April 1, 2002, p. A-1. Also see chap. 2 in this book.

16. See National Science Foundation, *Science and Engineering Indicators—2002*, vol. 1 (Arlington, VA: National Science Foundation, 2002), pp. 8-9.

17. Reported by an Eastman Chemical representative at the spring meeting of the Alliance's Financial Council II, March 21-23, 2002, Sarasota, FL.

CHAPTER 2

1. The assessment of the accelerated pace of economic globalization here is summarized from Ernest H. Preeg, *From Here to Free Trade: Essays in Post-Uruguay Round Trade Strategy* (Chicago: University of Chicago Press, 1998), pp. 1-44.

2. This issue is discussed in greater detail in Ernest H. Preeg, *Surging Yet Volatile Productivity Growth in U.S. Manufacturing Industry: The International Trade Dimension*, Economic Report 524 (Washington, DC: Manufacturers Alliance/MAPI, October 2001), pp. 5-7. Other reasons for the sectoral contrast are that many services are "nontradable" and some service industries are more highly protected.

3. See Preeg, *Surging Yet Volatile Productivty Growth*, pp. 8-12, for a fuller discussion of shifting comparative cost relationships in trade, including the declining relative importance of wage differentials.

4. GDP measured in "constant dollars" adjusts for changes over time in relative prices. The "current dollar" figures presented here, however, are the relevant measure for the issues discussed.

5. In keeping with current practices of disclosure, it is noteworthy that the Manufacturers Alliance/MAPI focuses heavily on such forward-thinking peer interaction through its 32 councils covering a wide range of manufacturing activities.

CHAPTER 3

1. U.S. Department of Labor, Bureau of Labor Statistics, "Projections to 2010," *Monthly Labor Review*, 124, no. 11 (November 2001), pp. 2-84.

2. The forecasting record of econometric models varies considerably, depending on the forecast horizon and the level of detail in the projection. An analysis of the forecasting record of the *Blue Chip* consensus forecast (central tendency of the approximately 50 forecasts that make up the *Blue Chip* survey over the years) by the Congressional Budget Office for the 1980s and 1990s finds that forecast accuracy improves with a longer forecast horizon. (Congressional Budget Office, *Evaluating*

CBO's Record of Economic Forecasts, July 30, 1999, at www.cbo.gov/showdoc.cfm?index=1486&sequence=0&from=1). The mean absolute error (the average of the forecast's errors without regard to arithmetic sign) for forecasts of nominal gross domestic product (GDP) was 1.0 percent for the two-year projections and 0.9 percent for the five-year projections. Similarly, the mean absolute error for the forecasts of inflation-adjusted GDP was 0.9 percent for the two-year projections and 0.5 percent for the five-year projections.

The U.S. Department of Labor, Bureau of Labor Statistics (BLS),does analyze its forecasting record for occupational employment over a 40-year time frame (Neal Rosenthal, "The Quality of BLS Projections: A Historical Account," *Monthly Labor Review*, May 1999), pp. 27-35. The BLS found that its projections of total employment over a ten-year time horizon were very accurate. Projections of major occupational groups were consistently in the correct direction, and rapid-growth and slow-growth projections for the major categories had been very accurate. However, as the level of detail gets more specific, the predictions have been less accurate. The BLS found that the accuracy of projections for occupations of large size was better than for occupations that were small in number. Nevertheless, the vast majority of occupations were projected in the correct direction.

3. The labor force participation rate of 67.2 percent in the United States is the highest among industrialized countries in the world. For example, the labor force participation rate in 2000 was 65.9 percent in Canada, 64.7 percent in Australia, and 62.0 percent in Japan. In Europe, the participation rate generally is substantially lower than in the United States. It was 56.0 percent in France, 57.9 percent in Germany, 47.8 percent in Italy, 61.5 percent in the Netherlands, 63.2 percent in Sweden, and 62.9 percent in the United Kingdom. The Europeans define the working age population as that between the ages of 15 and 65.

4. Richard Jackson, *The Global Retirement Crisis* (Washington, DC: Center for Strategic and International Studies, 2002), p. 12.

5. Paul S. Hewitt, "Depopulation and Aging in Europe and Japan: The Hazardous Transition to a Labor Shortage Economy," *Internationale Politik und Gesellschaft Online*, January 2002, p. 2.

6. Sylvester J. Schieber and Paul S. Hewitt, "Demographic Risk in Industrial Societies," *World Economics*, October-December 2000, p. 44.

7. For example, steel manufacturers sell steel to auto parts manufacturers, which then sell auto parts or components to auto assembly firms to produce a finished automobile. The auto manufacturers sell cars to dealers, which sell to the final user. Adding the output or sales at each of these steps would result in a total that is larger than the final sale to the end user. At each step in the supply chain, the output of one firm is input to another firm and is reflected in the sales price. The value of the product at each sale includes the prices of the previous inputs plus the value added at each stage.

8. One reason that manufacturing jobs declined more than output in percentage points from 1987 to 2000 is that jobs were outsourced to the service sector. For example, security workers and janitorial staff who receive paychecks from manufacturers are manufacturing workers. At other firms these functions are outsourced and the workers at the manufacturers' facilities are paid by security protection firms or outside janitorial service firms so they are classified as service industry workers. Similarly, workers employed through temporary employment agencies are service indus-

try workers even when they work in a manufacturing plant, office, or warehouse. Also, productivity growth in manufacturing has been higher than in the economy as a whole.

9. The services industry includes hotels and other lodging places; personal services; business services; auto repair, services, and parking; miscellaneous repair services; motion pictures; amusement and recreation services; health services; legal services; educational services; social services; membership organizations; and other services.

10. Mark A. Planting and Peter D. Kuhbach, "Annual Input-Output Accounts of the U.S. Economy-1998," *Survey of Current Business*, December 2001, p. 41.

11. Ibid., p. 70.

12. Consumption is calculated as domestic output, plus imports, less exports. Consumption is the dollar amount of product that is produced by domestic and foreign sources for use in the United States.

CHAPTER 4

1. Dale W. Jorgenson and Kevin J. Stiroh, in "Raising the Speed Limit: U.S. Economic Growth in the Information Age," in *Brookings Papers on Economic Activity*, vol. 2 (Washington, DC: Brookings Institution, 2000), table 2, p. 143, report that increasing capital quality contributed 1.0 percentage point to GDP growth in the late 1990s, compared to 1.2 percentage points to capital stock. Prior to the late 1990s, the contribution of capital quality ranged between one-fourth and one-third of the contribution of the capital stock.

2. See, for instance, Jeremy A. Leonard, *Taking Stock: The Role of Financial Market Structure in Economic Growth*, Economic Report 520 (Washington, DC: Manufacturers Alliance/MAPI, August 2001).

3. F. D. Gault, "Research and Development in a Service Economy," *Research Evaluation*, 7, no. 2 (1998), pp. 79-91.

4. See, for example, M. I. Nadiri, "Innovations and Technological Spillovers," Working Paper 4423 (Washington, DC: National Bureau of Economic Research, 1993).

5. Jason G. Cummins and Gianluca L. Violante, "Investment-Specific Technical Change in the U.S. (1947-2000): Measurement and Macroeconomic Consequences," *Review of Economic Dynamics*, 5, no. 2 (2002), pp. 243-284.

6. In the 1990s economic expansion, private fixed investment accounted for 25.1 percent of the increase in current-dollar GDP, compared to 12.9 percent in the 1980s expansion and 17.2 percent in the 1960s expansion. In addition, two-thirds of investment in the 1990s expansion consisted of equipment and software, much more than in prior expansions. See Thomas J. Duesterberg, *Manufacturing in the Era of the New Economy: Evidence for Sustainable Productivity Gains* (Washington, DC: Manufacturers Alliance/MAPI, 2000).

7. See, for example, Robert J. Gordon, "Has the 'New Economy' Rendered the Productivity Slowdown Obsolete?," working paper, Northwestern University and National Bureau of Economic Research, June 14, 1999.

8. Dale W. Jorgenson, Mun S. Ho, and Kevin J. Stiroh, "Lessons from the U.S. Growth Resurgence," prepared for the First International Conference on the Eco-

nomic and Social Implications of Information Technology, U.S. Department of Commerce, Washington, DC, January 27-28, 2003.

9. Spillover benefits cross international boundaries as well. For example, Bernstein and Mamuneas estimate that one-quarter of Canada's labor productivity growth since 1974 is attributable to spillovers from U.S. R&D efforts. See Jeffrey Bernstein and Theofanis Mamuneas, "The Contribution of U.S. R&D Spending to Manufacturing Productivity in Canada," paper presented at the Centre for the Study of Living Standards Conference on the Canada-U.S. Manufacturing Productivity Gap, January 2000.

10. Jeremy A. Leonard, "Assessing the Adequacy of Public Funding of ICT-Related R&D in Canada," report prepared for the Canadian Institute for Telecommunications Research, January 2001. This estimate includes returns from upstream basic and applied research performed at universities and government laboratories. Because business R&D is generally focused on applied product development and can be protected by secrecy and patents, spillovers from these activities are likely smaller in magnitude.

11. Bart Los and Bart Verspagen, "R&D Spillovers and Productivity: Evidence from U.S. Manufacturing Microdata," *Empirical Economics*, 25, Issue 1 (2000).

12. Ibid.

13. This interpretation of the role of innovation in economic growth is described in detail in William J. Baumol, *The Free Market Innovation Machine: Analyzing the Growth Miracle of Capitalism* (Princeton, NJ: Princeton University Press, 2002), chap. 8.

14. For instance, Edward N. Wolff estimates the economywide rate of return to R&D (including returns to the innovator) at 66 percent, compared to returns to the innovator of no more than 12.5 percent, yielding an implied spillover ratio of 0.8. See Edward N. Wolff, "Spillovers, Linkages, and Technical Change," *Economic Systems Research*, 9, March 1997, pp. 9-23.

15. Baumol, *The Free Market Innovation Machine*, discusses several examples of purely private R&D and technology alliances in chap. 6, pp. 86-92.

16. The Council on Competitiveness, in cooperation with Michael Porter, completed case studies of Wichita and four other clusters: San Diego, Pittsburgh, Atlanta, and Raleigh-Durham. See Michael E. Porter, *Clusters of Innovation: Regional Foundations of U.S. Competitiveness* (Washington, DC: Council on Competitiveness, 2001).

17. One example of availability of high-skill, low-wage labor is India, where a strong emphasis on computer science in universities has created a pool of high-skilled IT professionals. As a result, many U.S. companies have outsourced parts of their IT development and management function to India.

18. Joel Popkin, "Producing Prosperity: Manufacturing Technology's Unmeasured Role in Economic Expansion," report prepared for the Association of Manufacturing Technology, September 2000.

19. Thomas M. Tirpak, "Design-to-Manufacturing Information Management for Electronics Assembly," *International Journal of Flexible Manufacturing Systems*, 12, April 2000, pp. 189-205.

20. William Fulkerson, "Information-Based Manufacturing in the Informational Age," *International Journal of Flexible Manufacturing Systems* 12, April 2000, pp. 131-143.

21. Examination of input-output tables indicates that at least three-quarters of

outsourcing activity is undertaken by manufacturers. Thus, at least $160 billion of the $215 billion increase in outsourcing—or 1.6 percent of GDP—reflects a transfer of manufacturing activity into related service industries rather than a relative decline in manufacturing activity.

22. Thijs Ten Raa and Edward N. Wolff, "Outsourcing of Services and the Productivity Recovery in U.S. Manufacturing in the 1980s and 1990s," *Journal of Productivity Analysis*, 16:2 (September 2001), pp. 149-165.

CHAPTER 5

1. Tom Peters, *Liberation Management: Necessary Disorganization for the Nanosecond Nineties* (New York: Alfred A. Knopf, 1992), p. 650.
2. John Kay, "Keeping Up with the Market," *The Economist: The Future Surveyed*, September 11, 1993, p. 66.
3. Michael E. Porter, *Competitive Strategy: Techniques for Analyzing Industries and Competitors*, rev. ed. (New York: The Free Press, 1998), pp. 35-37.
4. Kenichi Ohmae, *The Borderless World: Power and Strategy in the Interlinked Economy* (New York: Harper Business, 1990), pp. 43-44.
5. Southwood J. Morcott, "Today's Automotive-Supply Industry: Evolution or Revolution?" (Washington, DC: Manufacturers Alliance/MAPI, April 2000).
6. Clayton M. Christensen, Michael Raynor, and Matt Verlinden, "Skate to Where the Money Will Be," *Harvard Business Review*, November 2001, pp. 73-81.
7. Paul Roemer, "Ideas and Things," *The Economist: The Future Surveyed*, September 11, 1993, p. 72.
8. Robert O'Harrow, Jr., "Next: An ID Chip Planted in Your Body?," *The Washington Post*, December 19, 2001, p. E-1.
9. Beth Baker, "Doctor in the House," *The Washington Post*, December 18, 2001, p. F-1.
10. Neil Irwin, "This Little Slinky Goes to Market," *The Washington Post*, January 13, 2002, p. H-1.
11. "The Year in Ideas," *New York Times Magazine*, December 9, 2001, p. 110.
12. U.S. Department of Labor, *Report on the American Workforce* (Washington, DC: U.S. Department of Labor, 1999), p. 18. Available at www.bls.gov/opub/rtaw/pdf/rtaw1999.pdf.
13. Ibid., p. 20.
14. Angela Clinton, "Flexible Labor: Restructuring the American Work Force," *Monthly Labor Review*, August 1997, pp. 3-17.
15. Steve Liesman, "Better Machine Tools Give Manufacturers Newfound Resilience," *The Wall Street Journal*, February 15, 2001, p. A-1.
16. Tim Hindle, "Back to Basics," *The Economist*, March 9, 2002.

CHAPTER 6

1. To keep this discussion tractable, it is focused mainly on the technology and application of automation for firms that include manufacturing somewhere in the supply chain for their primary products. Though in some respects there may be a

greater potential for applying automation in certain service sectors, that question is beyond the scope of this book.

2. The importance of these objectives for manufacturing strategy was adapted from the second chapter of Paul Kenneth Wright's *21st Century Manufacturing* (Englewood Cliffs, NJ: Prentice-Hall, 2001).

3. A good discussion of the difference between TCA and ABC can be found in Peter F. Drucker, *Management Challenges for the 21st Century* (New York: Harper Business, 1999).

4. An excellent description of flow manufacturing, its historical evolution, and its business implications, is provided by H. Thomas Johnson and Anders Broms, *Profit Beyond Measure* (New York: The Free Press, 2000).

5. National Institute for Standards and Technology, Manufacturing Engineering Laboratory, "Research and Engineering of Intelligent Systems," www.mel.nist.gov/proj/reis.htm.

6. Robert Filippini, Andrea Vinelli, and Chris Voss, "Paths of Improvement in Plant Operations," in *High Performance Manufacturing*, Roger G. Schroeder and Barbara B. Flynn, eds. (New York: John Wiley and Sons, 2001).

7. Ibid., p. 22.

CHAPTER 7

1. These figures, based on the SITC definition of manufactures in the table, differ slightly from the WTO definition of manufactures presented in chap. 2.

2. Gordon H. Hanson, Raymond J. Mataloni, Jr., and Matthew J. Slaughter, "Expansion Strategies of US Multinational Firms," draft working paper, U.S. Department of Commerce, Bureau of Economic Analysis, April 2001.

3. The historical cost of book-value estimates of foreign direct investment is simply the accumulated cost of the investments when they were made. These are the only figures available that contain detail by country and industry. For several purposes, such as determining the return on investment in the current year, it would be better to have either the replacement or market value of the assets. Such figures are unavailable. Nevertheless, historical cost figures provide a suitable basis for analyzing changing patterns of foreign direct investment by country and industry.

4. For an overview of these issues, see David Dollar and Aart Kraay, "Trade, Growth, and Poverty," World Bank Working Paper, June 2001.

5. OECD, *The New Economy: Beyond the Hype* (Paris: OECD, 2001).

6. United Nations Population Division, *World Urbanization Prospects*, 2001 Revision, March 2002.

7. Static gains from trade derive from comparative cost advantages in existing plants and operations, while dynamic gains result mainly from new investment, with embedded new technology and other cost savings. Dynamic gains from trade are estimated to be roughly three to four times larger than the classic static gains, and should be even more dominant in the current U.S.-Mexican relationship.

8. For example, in the MAPI/NAM survey, *U.S. Manufacturing Industry's Impact on Ethical, Labor, and Environmental Standards in Developing Countries* (Washington, DC: MAPI/NAM, 2001), about half of the companies with production facilities in Mexico reported environmental standards higher than Mexican national standards, including specific examples of U.S. standards.

9. A full presentation of the issues discussed here is contained in Ernest H. Preeg, *The Trade Deficit, the Dollar, and the U.S. National Interest* (Indianapolis, IN: Hudson Institute, 2000).

10. Actually, about 80 percent is consumption and 20 percent investment. See ibid., chap. 4, and "A Rose Tinted View of the Deficit," *Financial Times*, June 22, 2000.

11. For a more detailed assessment of this subject, see the May 1, 2002, testimony of Ernest H. Preeg before the Senate Banking Committee, "Chinese Currency Manipulation," available at www.mapi.net.

12. In effect, the $40 billion central bank purchases offset almost all of the upward pressure on the currency from the FDI inflow, and was twice as large as the trade surplus effect. A frequent misunderstanding is to relate ***net*** central bank purchases of dollars to ***gross*** trade and financial flows, whereas the relevant figures are the ***net*** flows.

CHAPTER 8

1. Ronald Coase, "The Nature of the Firm," *Economica*, n.s. IV (1937): 386-405.

2. Bengt Holmström and John Roberts, "The Boundaries of the Firm Revisited," *Journal of Economic Perspectives*, 12, no. 4 (Fall 1998), pp. 73–94.

3. In contrast, the natural gas industry historically was not vertically integrated, even though the nature of the business was very similar to that of oil. The various stages of the natural gas industry were subject to extensive rate regulation by different authorities, thereby constraining opportunistic behavior as well as making it more difficult to gain regulatory approval for integration.

4. Benjamin Klein, Robert Crawford, and Armen Alchian, "Vertical Integration, Appropriable Rents, and the Competitive Contracting Process," *Journal of Law and Economics*, 21 (1978), pp. 297-326.

5. Benjamin Klein, "Fisher-General Motors and the Nature of the Firm," *Journal of Law and Economics*, XLIII, no. 5 (2000), pp. 105-141.

6. A number of empirical studies in the 1970s and early 1980s looked for evidence on whether highly concentrated industries, i.e., those that might be less than fully competitive, earned above-normal profits. For background on this debate, see Harold Demsetz, "Two Systems of Belief About Monopoly," in *Industrial Concentration: The New Learning*, Harvey Goldschmid, Michael Mann, and J. Fred Weston, eds. (Boston: Little, Brown, 1974), pp. 164-184.

7. The extent of competitive pressures felt by firms is not some absolute that lends itself to measurement. In the economic model of "perfect competition," firms take the market price as a given and expand production until their marginal costs equal this price. There is no competition in the sense that firms engage in rivalry.

8. Timothy Aeppel, "The Dollar's Strength Tests the Ingenuity of U.S. Manufacturers," *The Wall Street Journal*, January 22, 2002, p. A-1.

9. Ibid., p. A-3.

10. J. R. Hicks, "Annual Survey of Economic Theory: The Theory of Monopoly," *Econometrica*, 3 (1935), reprinted in George J. Stigler and Kenneth E. Boulding, *Readings in Price Theory*, vol. 6 (Chicago:Richard D. Irwin, 1952), p. 369.

11. For some evidence that deregulation has lowered the costs of goods and ser-

vices provided by regulated industries in the United States, see George Winston, "Economic Deregulation: Days of Reckoning for Microeconomists," *Journal of Economic Literature*, 31, no. 3, September 1993, pp. 1263-1289.

12. In contrast, nonresidential investment grew by an annual average rate of 4.3 percent.

13. Total R&D spending in 2000, including that undertaken by the federal government, was equal to 2.7 percent of GDP, up slightly from 2.5 percent in 1959.

14. William J. Baumol, *The Free-Market Innovation Machine: Analyzing the Growth Miracle of Capitalism* (Princeton, NJ: Princeton University Press, 2002), pp. 2-3.

15. Baumol, along with a number of his colleagues, including Robert Willig and John Panzar, formally developed the notion of contestability in a series of books and articles.

16. One recent example is Black & Decker's decision to shut down three manufacturing plants in the United States and move production to low-cost locations in Mexico, China, and the Czech Republic. See Martha McNeil Hamilton, "Black & Decker to Shut Plants," *The Washington Post*, January 30, 2002, pp. E-1, E-3.

17. U.S. Department of Labor, Bureau of Labor Statistics, "International Comparisons of Labor Productivity and Unit Labor Costs in Manufacturing, 2000" (Washington, DC: Bureau of Labor Statistics, 2002), pp. 12, 23.

18. Gordon H. Hanson, Raymond J. Mataloni, Jr., and Matthew J. Slaughter, "Expansion Strategies of U.S. Multinational Firms," draft working paper, U.S. Department of Commerce, Bureau of Economic Analysis, April 2001.

19. "The Ins and Outs of Outing," *The Economist*, August 31, 1991, pp. 54-56.

20. Holmström and Roberts, "The Boundaries of the Firm Revisited."

21. See "A Matter of Choice," *The Economist*, December 22, 2001, pp. 74-76; and Klein, "Fisher-General Motors and the Nature of the Firm," where the importance of reputation is discussed.

22. "The Ins and Outs of Outing," p. 55.

23. John McLaren, "Globalization and Vertical Structure," *American Economic Review*, 90, no. 5, December 2000, pp. 1239-1254.

24. For an overview of the motivations for the wave of mergers and acquisitions during the 1990s, see Daniel J. Meckstroth, *An Analysis of Merger and Acquisition Activity in the United States* (Washington, DC: Manufacturers Alliance/MAPI, 1999).

25. Acquisitions motivated by desire to achieve economies of scope are different from the conglomerate mergers of the 1960s and 1970s, where the stated rationales were portfolio diversification and the achievement of synergies between two firms.

26. John Graham, Michael Lemman, and Jack Wolf, "Does Corporate Diversification Destroy Value?," *Journal of Finance*, 57, April 2002, pp. 695-720.

27. Patrick Bolton and David S. Scharfstein, "Corporate Finance, the Theory of the Firm, and Organizations," *Journal of Economic Perspectives*, 12, no. 4 (Fall 1998), pp. 95-114.

28. Charles J. Hadlock, Michael Ryngaert, and Shawn Thomas, "Corporate Structure and Equity Offering: Are There Benefits to Diversification?," *Journal of Business*, 74, no. 4 (2001), pp. 613-634.

29. Graham, Lemman, and Wolf, "Does Corporate Diversification Destroy Value?"

30. There are questions about how good the data on industry capacity are and

what they measure. Nonetheless, the magnitude of the increase suggests that there was a significant expansion in the late 1990s.

31. Joann Muller, with Kathleen Kerwin and David Welch, "Autos: A New Industry," *Business Week* 15 July, 2002, pp. 98-106.

32. Todd Zaun, Scott Miller, and Joseph B. White, "Honda Aims to Export Cars from China," *The Wall Street Journal* 11 July, 2002, p. A-12.

33. Change by its very nature creates winners and losers. Clearly, some autoworkers and the communities in which they live have borne costs as production has shifted around the world and in the United States. In addition, many firms that supply the automobile manufacturers are under intense pressure to reduce their costs in order to retain their supplier relationship with the manufacturers.

34. Penetration rates, however, do not necessarily measure the extent to which households own multiple units of appliances. Many households have more than one television set and an increasing number have two or more refrigerators and computers.

35. "Whirlpool Corporation Announces Key Steps in Extension of Global Business Strategy," *ScreamingMedia, Business Wire* 6 January, 2000, http://industry.java.sun.com/javanews/stories/story2/0,1072,21774,00.html.

36. See India Infoline at www.Indiain.com/sect/whtg/ch05.html.

37. See www.projectshub.com/projects.

CHAPTER 9

1. William J. Baumol, *The Free Market Innovation Machine: Analyzing the Growth Miracle of Capitalism* (Princeton, NJ: Princeton University Press, 2000), chap. 2.

2. Joe Kirwin, "EU R&D Continues to Lag Behind U.S. as Member States' Private Spending Sags," Bureau of National Affairs, *Daily Report for Executives*, June 28, 2002, p. A-3.

3. See Gary and Aldona Robbins, *Manufacturing, Taxes, and the Longest Economic Expansion in Modern U.S. History* (Arlington, VA: Manufacturers Alliance/MAPI, 1999).

4. See Glenn Simpson, "A New Twist in Tax Avoidance: Firms Send Best Ideas Abroad," *The Wall Street Journal*, June 24, 2002, p. A-1.

5. International Intellectual Property Association, www.iipa.com.

6. Andrew S. Grove, "Stigmatizing Business," *The Washington Post*, July 17, 2002, p. A-23.

7. See Felix Rohatyn, "An Agenda for Corporate Reform," *The Wall Street Journal*, June 24, 2002, p. A-16.

8. For a discussion of the value of international accounting "principles," see Walter Wriston, "The Solution to Scandals? Simpler Rules," *The Wall Street Journal*, August 5, 2002, p. A-10. See also John S. McClenahen, "GAAP Goodbye? PwC's CEO Wants to Scrap Rules-Based Accounting for Global Guidelines," *IndustryWeek*, August 2002, pp. 16-18.

9. We have explored this problem in depth in: Frederick T. Stocker, ed., *I Pay, You Pay, We All Pay: How the Growing Tort Crisis Undermines the U.S. Economy and the American System of Justice* (Arlington, VA: Manufacturers Alliance/MAPI, 2003).

10. See R.W. Judy and Carol D'Amico, *Workforce 2020: Work and Workers in the 21st Century* (Indianapolis, IN: Hudson Institute, 1997), pp. 81-85.

11. According to a recent tally, at the end of 2001 there were 4,509 regulations in process, of which 149 met the threshold of $100 million in economic impact. Economically significant rules did decrease slightly, by 5.7 percent, from 2000 to 2001. See Clyde Wayne Crews, "Ten Thousand Commandments: An Annual Snapshot of the Federal Regulatory State." (Washington, D.C.: Cato Institute, 2002), p. 1.

12. Baumol, *Free Market Innovation Machine*, p. 119. See his discussion of the issue on pp. 114-119.

13. For a discussion of this process, see Thomas J. Duesterberg and Kenneth Gordon, *Competition and Deregulation in Telecommunications: The Case for a New Paradigm* (Indianapolis, IN: Hudson Institute, 1997).

14. For a longer discussion, see Thomas J. Duesterberg and Jeremy Leonard, *The Telecommunications Sector and Economic Recovery* (Arlington, VA: Manufacturers Alliance/MAPI, 2001), pp. 1-8. See also Peter S. Goodman, "Giant Phone Companies Offer Stable, Well-Funded Option," *The Washington Post*, July 8, 2002, p. A-1.

15. On the poor business models and the role of regulation, see Peter Huber, "Washington Created WorldCom," *The Wall Street Journal*, July 1, 2002, p. A-14, and Robert Samuelson, "Sleaze and the Slump," *The Washington Post* 3 July, 2002, p. A-23.

16. Duesterberg and Leonard, *The Telecommunications Sector and Economic Recovery*, pp. 9-11.

17. Alfred E. Kahn, *Letting Go: Deregulating the Process of Deregulation* (East Lansing: Institute of Public Utilities and Network Industries, Michigan State University, 1998).

18. Jeffrey Eisenach, "Computer Industry Flexes Its Muscle," *Intellectual Capital-Com*, January 28, 1999.

19. See Thomas J. Duesterberg, *Broadband Access: Do We Need a Regulatory Solution?* (Washington, DC: Manufacturers Alliance/MAPI, 2000).

20. For a full presentation of this initiative, see Ernest H. Preeg, *From Here to Free Trade in Manufactures: Why and How* (Arlington, VA: Manufacturers Alliance/MAPI, 2003).

21. A full presentation of this strategy is contained in Ernest H. Preeg, "Currency Manipulation to Gain an Unfair Competitive Advantage: The Case Against Japan and China," contained in *Dollar Overvaluation and the World Economy* (Washington, DC: Institute for International Economics, 2003), edited by C. Fred Bergsten and John Williamson, pp. 267-284.

22. Baumol, *Free-Market Innovation Machine*, p. viii.

Bibliography

Aeppel, Timothy. "The Dollar's Strength Tests the Ingenuity of U.S. Manufacturers." *The Wall Street Journal*, January 22, 2002: A-1.

Baker, Beth. "Doctor in the House." *The Washington Post*, December 18, 2001: F-1.

Baumol, William J. *The Free Market Innovation Machine: Analyzing the Growth Miracle of Capitalism*. Princeton, NJ: Princeton University Press, 2002.

Bernstein, Jeffrey, and Theofanis Mamuneas. "The Contribution of U.S. R&D Spending to Manufacturing Productivity in Canada." Paper presented at Centre for the Study of Living Standards Conference on the Canada-U.S. Manufacturing Productivity Gap, January 2000.

Bolton, Patrick, and David S. Scharfstein. "Corporate Finance, the Theory of the Firm, and Organizations." *Journal of Economic Perspectives*, 12 (4) (Fall 1998): 95–114.

Christiansen, Clayton M., Michael Raynor, and Matt Verlinden. "Skate to Where the Money Will Be." *Harvard Business Review*, November 2001, pp. 73-81.

Clinton, Angela. "Flexible Labor: Restructuring the American Work Force." *Monthly Labor Review*, August 1997.

Coase, Ronald. "The Nature of the Firm." *Economica n.s.* (1937): 386–405.

Crews, Clyde Wayne. *Ten Thousand Commandments: An Annual Snapshot of the Federal Regulatory State*. Washington, DC: Cato Institute, 2002.

Cummins, Jason G., and Gianluca L. Violante. "Investment-Specific Technical Change in the U.S. (1947–2000): Measurement and Macroeconomic Consequences." *Review of Economic Dynamics*, 5 (2) (2002): 243-284.

Davis, Bob. "Why Europe Trails U.S. in High-Tech Innovation." *The Wall Street Journal*, April 1, 2002: A-1.

Demsetz, Harold. "Two Systems of Belief About Monopoly." In *Industrial Concentration: The New Learning*, edited by Harvey Goldschmid, Michael Mann, and J. Fred Weston, 164–184. Boston: Little, Brown, 1974.

Dollar, David, and Aart Kraay. "Trade, Growth, and Poverty." Working paper, World Bank, June 2001.

Drucker, Peter F. *Management Challenges for the 21st Century*. New York: Harper Business, 1999.

Duesterberg, Thomas J. *Broadband Access: Do We Need a Regulatory Solution?* Washington, DC: Manufacturers Alliance/MAPI, 2000.

Duesterberg, Thomas J. *Manufacturing in the Era of the New Economy: Evidence for Sustainable Productivity Gains*. Washington, DC: Manufacturers Alliance/MAPI, 2000.

Duesterberg, Thomas J., and Kenneth Gordon. *Competition and Deregulation in Telecommunications: The Case for a New Paradigm*. Indianapolis, IN: Hudson Institute, 1997.

Duesterberg, Thomas J., and Jeremy A. Leonard. *The Telecommunications Sector and Economic Recovery*. Washington, DC: Manufacturers Alliance/MAPI, 2001.

Eisenach, Jeffrey. "Computer Industry Flexes Its Muscle." *Intellectual Capital-Com*, January 28, 1999.

Evans, Michael K. "U.S. Headed for 'Hollow' Economy: Manufacturing Leads the Way for Plunging Profits." *IndustryWeek*, August 2002, p. 80.

Filippini, Robert, Andrea Vinelli, and Chris Voss. "Paths of Improvement in Plant Operations." In *High Performance Manufacturing*, edited by Roger G. Schroeder and Barbara B. Flynn. New York: John Wiley and Sons, 2001.

Fulkerson, William. "Information-Based Manufacturing in the Informational Age." *International Journal of Flexible Manufacturing Systems*, April 2000.

Gault, F. D. "Research and Development in a Service Economy." *Research Evaluation*, 7 (2) (1998).

Goodman, Peter S. "Giant Phone Companies Offer Stable, Well-Funded Option." *The Washington Post*, July 8, 2002: A-1.

Gordon, Robert J. "Has the 'New Economy' Rendered the Productivity Slowdown Obsolete?" Working paper, Northwestern University and National Bureau of Economic Research, June 14, 1999.

Graham, John, Michael Lemman, and Jack Wolf. "Does Corporate Diversification Destroy Value?" *Journal of Finance*, April 2002.

Grove, Andrew S. "Stigmatizing Business." *The Washington Post*, July 17, 2002: A-23.

Hadlock, Charles J., Michael Ryngaert, and Shawn Thomas. "Corporate Structure and Equity Offering: Are There Benefits to Diversification?" *Journal of Business*, 74 (4) (2001): 613–634.

Hamilton, Martha McNeil. "Black & Decker to Shut Plants." *The Washington Post*, January 30, 2002: E-1, E-3.

Hanson, Gordon H., Raymond J. Mataloni, Jr., and Matthew J. Slaughter. "Expansion Strategies of US Multinational Firms." Draft working paper, U.S. Department of Commerce, Bureau of Economic Analysis, April 2001.

Hewitt, Paul S. "Depopulation and Aging in Europe and Japan: The Hazardous Transition to a Labor Shortage Economy." *Internationale Politik und Gesellschaft Online*, January 2002: 2.

Hicks, J. R. "Annual Survey of Economic Theory: The Theory of Monopoly." *Econometrica*, 3 (1) (1935), as reprinted in George J. Stigler and Kenneth E. Boulding, *Readings in Price Theory*, vol. 6, 369. Chicago: Richard D. Irwin, 1952.

Hindle, Tim. "Back to Basics." *The Economist*, March 9, 2002.

Holmström, Bengt, and John Roberts. "The Boundaries of the Firm Revisited." *Journal of Economic Perspectives*, 12 (4) (Fall 1998): 73–94.

Huber, Peter. "Washington Created WorldCom." *The Wall Street Journal*, July 1, 2002: A-14.

Irwin, Neil. "This Little Slinky Goes to Market." *The Washington Post*, January 13, 2002: H-1.

Jackson, Richard. *The Global Retirement Crisis*. Washington, DC: Center for Strategic and International Studies, 2002.

Johnson, H. Thomas, and Anders Broms. *Profit Beyond Measure*. New York: The Free Press, 2000.

Jorgenson, Dale W. "Projecting Productivity Growth." Presentation to the Machinery Institute, June 17, 2002.

Jorgenson, Dale W., Mun S. Ho, and Kevin J. Stiroh. "Lessons from the U.S. Growth Resurgence." Prepared for the First International Conference on the Economic and Social Implications of Information Technology, U.S. Department of Commerce, Washington, DC, January 27-28, 2003.

Jorgenson, Dale W., and Kevin J. Stiroh. "Raising the Speed Limit: U.S. Economic Growth in the Information Age." In *Brookings Papers on Economic Activity*, vol. 2. Washington, DC: Brookings Institution, 2000.

Judy, R. W., and Carol D'Amico. *Workforce 2020: Work and Workers in the 21st Century*. Indianapolis, IN: Hudson Institute, 1997.

Kahn, Alfred E. *Letting Go: Deregulating the Process of Deregulation*. East Lansing: Institute of Public Utilities and Network Industries, Michigan State University, 1998.

Kay, John. "Keeping Up with the Market." *The Economist: The Future Surveyed*, September 11, 1993, p. 66.

Kirwin, Joe. "EU R&D Continues to Lag Behind U.S. as Member States' Private Spending Sags." Bureau of National Affairs, *Daily Report for Executives*, June 28, 2002: A-3.

Klein, Benjamin. "Fisher-General Motors and the Nature of the Firm." *Journal of Law and Economics*, XLIII (2000): 105–141.

Klein, Benjamin, Robert Crawford, and Armen Alchian. "Vertical Integration, Appropriable Rents, and the Competitive Contracting Process." *Journal of Law and Economics*, 21 (1978): 297–326.

Leonard, Jeremy A. "Assessing the Adequacy of Public Funding of ICT-Related R&D in Canada." Report prepared for the Canadian Institute for Telecommunications Research, January 2001.

Leonard, Jeremy A. *Taking Stock: The Role of Financial Market Structure in Economic Growth*. Washington, DC: Manufacturers Alliance/MAPI, 2001.

Liesman, Steve. "Better Machine Tools Give Manufacturers Newfound Resilience." *The Wall Street Journal*, February 15, 2001: A-1.

Los, Bart, and Bart Verspagen. "R&D Spillovers and Productivity: Evidence from U.S. Manufacturing Microdata." *Empirical Economics*, 25 (1) (2000).

Manufacturers Alliance/MAPI and National Association of Manufacturers. *U.S. Manufacturing Industry's Impact on Ethical, Labor, and Environmental Standards in Developing Countries*. Washington, DC: Manufacturers Alliance/MAPI and NAM, 2001.

McClenahen, John S. "GAAP Goodbye? PwC's CEO Wants to Scrap Rules-Based Accounting for Global Guidelines." *IndustryWeek*, August 2002, pp. 16–18.

McLaren, John. "Globalization and Vertical Structure." *American Economic Review*, 90 (5) (December 2000): 1239–1254.

Meckstroth, Daniel J. *An Analysis of Merger and Acquisition Activity in the United States*. Washington, DC: Manufacturers Alliance/MAPI, 1999.

Morcott, Southwood J. *Today's Automotive-Supply Industry: Evolution or Revolution?* Washington, DC: Manufacturers Alliance/MAPI, 2000.

Muller, Joann, with Kathleen Kerwin and David Welch. "Autos: A New Industry." *Business Week*, July 15, 2002, pp. 98–106.

Nadiri, M. I. "Innovations and Technological Spillovers." National Bureau of Economic Research, working paper 4423, 1993.

National Science Foundation. *Science and Engineering Indicators—2002, vol. 1*. Washington, DC: National Science Board, 2002.

O'Harrow, Robert. "Next: An ID Chip Planted in Your Body?" *The Washington Post*, December 19, 2001: E-1.

Ohmae, Kenichi. *The Borderless World: Power and Strategy in the Interlinked Economy*. New York: Harper Business, 1990.

Organization for Economic Cooperation and Development. *The New Economy: Beyond the Hype*. Paris: OECD, 2001.

Organization for Economic Cooperation and Development. *International Investment Perspectives*. "Trends and Recent Developments in Foreign Direct Investment." Paris: OECD, September 2002.

Peters, Tom. *Liberation Management: Necessary Disorganization for the Nanosecond Nineties*. New York: Alfred A. Knopf, 1992.

Planting, Mark A., and Peter D. Kuhbach. "Annual Input-Output Accounts of the U.S. Economy–1998." *Survey of Current Business*, December 2001, p. 41.

Popkin, Joel. "Producing Prosperity: Manufacturing Technology's Unmeasured Role in Economic Expansion." Report prepared for the Association of Manufacturing Technology, September 2000.

Porter, Michael E. *Competitive Strategy: Techniques for Analyzing Industries and Competitors*. Revised edition. New York: The Free Press, 1998.

Porter, Michael E. *Clusters of Innovation: Regional Foundations of U.S. Competitiveness*. Washington, DC: Council on Competitiveness, 2001.

Preeg, Ernest H. *From Here to Free Trade: Essays in Post-Uruguay Round Trade Strategy*. Chicago: University of Chicago Press, 1998.

Preeg, Ernest H. "A Rose Tinted View of the Deficit." *Financial Times*, June 22, 2000.

Preeg, Ernest H. *The Trade Deficit, the Dollar, and the U.S. National Interest*. Indianapolis, IN: Hudson Institute, 2000.

Preeg, Ernest H. *Surging Yet Volatile Productivity Growth in U.S. Manufacturing Industry: The International Trade Dimension*. Washington, DC: Manufacturers Alliance/MAPI, 2001.

Preeg, Ernest H. "Free Trade in Manufactures as the Central Objective for the Doha Multilateral Trade Negotiations." Presented to the Office of the U.S. Trade Representative, April 30, 2002. Available at www.mapi.net.

Preeg, Ernest H. "Currency Manipulation to Gain an Unfair Competitive Advantage: The Case Against Japan and China," contained in *Dollar Overvaluation and the World Economy* (Washington, DC: Institute for International Economics, 2003), edited by C. Fred Bergsten and John Williamson, pp. 267-284.

Preeg, Ernest H. *From Here To Free Trade in Manufactures: Why and How* (Arlington, VA: Manufacturers Alliance/MAPI, 2003).

Raa, Thijs Ten, and Edward N. Wolff. "Outsourcing of Services and the Productivity Recovery in U.S. Manufacturing in the 1980s and 1990s." *Journal of Productivity Analysis*, 16 (2) (September 2001): 149-165.

Robbins, Gary, and Aldona Robbins. *Manufacturing, Taxes, and the Longest Economic Expansion in Modern U.S. History*. Washington, DC: Manufacturers Alliance/MAPI, 1999.

Roemer, Paul. "Ideas and Things." *The Economist: The Future Surveyed*, September 11, 1993, p. 72.

Rohatyn, Felix. "An Agenda for Corporate Reform." *The Wall Street Journal*, June 24, 2002: A-16.

Rosenthal, Neal. "The Quality of BLS Projections: A Historical Account." *Monthly Labor Review*, May 1999, pp. 27–35.

Samuelson, Robert. "Sleaze and the Slump." *The Washington Post*, July 3, 2002: A-23.

Schieber, Sylvester J., and Paul S. Hewitt. "Demographic Risk in Industrial Societies." *World Economics*, October-December 2000, p. 44.

Schwartz, Peter, Peter Leyden, and Joel Hyatt. *The Long Boom: A Vision for the Coming Age of Prosperity*. New York: Perseus, 2000.

Scott, Robert. "Fast Track to Lost Jobs: Trade Deficits and Manufacturing Decline Are the Legacies of NAFTA and WTO." Briefing paper, Economic Policy Institute, 2002. Available at www.epinet.org.

Simpson, Glenn. "A New Twist in Tax Avoidance: Firms Send Best Ideas Abroad." *The Wall Street Journal*, June 24, 2002: A-1.

Stocker, Frederick T., ed., *I Pay, You Pay, We All Pay: How the Growing Tort Crisis Undermines the U.S. Economy and the American System of Justice*, Arlington, VA: Manufacturers Alliance/MAPI, 2003.

Tassey, Gregory. *R&D and Long-Term Competitiveness: Manufacturing's Central Role in a Knowledge-Based Economy*. Washington, DC: National Institute of Science and Technology, 2002.

Terborgh, George. *The Bogey of Economic Maturity*. Chicago: Machinery and Allied Products Institute, 1945.

Thornhill, John. "Asia Awakes: The Region's Middle Classes Are Spending and Borrowing More." *Financial Times*, April 2, 2002, p. 14.

Tirpak, Thomas M. "Design-to-Manufacturing Information Management for Electronics Assembly." *International Journal of Flexible Manufacturing Systems*, 12 (2000): 189–205.

Tonelson, Alan. *Race to the Bottom*. New York: Westview Press, 2000.

United Nations. *World Urbanization Prospects*. 2001 revision. New York: United Nations, Department of International Economic and Social Affairs, 2002.

U.S. Department of Labor. Bureau of Labor Statistics. *International Comparisons of Labor Productivity and Unit Labor Costs in Manufacturing, 2000*. Washington, DC: Bureau of Labor Statistics, 2002.

Winston, George. "Economic Deregulation: Days of Reckoning for Microeconomists." *Journal of Economic Literature*, 31 (3) (September 1993): 1263–1289.

Wolff, Edward N. "Spillovers, Linkages, and Technical Change." *Economic Systems Research*, 9:1 (March 1997).

Wright, Paul Kenneth. *21st Century Manufacturing*. Englewood Cliffs, NJ: Prentice-Hall, 2001.

Wriston, Walter. "The Solution to Scandals? Simpler Rules." *The Wall Street Journal*, August 5, 2002: A-10.

Zaun, Todd, Scott Miller, and Joseph B. White. "Honda Aims to Export Cars from China," *The Wall Street Journal*, July 11, 2002: A-12.

Zimmerman, Fred, and Dave Beal. *Manufacturing Works: The Vital Link Between Production and Prosperity*. Dearborn, MI: Dearborn Trade Publishing, 2002.

Index

About the Editors and Contributors

THOMAS J. DUESTERBERG, co-editor, is President and Chief Executive Officer of Manufacturers Alliance/MAPI (the Alliance). He previously served as Senior Fellow and Director, Washington office, of the Hudson Institute. Prior to that he held the position of Assistant Secretary for International Economic Policy at the U.S. Department of Commerce, and worked as a senior staff aide in the U.S. Senate and U.S. House of Representatives. He is the author of numerous articles and books on trade, comparative economics, and technology regulation. He is co-editor of *Riding the Next Wave: Why the Next Century Will Be a Golden Age for Workers, the Environment, and Developing Countries* (2001). His work has appeared in the *Wall Street Journal, New York Times*, *Los Angeles Times*, *Financial Times*, *Washington Quarterly*, and numerous other publications. He is a graduate of Princeton University and holds a Ph.D. in history from Indiana University.

ERNEST H. PREEG, co-editor, is currently Senior Fellow in Trade and Productivity at the Alliance. Prior to that he was a Senior Fellow at the Hudson Institute and held the Scholl Chair in International Business at the Center for Strategic and International Studies. His career in government included the positions of Ambassador to Haiti; Executive Director, Economic Policy Group, White House Staff; Chief Economist, Agency for International Development; and Deputy Assistant Secretary of State for International Finance and Development. He is the author of 14 books on trade and international economic issues, the most recent being *The Trade Deficit, the Dollar, and the U.S. National Interest* (2000), and *From Here To Free Trade in Manufactures: Why and How* (2003). His work has appeared in the *Wall Street Journal*, *Financial Times, Washington Post*, and *Washington*

Times. He has a B.S. in marine transportation from the New York State Maritime College and a Ph.D. in economics from the New School for Social Research. He began his working career in the U.S. merchant marine, rising to chief mate, oceans.

DANIEL J. MECKSTROTH is Chief Economist for the Alliance. Prior to coming to the Alliance, he served as Supervisor of Economic Analysis at Armco, Inc. At the Alliance, he publishes a quarterly analysis of selected industrial indicators and has written on a wide variety of topics, including the evolution of e-business, an analysis of merger and acquisition activity in the United States, and employment and economic growth in the United States. He directs the Purchasing and E-Business councils of the Alliance. He holds a B.B.A. from Eastern Kentucky University and a Ph.D. in economics from the University of Cincinnati.

JOSEPH V. KENNEDY is General Counsel for the Permanent Subcommittee on Investigations, Government Affairs Committee, United States Senate. Prior to this Dr. Kennedy was an attorney/economist at the Manufacturers Alliance/MAPI and directed its councils on Strategic Planning and Development, Supply Chain Logistics, and Research and Innovation. He previously served as an economist for the Committee on Budget of the U.S. House of Representatives, an attorney for a large law firm, and a budget examiner for the U.S. Office of Management and Budget. His research interests include corporate strategic planning, innovation, and regulation. For the Alliance he wrote on the impact of information technology on manufacturing, global warming, encryption, and tax issues. Kennedy holds a B.S.F.S. from Georgetown University, a Ph.D. in economics from George Washington University, and a J.D. and M.S. from the University of Minnesota.

JEREMY A. LEONARD is economic consultant to the Alliance, a position he has held since 1997. Leonard resides in Montreal and writes regularly for the Alliance and for Canadian publications on the state of the Canadian economy, productivity, economic growth, innovation, and regulation of technology. His publications for the Alliance include the role of financial market structure in economic growth; the role of information technology investment in recent U.S. economic performance; U.S. electricity deregulation and its importance to manufacturers; and biannual reviews of the Canadian economy. Leonard has a B.A. from the University of Pennsylvania and an M.A. in economics from McGill University.

JEFFREY F. WERLING is President, Inforum, in the Department of Economics at the University of Maryland. Inforum is a research organization dedicated to improving business forecasting and government policy analysis. Dr. Werling worked previously as an economist for the Manufacturers Alliance/MAPI. With MAPI he managed the Marketing, Manufacturing, and Information Systems Councils. His research included reports on global economic developments and the development of new manufacturing techniques and their implications for global manufacturing. Prior to joining the Alliance, Werling was Director of International Consulting at the WEFA Group, an economic forecasting and consulting firm. For his doctoral dissertation, he worked under a fellowship from the Spanish government to direct the development of a macroeconomic, multisectorial model of Spain at the Fundación Tomillo, in Madrid, Spain. Dr. Werling has a B.S. in mineral economics from Pennsylvania State University and an M.A. and Ph.D. in economics from the University of Maryland.

DONALD A. NORMAN joined the Alliance in 2000 and directs its three Financial councils. He previously was Research Manager at the American Petroleum Institute and an economist at the U.S. Federal Trade Commission. His research interests include financial markets, antitrust, regulation, energy conservation, and the restructuring of the electric power industry. Norman holds a B.A., M.A., and Ph.D. in economics from the University of California at Los Angeles and an M.B.A. in finance from George Mason University.